Small Business, Education, and Management

T0289901

This book examines the life and times of John Bolton, a Cambridge graduate who graduated as a Baker Scholar from Harvard Business School and returned to Britain to quickly chair Solartron, one of the outstanding early British electronics companies in the 1950s.

John Bolton also enjoyed a career of public service and private good works. He led the founding of the Foundation for Management Education, which had an extremely influential role in the development of management education in Britain, and chaired the 1968–71 Committee of Inquiry on Small Firms, resulting in what is now generally called the Bolton Report. The Bolton Report became and continues to be the starting point for analysis of the sector at a time when small business is again being seen as a major contributor to the British economy and has revolutionized attitudes and policy toward the small business sector at all levels.

Bolton's career covered a range of different dimensions of mid- to late-20th-century industrial and public life in Britain, and the history is as much about these as it is of the man himself. The intention of this book is to illuminate the institutions in which Bolton worked as well as to paint a picture of his own role.

Andrew Thomson was Emeritus Professor at The Open University, UK.

Routledge International Studies in Business History

Series editors: Ray Stokes and Matthias Kipping

Photo 1   The Committee of the Royal Commission on Local Government for England, 1966–69

Small Business, Education, and Management

The Life and Times of John Bolton

Andrew Thomson
with the assistance of Athalie Haylor

Routledge
Taylor & Francis Group

NEW YORK AND LONDON

First published 2016
by Routledge
711 Third Avenue, New York, NY 10017

and by Routledge
2 Park Square, Milton Park, Abingdon, Oxon OX14 4RN

First issued in paperback 2018

*Routledge is an imprint of the Taylor & Francis Group,
an informa business*

Library of Congress Cataloging-in-Publication Data
CIP data has been applied for.

ISBN 13: 978-1-138-34007-7 (pbk)
ISBN 13: 978-1-138-79000-1 (hbk)

Typeset in Sabon
by Apex CoVantage, LLC

To Eloise

This book is dedicated to the memory of Andrew Thomson, a trusted and respected colleague who is greatly missed.

Contents

Tables

Photographs

Prologue

This book is about the 'times' as well as the life of John Bolton and thus requires to be seen in a wider frame of reference, insofar as the times helped to make him who he was, while he in turn contributed to shaping them. Such a frame of reference is important for a 21st-century audience, because although the events covered are well within the last century, much of the political, economic, social, and moral grounding on which the story is based has changed, very substantially albeit often subtly, beyond easy recognition. A prologue is an opening to a story that establishes the setting and provides background, hence the title of this introduction to the book, covering the period of Bolton's life from 1920–2003.

The interwar years were not an ideal period for growing up in Britain, especially where the traditional industries were in decline, or for those without a breadwinner in a steady job, as was the case for the Boltons after the father's death in 1933. The Great Depression and the two World Wars were the key events of the first half of the 20th century, with a massive social and psychological impact on the generations that experienced them. At the time of writing, much is rightly being made of 2014 as the final celebrations of the Normandy landings in 1944 and the start of the First World War in 1914. If the First World War was the 'war to end wars', the Second was the people's war, the war of good against evil, with those who fought it now lauded as 'the greatest generation', not only for their success in winning it but because of the moral standards they exhibited in doing so. And in its aftermath too, that morality was a feature of how the survivors felt and behaved, both collectively and individually. The sense of being all in it together was a central focus of the wartime period, and it helped to generate the Beveridge Report and a strong sense of a social contract irrespective of party political differences. People in the War had shared strong experiences, perhaps most powerfully evoked in Steven Ambrose's *Band of Brothers* (1992), an American Army story of the unifying force of war in a citizen army, but applicable in many other situations such as John Bolton's British Navy destroyer HMS Wilton. It was not just on the battlefields. Rationing worked well and was seen to be fair and there was a general belief that the war economy had been successful under state controls. Thus, as Stone

(2010: 9) noted 'For the State to take over, to plan and develop a welfare state therefore seemed sensible'. The Cold War helped to continue wartime attitudes of being in it together. Empathy came easily in such a context, and so did service to the country as a duty. These were to be ongoing characteristics of John Bolton's career.

The immediate post–World War II period, under a Labour Government, saw a first stage of transforming Britain, characterized by widespread nationalization of basic industries, together with the setting up of the Welfare State. But there was also continued rationing combined with shortages of many basics, while the cost of the War continued to be felt. Even so, in 1950, when Bolton returned from Harvard, Britain's situation as a leading industrial power was ostensibly more favourable than anywhere else except the United States. She accounted for a quarter of world exports of manufactures, more than double the share of France, her nearest competitor other than the United States; in addition her GDP per head was 'a third higher than France's, two-thirds higher than West Germany's, twice Italy's, and nearly four times higher than Japan's' (Barnett 2001: 346). But this was to prove a false illusion of economic strength and over the next four decades Britain was to slip relative to these competitors in terms of output, exports, and GDP. As we will see, John Bolton himself developed some ideas about the underlying weaknesses in his research for Harvard Business School, but they have been well catalogued by Barnett (2001), one of their most severe critics, in the last of his *Pride and Fall* sequence: a heavy commitment to defence expenditure with the calls of the colonial empire and the outbreak of the Korean War, an ongoing balance of payments problem, poor infrastructure and logistics, shortages of key components for an industrial reinvestment programme such as ball-bearings, and an over-dependence on old industries and a lack of growth in new ones (although Bolton's Solartron was a notable exception). Cultural snobberies did not help, with a preference for finance over industry, for pure science over technology, and for experimental computer development rather than commercially oriented ones and indeed a lack of interest in business machines and business techniques more generally. Education had little or no interest in industry at any level from management to the shop floor. Marketing was a rarity outside a few fast-moving consumer goods industries. Where there were successes, like the Morris Minor or the Land Rover, they were not pursued with any vigour. The Anglo-American Council on Productivity sent 47 industry teams and 21 specialist teams to the United States to study productivity (Brech, Thomson, and Wilson 2010: 145) and their reports were almost universally damning of British industry practices but they had little impact on a British industry which did not want to listen.

Of particular relevance to this book were severe institutional problems in industry. A key issue according to the doyen of business history, Alfred Chandler (1990), was the persistence of what he calls personal capitalism (and which Quail (2000) has called proprietorial capitalism) in which both

the governance and the culture are personally managed within a family structure and there is little in the way of a hierarchy of professional management.
Companies were largely responsible only to their own boards of directors,
who were self-perpetuating oligarchies operating on consensus. It was this
slow transition to professional management and its counterpart managerial
capitalism (with a number of exceptions such as BP, Shell, Unilever, and
ICI) which differentiated Britain from the United States and Germany well
after World War II and into the 1960s, whereas the others had moved into
managerial capitalism in the 1920s.

There was a recognition at the national level of things going wrong from
the mid-1950s, together with the feeling that something needed to be done
by the state in the absence of other active parties. This led to corporatism as
a second stage of transformation. Peter Thorneycroft as a new Chancellor
of the Exchequer accepted that the only source of future strength could lie in
'great and prosperous and expanding industries. All else is vanity' (Barnett
2001: 515). His prime minister, Harold Macmillan, was himself a prototype
corporatist based on his experiences as MP for Stockton in the interwar
period. Corporatism saw the need for big companies to compete on the
world stage and was prepared to use the institutions of the state to achieve
them. Size became important for its own sake, especially through horizontal
mergers, both to compete on world markets and as a mechanism for mod-
ernization. The Conservatives took the first step by creating the National
Economic Development Council, the National Economic Development
Office, and the industry-based 'little Neddies' in 1962. Then the Labour
Government between 1964 and 1970 set up various institutions of tripartite
organization: the National Plan, the Industrial Reorganization Corporation,
and the National Board for Prices and Incomes were amongst these. The
outcome was the state-led reorganization of many large industries beyond
those already nationalized. These developments were not unique to Britain,
and indeed were partly based on French indicative planning. Moreover the
influential Harvard economist J. K. Galbraith in *The New Industrial State*
(1967) as well as the Reith Lectures of 1966 gave academic support to these
positions.

The concept of the 'Establishment' was also part of the image of the times,
perhaps made most famous by Anthony Sampson in his *Anatomy of Britain*
series. Within the Establishment, managers were treated with suspicion as
representing 'the antithesis of the old knightly ideals' (1965: 506) and even
though managers were becoming more important and Sampson could at
least ask the question of whether managers could constitute a profession,
there was still a sense of conflict between the amateurs and the professionals,
or what Coleman (1973) called the 'gentlemen and players', taking a crick-
eting analogy. Sampson saw consultants as the 'shock troops of industry'
(1965: 510) and certainly the 1960s was also the period of the transition
to the structures of managerial capitalism in Britain, largely engineered by
McKinsey and other American consultancies, as well as supported by the

corporatist state. This was just as well, because the companies did not have many ideas of their own and the universities were very far from providing any intellectual underpinnings.

But the underlying problems were not solved by corporatism and the 1970s oil crises uncovered them, leading to a third stage of transformation in the 1980s, away from collectivism and the state, toward individualism and the free market. Industrially too, the tide was turning toward financial capitalism and away from managerial capitalism. Economics changed from stakeholder to shareholder capitalism and to a neoliberal, monetarist ideology. Within the organization, the large-scale hierarchies associated with managerial capitalism were slimmed down and de-layered, while the 'organization man' and the corporate career of Whyte's eponymous book (1956) disappeared for the majority of managers. Looking externally, organic growth with control by the board of directors under managerial capitalism was replaced by more aggressive positions by investor organizations through dependence on the equity markets and transactional strategies. The investor organizations tended not to be committed to long-term ownership, but rather sought to maximize short term profit, to the detriment of investment. The share price became the measure of success. What Chandler (1990: 625) called 'an institutionalized market for corporate control' came to dominate. The financial services sector became much more important than manufacturing, and after the deregulation 'Big Bang' of 1987, the era of gentlemanly service in the City of London came to an end. At the national level the feature of the 1980s was a move to privatization and deregulation through the sale of state-owned industries and council houses to provide a property-owning, shareholding democracy. The intellectual argument was the triumph of the market, initiated in the Conservative Party by Keith Joseph but taken on board by Margaret Thatcher. Throughout the whole period Europe was an ongoing issue, initially 'missing the bus', then catching it with reservations and never making a fist of being a full member.

Another part of this change was an attack on existing attitudes; in a much-quoted book, the American Martin Wiener (1981) explored the English ambivalence to modern industrial society, revealing a pervasive middle- and upper-class frame of mind hostile to industrialism and economic growth, while the successful in the industrial class had willingly subjected themselves to a process of gentrification, becoming chiefly concerned with emulating the traditional upper middle class. Sir Peter Parker put it very simply (Parker 1989: 118) 'we are an industrial society with an anti-industrial culture'. Margaret Thatcher strongly supported Wiener's hypothesis, which was particularly amenable to the social and economic climate of the time: industrial decline and an increasing reliance upon financial services. This view was not unchallenged (see Rubinstein 1994 and Thompson 2001) but it had a wide immediate impact.

While these economic, political, and structural changes were taking place, the social transformation of British life during the second half of the 20th century was tabulated by Rosen (2003):

- an increase in the standard of living, especially in rates of car and home ownership;
- more higher education, especially for women;
- more women in the workforce;
- a more diverse society, even though there had always been waves of immigrants;
- the impact of the digital revolution;
- a new youth culture based largely on America;
- the rise of mass communication largely through television, but later the Internet;
- the losing by labour in the battle with capital and the beginnings of a rise in inequality;
- a liberalizing of social values in areas like the death penalty, homosexuality, and abortion;
- a decline in support for hitherto popular institutions such as the police, religion, politics, marriage, and the unions; and
- an increase in individualism, both in relation to collectivism and toward others, with a rise in narcissism and a decline in empathy.

This prologue has chronicled the change from personal to managerial to financial capitalism and from nationalization to corporatism to privatization within a period of less than 50 years. Thus by the end of the period the economic structure, the system of capitalism, and the attitudes toward public services, the self, and others were very significantly different than at the start, providing a context for what was happening in the wider British setting during Bolton's life and career, to which we will now turn.

Preface and Acknowledgements

Biographies are one of the best ways of understanding history. Indeed Ralph Waldo Emerson wrote 'There is properly no history; only biography' (The History Guide, n.d.), and Thomas Carlyle followed by arguing not only that biography is a part of history but that the lives of great human beings are essential to our understanding of society and its institutions. There are of course different types of biographies, but this one views John Bolton through the lens of what he did for society as one of the key people who helped to make management what it is today in Britain. Indeed this was why it was written, as a contribution to the history of management and as a way of recognizing one of the giants on whose shoulders the present has been created. John Bolton needs to be thanked, not only for what he did, but for the generous, optimistic, and self-effacing way in which he did it, providing a role model for others. Most biographies in management are written about people who lead great companies, important in their particular industry but rarely influencing the wider industrial and commercial scene. John Bolton did lead a most interesting company, but this was for only a relatively short period in his career, the majority of which was spent in a broader context of public service and management institutions. Emerson also argued that an institution was the lengthened shadow of one man and Bolton certainly cast his shadow on at least two key dimensions of British management, with significant contributions to several others.

The availability of sources can influence a biography. Bolton kept no diary or even a personal scrapbook, wrote no sets of letters to family or other correspondents, no reports to employers, no published works on his thoughts or philosophy. But whether it was him or more likely his secretaries/personal assistants, a great deal of ephemera in the way of newspaper and magazine cuttings, letters inward and outward, annual reports, and handwritten cards or typed drafts for speeches did find their way into boxes. After his death, these passed into the possession of his daughter, Athalie, and have formed the main basis for this biography. Beyond those, published sources and contacts with individuals have provided additional information.

Of those who assisted with the book, Bolton's daughter Athalie Haylor was exceptional. She provided the key archives without which the book would not have been possible, and having been devoted to her father, she became almost as devoted to the cause of the book, providing contacts, some by diligent researching of the Internet, commenting on the drafts for accuracy and perspective, and acting as an editor of punctuation and spelling. Her husband Brian and her daughter Eloise, to whom this book is dedicated for lighting up the later years of Bolton's life, helped to make me feel welcome in their family. Bolton's son Nicholas, who sadly died while this book was being written, was also invaluable in providing support and contacts in the early stages of the book. Next there are others who worked with him or knew him: Marc Verstringhe, Tony Kelly, Chrissie Napier, Peter Butler, Peter Curry, Mike Parson, Stella and Gordon Pasley, Richard Long, Tina Willbanks, and perhaps most importantly in this group, Graham Bannock as the Director of Research and David Hartridge as the Committee Secretary for Bolton's 'magnum opus', the Committee of Inquiry into Small Firms. Robert Blackburn, David Storey, Colin Gray, and Richard Blundel were very helpful on the more academic side of small firms, Christopher Saunders gave a valuable perspective on Harvard Business School as a fellow MBA student and joint Baker Scholar in Bolton's Class of 1950, Allan Williams gave useful information from his graduate work on Solartron, and David Musson gave advice about the book itself as well as invaluable initial contacts. I would also like to acknowledge Philip Nind, an outstanding secretary of the Foundation for Management Education, who died just as the book was being started. In addition, several organizations: the Chartered Management Institute, the Foundation for Management Education, the Engineering Industries Association, and Surrey University provided valuable information about Bolton's role with them. I would also like to give thanks to Routledge as publishers and particularly to the successive editors Laura Stearns for her initial faith in the potential of the book and later David Varley for following it through to the contract stage, to Jabari LeGendre as editorial assistant, and to their referees in the assessment of this book. Finally, I would like to thank Edward Brech for his inspirational role in fostering the study of management history in Britain, and for his desire that this book should be written.

Andrew Thomson
Waitangi
13 September 2014

1 Formative Years

Family Background
Schools
Accountancy Articles
World War II
Cambridge
Marriage
Harvard Business School
Research in Britain

FAMILY BACKGROUND

John Eveleigh Bolton, often known as JEB, was born on 17 October 1920, the middle of three children, Nigel being almost five years older and Ethelwyn Mary some three years younger. The unusual name 'Eveleigh' was a family name from some two generations previous when John's grandmother had a half-brother called 'Eveleigh'. His parents Ernest and Edith both came from Wednesbury in the West Midlands. His father was associated with railways, in part because his stepmother thought that a railway company was a better place to work in than a factory, while his mother was the daughter of a coachbuilder, Mr. J. B. Duckhouse. Ernest entered railway service for the London and North Western in 1898 and was appointed assistant delivery clerk at Wednesbury in 1900. In 1910 he was made staff clerk at Great Bridge before being transferred to the staff department at Wolverhampton in 1917. In 1927 he was appointed staff clerk to the Leeds district goods manager in the London Midland and Scottish and in 1932 was promoted to the position of cartage assistant. He had been a prominent member of the old Wednesbury YMCA and a keen cricketer. He was also prominent in ambulance work, being district secretary of the LMS ambulance competition and in recognition of his work was made a serving officer of the Order of St John of Jerusalem in England. Another of his interests was life-saving, in which he was at one time an instructor at the West Bromwich baths. After taking up his appointment at Leeds, he continued his ambulance and sports activities and served on the Executive Committee of the Burley-in-Wharfedale Sports Club. At his death the LMS Magazine noted that 'he was a man who never spared himself and by his death the Company has lost a loyal and conscientious servant'.

In 1929, after the move from Wolverhampton to Yorkshire the family went to live in Burley-in-Wharfedale, an attractive village on the banks of the River Wharfe and close to the Yorkshire Dales, about 20 kilometres from the centre of Leeds. They moved into what had once been the stationmaster's house; John's sister remembers those early days with nostalgia:

> A positive factor was the beautiful countryside which was wonderful for children. There were always so many interesting things to do. John taught me to climb trees and to walk along the tops of five-bar gates and dry-stone walls. He showed me how to 'tickle' fish in the streams and taught me the names of the many wildflowers in the fields. On one occasion he took me to play with his friends who were all boys: their immediate response was 'oh! she's a girl!' John's response was 'she is alright; I have trained her!' These idyllic early years—for both of us—came to an abrupt halt when after a short illness my father died on 15 October 1933.

Their father's death in Leeds Infirmary at the young age of 49, just two days before John's 13th birthday, left their mother to bring up the three children. Fortunately, they were a close, friendly family and all of them had to be very strong and courageous, helping each other as much as they could. Mrs. Bolton was not a tough or bossy woman but very generous and gentle, dedicated to the well-being of her children. The important factors were her intelligence and her very strong character—very determined and dedicated.

The family moved back to Wolverhampton in 1935 but these were difficult times for them without a traditional breadwinner, while the economy was still feeling the effects of the Great Depression. Nevertheless Mrs. Bolton's family of five sisters was very helpful and they were surrounded by many other friendly people, which was an influence for the good. All three children did well at school. Nigel went on to become a doctor and Ethelwyn Mary, who was a gifted mathematician, became a scientific officer in the Scientific Civil Service working in munitions quality control and later guided projectiles. It would have been unusual for all three children to achieve this level of academic success in those days, when very few children went on to secondary school examinations; perhaps one child in a family but not all three. It says much for Mrs. Bolton, especially in the circumstances of her husband's death. John, like his mother, was a strong and determined character. His sister remembers him as being a leader not a follower, not bossy but with an uncanny knack of making the right decisions.

SCHOOLS

After the move to Leeds in 1929 John and his sister went to Burley Wood-head School on the edge of the moors and close to Ilkley. It was an interesting little school, founded in 1832 to serve the hamlet of Burley Woodhead as well as the village of Burley-in-Wharfedale and the surrounding area. Miss Swithenbank was the wonderful headmistress; when John moved on to Ilkley Grammar school the mathematics master wrote to Miss Swithenbank to congratulate her on the way she had taught mathematics to John.

Ilkley Grammar School, which John attended from 1930 to 1935, was an old foundation. An endowment of £100 was made by George Marshall in 1601 to fund the salary of a schoolmaster—at the time, one William Lobley. Payments to Lobley were fitful, and the executors of Marshall's estate had to go to law to rectify the situation; the date of settlement of the issues—1607—is now taken as the date of origination of the school. On the 2 January 1635, a group of townspeople signed an undertaking to erect a dedicated schoolhouse, and records indicate that by April 1637 this had been built. The building, in Church Street, still exists and is now a listed building, converted into a shop. John had always been good scholastically, and by the end of his stay in 1935 he had passed the Northern Universities School Certificate.

From 1935 to 1937 he attended Wolverhampton Grammar School and continued to do well scholastically, as well as being active in sports. Wolverhampton Grammar School was one of the ancient grammar schools, a century older than Ilkley, founded in 1512 by Sir Stephen Jenyns, a master of the ancient guild of Merchant Taylors, who was also Lord Mayor of London in the year of Henry VIII's coronation. Jenyns was born in the city of Wolverhampton in 1448. In the year 1519 he was one of the wealthiest men in the country and is reported to have paid more tax than any other person in that year. In 1875, the school moved to its present site on Compton Road from its previous site on John Street in the centre of Wolverhampton. It is also not without other famous alumni, Lord Normanbrook, head of the British Civil Service in the late 1950s and early 1960s, and Sir Mervyn King, Governor of the Bank of England from 2003–2013, being two of the most notable.

Whilst at Wolverhampton Grammar School, John distinguished himself in physics and mathematics, taking the Cambridge Higher School Certificate in both subjects, although his reference from the senior mathematics master, Mr. Sheen, was somewhat bland:

> John Eveleigh Bolton has been my pupil during the past two years. His work has been at all times neat and careful and he has shown himself to be capable of sustained effort and of good work. His manner is pleasant and in my dealings with him I have found him honest and trustworthy.

In addition, John was an active sportsman while at school, being best at cricket (as might be expected given his father's interest), winning his 2nd XI colours, and also tennis.

ACCOUNTANCY ARTICLES

When John left school in 1937 he became articled to a firm of accountants, Bernard S. Richardson of 195 Wolverhampton Street, Dudley, to train as a chartered accountant. At that time articles were for a period of five years, and included attendance at Wolverhampton Technical College and further study through the Accountancy Correspondence College. However after starting his articles in September 1937 the War intervened and in December 1940, at the age of 20, he joined the Royal Navy. Just before doing this, however, he had taken the Intermediate Examination of the Institute of Chartered Accountants, which he passed with distinction, with his name appearing high on the list of successes, placing him 40th out of 260 candidates. At this time the examinees were graded in order and the results published in the newspapers. Moreover, Mr. Richardson, the principal of the firm, was later to say of him:

> From the commencement of his service with me, Mr. Bolton showed considerable promise of being able to undertake responsibility, so that in less than the usual time he was doing work of a senior clerk though young in years, and was able to acquire a varied experience in relation to the accounts of different types of businesses, including those of a Local Authority, namely, the County Borough of Dudley.
>
> Mr. Bolton always impressed me as a gentleman of outstanding ability with a strong personality and a manner both engaging and frank. His character is excellent.

This experience was undoubtedly extremely valuable in later life. And to be a senior clerk, supervising audits, by the time he was 20, was an indication of a rare skill.

WORLD WAR II

John joined the Navy, not because he was a natural sailor but probably because the Navy often appeared to offer a more interesting, varied, and adventurous life than either of the other two services. He also caustically noted that drowning was the least traumatic way to die in war. He joined as an Ordinary Seaman in December 1940, but was commissioned in the Royal Naval Volunteer Reserve (RNVR) in November 1941 and gained promotion to Lieutenant in October 1943, serving as Executive and Navigating Officer in destroyers until mid-1946.

The three main destroyers on which Bolton served were the *Bedouin*, the *Wilton*, and the *Childers*. In these ships, mainly used on convoy escort duties, the manoeuvrability and speed of the destroyers was their greatest strength. As an officer he gained experience in the management of men from all stations of life. And like many men in similar situations, his wartime experiences were very important to him throughout the rest of his life. He was on the *Bedouin* as an Ordinary Seaman until he was commissioned. The *Bedouin* was mainly involved in operations in Northern waters against enemy shipping, but was also engaged in the hunting of the Bismarck, and was slightly damaged in the Battle of Narvik. The *Bedouin* was sunk in the Mediterranean in August 1942 after John had left her.

His main ship, from February 1942 until March 1945, was HMS *Wilton*, a Type II HUNT-Class Escort Destroyer launched in October 1941. This large class of destroyers had a length of 279' 10", a beam of 31' 6", a draught of 8' 3" and a speed of 27 knots or 31 mph, with a complement of 164. The *Wilton* was named after a hunt in Dorset. One of the lessons learned at the expense of many lives and the loss of many merchant ships was that the survival of Great Britain in war depended on the safe passage of shipping to and from the United Kingdom. This requirement was satisfied when after much reluctance the convoy system was introduced in 1917. Ships in convoy then had to be escorted by warships able to counter the threat of submarines and surface craft. By 1938 it was clear that the Royal Navy did not have sufficient suitable ships to meet this obvious threat, to which a third dimension had also been added. The use of aircraft by any enemy to attack shipping simply made the need for escorts of even greater importance.

For this reason a new class of Escort Destroyers was authorised. These ships were needed to be available for service without an inordinate delay and had to be armed to deal with the submarine, surface, and air threats. They were designed to carry two or three twin, four-inch gun mountings capable of dealing with the submarine, surface, and aircraft threats. For anti-submarine attacks the design called for 60 depth charges with two throwers and two sets of rails. The speed requirement called for in the build specification was between 28 and 30 knots. In all, 86 HUNT Class were built and, apart from the differences in gun and torpedo fits, had the same type of propulsion machinery with a shaft horsepower of 19,000 driving two shafts. A larger complement of 168 was required in the ships with three twin mountings or with the torpedo tubes.

Once in service the HUNT Class played a vital part in sea operations. Their four-inch armament with a dual purpose anti-aircraft and surface capability made them effective escorts. All types did however have the disadvantage of requiring frequent fuelling during long voyages, as for example when used for escorting Russian convoys. They were not comfortable ships and their accommodation was cramped. The first ships completed were used for coastal convoy escorts but as more became available the HUNT Class were deployed in the Mediterranean and in the Arctic. A heavy price was paid for the contribution made. Nineteen ships were lost in action and a further six damaged beyond economic repair with 17 others being out of operational use due to action damage which needed many months under repair.

With the *Wilton* Bolton participated in some of the most intense naval operations of World War II. The Arctic convoys to Russia were particularly gruelling due to the extremely cold conditions, which got down to 60 degrees below freezing. John once told his sister that there was no point in taking a hot drink up to the bridge as it would have frozen before getting there; she made him a pair of silk gloves to go underneath his normal pair to help keep out the cold. The cold was not just a problem for people; it was critical to keep the upper deck clear of ice and snow by means of axes and steam hoses or the ship could become top heavy. Moreover in the frequent gales the seas became violent with huge waves, making the ships roll as much as 30 degrees to port or starboard, with some even turning over.

Of the Russian convoys which *Wilton* escorted as part of the 6th Destroyer Flotilla, namely Convoys 13, 14, 17, and 18, Convoy PQ17 in June–July 1942 was one of the worst maritime disasters of the War, in that of 36 merchant ships which set out, only two returned. The largest of the German capital ships including the *Tirpitz* were located in the north of Norway, and for fear of them the Admiralty decided to withdraw support from the convoy when it was above the North Cape, ordering it to disperse, with disastrous results. Roger Hill DSO, DSC, RN, in command of another destroyer, HMS *Ledbury*, admitted that he had never come to terms with leaving the convoy without protection, echoed in his excellent book *Destroyer Captain* (1975):

> There were 23 ships sunk in that PQ17, 190 seamen killed, 400–500 aircraft were lost, about 300 tanks and 100,000 tons of war material. That's what resulted from that Admiralty signal. It was really terrible, even now I have never got over it, because for the Navy to leave the Merchant Navy like that was simply terrible. The American cruiser people ashore, of course they just said 'The Limeys are yellow' and they all had fights and had to have leave on different nights and so on, and the *Tirpitz* was not within three or four hundred miles of the convoy. She came out eventually, but not that day, the next day I think, or the following day. She was sighted by a submarine which made a signal, the Germans intercepted that signal and called her straight back to harbour. There was no threat to the convoy at all except from the air and all these poor merchant ships, one merchant ship signalled 'I can see 7 submarines approaching me on the surface' and there was continual air attack. It was simply awful.

It would be very surprising if John Bolton and the crew of the *Wilton* did not feel exactly the same as Hill.

Almost immediately after this, in August 1942 the *Wilton* participated in Operation Pedestal to force supplies through to save Malta from having to surrender. Malta had had a very difficult time due to its strategic location, and in April 1942 had been awarded a collective George Cross for its courage and determination during the siege in the early part of the War, which Operation Pedestal was designed to break. Fourteen of the fastest merchant ships available were supported by the largest task force for any convoy during the War, including two battleships, four aircraft carriers, seven cruisers, and 33 destroyers. In spite of this support, the Germans and Italians also realized the convoy's significance and relentlessly attacked with aircraft, surface ships, and submarines, with *Wilton* herself being dive-bombed nine times on August 11–12, although only receiving superficial damage. The aircraft carrier *Eagle* and two cruisers were lost, as well as nine of the merchant ships, and other naval ships were badly damaged. But five merchant ships managed to reach Malta, including the *Ohio*, the largest tanker then afloat, which survived the worst of the pounding and was towed into Valetta Harbour lashed between two destroyers, finally sinking just as the last of her fuel was recovered. Although a serious tactical defeat, the supplies which did get through enabled Malta to stay in the War and act as a base from which to attack German supply lines to North Africa, turning it into a significant strategic victory.

After Operation Pedestal the *Wilton* stayed mainly in the Mediterranean and there were other key contributions which *Wilton* made: supporting Allied landings in both North Africa and Sicily; attacking the U443 and U223 with depth charges in conjunction with other destroyers, blockading Tunisia to prevent the escape of enemy forces; and providing naval gunfire to support the capture of Corfu and attacking an enemy motorboat base on the island of Lussinpiccolo, both in the Adriatic. In this latter engagement, the *Wilton* went in to point-blank range to destroy enemy gun emplacements and was slightly damaged by machine-gun fire. On December 12, 1944, she landed a reconnaissance party of Army and RAF personnel for a survey of the airfields at Zadar in Dalmatia and later also took Field Marshal Alexander to Greece. There were several times when the ship was subject to air or submarine attacks, and on November 9, 1942, she was lucky when a torpedo passed under the ship during close support duties for the landings at Algiers. Bolton himself served variously as watch-keeping, anti-submarine, navigator, and signals officer until March 1945.

Many years later, a new *Wilton* was commissioned in 1973, this time a minehunter and indeed the largest vessel yet built in glass-reinforced plastics. John and Gay could not attend the commissioning, but instead they were very happy to host a reunion of some of those who had served on the previous *Wilton* at a lunch at Brook Place. The reunion was such a success that another was held three months later in Captain Northey's house. Lt. Pat Fletcher sent his apologies but also some recollections in 1973 of his time on the *Wilton*, including:

> The ship's company of 180 lived in extremely cramped conditions, many of them having to sleep on the decks or on some tables as there was not

enough room for them to sling hammocks. The mess decks, heads and bathrooms were very crowded, crude and inadequate by present day standards. The food was plentiful but inevitably monotonous. But in comparison the weather was in general reasonably pleasant, even in winter.

After the *Wilton*, John had a short period on HMS *Javelin* as navigating officer returning from the Mediterranean. Finally, HMS *Childers* gave him experience of a different sort in supervising parts of the construction of destroyers and in Naval accounting methods prior to and during its launch in 1945, after which he served on her as navigating officer, again in the Mediterranean, until leaving the Navy in 1946. As he put it of his experiences, in the Navy he learned to say 'Sir' with 60 different shades of meaning, and talked in a letter about frequently 'scampering up to the crow's nest' of a destroyer in the Atlantic in 1941. He was awarded the Distinguished Service Cross in June 1945 on the recommendation of his commanding officer on HMS *Wilton*, Lieutenant Commander G. G. Marten DSC, who was later to become Naval Equerry to His Majesty King George VI. Marten wrote the following testimony in support of John's application to Harvard:

> Naturally I got to know him very well, and without hesitation I can give you a good report of him as far as the qualities required in a naval officer are concerned. Of his intellectual ability it is not easy for me to judge, but to the extent that his duties called for intellectual abilities he showed it, and in his interests and reading I remember that he was enterprising and always seeking after knowledge.
>
> In my eyes his outstanding quality was reliability, both in his work and as a man, and a good many nights I slept the better for it. He is extremely thorough and orderly-minded, and so completely trustworthy that I know he would never let anyone down. Nothing was too much trouble for him, even when he was tired, and I always considered myself exceptionally fortunate to have such a man as one of my officers. Always extremely loyal to me and to his shipmates, secret or confidential information was always absolutely safe with him, and his honesty and integrity are beyond question.
>
> He is a pleasant personality—quiet, well-mannered and easy for anyone to get on with, and with it he has plenty of strength of character and sound judgment. As an officer he has the invaluable quality of never getting flustered, either in his day-to-day work or in action. For his coolness, as much as his efficiency, I recommended him twice for a decoration. . . .
>
> I am very glad to be able to give you such a good report of him, and having known him so well I can assure you that in him you have a really first class chap.

Bolton was awarded the DSC for 'gallantry in the face of the enemy and setting an example of wholehearted devotion to duty that upheld the highest tradition of the Royal Navy'. In addition, his accelerated promotion to Lieutenant in October 1943 was another measure of his performance. He also had very positive reports from his various captains on the *Wilton* and the *Childers*, all saying that he had conducted himself 'to my entire satisfaction'. His first captain on the *Wilton*, Lt. Cdr. Mowbray, called him 'a very keen and promising young officer with plenty of brains and intelligence', while Lt. Cdr. Marten, his second captain on the *Wilton* noted of him:

> A thorough and conscientious officer, at all times unflurried by events. An exceptional, capable navigator and experienced A/S officer with a great interest in both departments. Has been a strong and steady influence in the ship, and after three years has shown no sign of slackening in zeal and devotion to duty.

Lt. Cdr. Bailey of the *Childers* called him 'a most conscientious officer and an efficient navigator', and in a personal letter in May 1946, wrote:

> I trust that you had a good trip home and that you are enjoying your well-earned leave. You certainly worked like a Trojan aboard here and I have missed your discerning eye a lot. As for your Data Book, that will be a monument to you until the day that this ship reaches the scrap heap.

As well as these professional attributes and compliments, he had a useful ability to entertain his colleagues by 'riffing' jazz on the piano, and hence earned himself the nickname of 'Bing'. By any standards, he had 'a good war'. His date of release from service was July 30, 1946.

The War was not without profit for Bolton. His work as a navigator made him familiar with radio and radar and stimulated his interest in electronics. Moreover, his interest in small businesses grew as a result of serving in small ships with a complement of less than 200 people where companionship and flexibility of mind were essential to efficient operation.

CAMBRIDGE

After his naval service ended in the middle of 1946 Bolton decided to go to Cambridge, rather than going back to his accountancy articles. On his return to civilian life, he was uncertain about his future and talked things over with his old friend Charles Hayward, who was to play an important role when he was with Solartron. He had first met Hayward, a prosperous industrialist with origins in Wolverhampton, back in 1936 when John was 16 and taking his Higher School Certificate in mathematics and physics before becoming articled to a chartered accountant. As a result of these discussions on demobilization he decided to go up to Trinity College Cambridge to read economics. John always wanted nothing less than the best and gained admission on the strength of his own academic achievements and an excellent and gallant war record. However it was also, if not mainly, his drive, his persistence, and his determination never to take 'no' for an answer that won the day. There had been no previous family connection with either Cambridge or Trinity, but John's son Nicholas was also to go to Trinity (and obtain a first in engineering), as did his sister's three sons, so that Trinity became something of a family college. He read economics from 1946–1948; these were the days before business management was considered a 'proper' subject of study at most British universities. John financed himself through a service scholarship, and like many servicemen took his honours degree in two years. Cambridge in that period was a very exciting place, full of people with exceptional talents, many of whom, like John, had outstanding war records.

Trinity was founded in 1546 and is the largest college in Cambridge, with strong Royal Family connections and indeed considered aristocratic. Nevertheless it has high academic standards and boasts connections with 32 Nobel Prize winners to say nothing of many other eminent alumni such as Sir Isaac Newton. John was certainly interested in his subject, as manifested by becoming President of the Economic Society at the University, but he was also very active in the wider aspects of university life. He participated in debates, played squash and rowed. He was later to remember:

> my only real success on the river at Cambridge. It was in the Lent 'bump' races and I rowed in an ex-servicemen's gentlemen's eight—that meant we didn't train and most of us smoked. By a superhuman effort we managed to bump the boat in front of us on four successive nights as we climbed the 'ladder' and 'won our oars'. As we slumped, exhausted over our oars, our coach bicycled up and said 'Well done! You did everything wrong, but you must have done it a damn sight harder than the other chaps.'

But perhaps his most important contributions were in organizational roles as Treasurer of the Trinity College Student Union, Treasurer of the College Boat Club, and for two years as Joint Treasurer of the Boat Club's May Ball Committee. These treasurer roles obviously linked back to the skills he had developed in his accountancy articles, and were ones which few undergraduates would have possessed as well as not being popular due to their 'boring' if necessary requirements. Still, to be treasurer of all three bodies indicates that his skills were recognized, as well as showing commitment on his part. David Hinks, the Junior Bursar of Trinity, who had an oversight of these student activities, commented on his contribution, again in a reference in support of his application to Harvard:

> In all these capacities, and particularly in the last (because in that case the management of quite a large enterprise, with a turnover of some

thousands of pounds, is carried on almost entirely by the undergraduates with very general supervision from me) he has plainly shewn me that he has a gift for the business-like conduct of affairs, and a power of accountancy, far above what I should expect to find in the men who usually fill these positions. I rate his competence very high, and say with confidence that he is peculiarly capable of profiting by a course in Business Administration such as Harvard can provide.

Following up on these business interests, during his Cambridge vacations he visited various manufacturing plants and in the summer of 1948 he worked as a senior clerk for a chartered accountant probably returning to Richardson's, possibly considering whether he might go back to the profession if his Harvard application did not succeed, or perhaps just to earn some money during the vacation.

But Bolton's chief recollection of Cambridge was an intellectual shock which altered his attitude to the world around him, according to a profile of him in the New Scientist in 1958. He was reading an essay in his last term when his supervisor interrupted him. 'Bolton, you are telling me what Keynes thought' he said, 'But it is all here in his book [taking the book off the shelf and leafing through it], in his beautiful prose. Bolton, I want to know what *you* think' [pointing a finger at him]. A commonplace rebuke, no doubt, but Bolton never forgot it, and tried to put it into action. Indeed he was later to say that it was the single most important thing that he learned at Cambridge.

Of his degree papers, Sraffa wrote to him saying 'It appears that you did poor standard papers in Essay, Principles and Money, but good standard papers in both Industry and Labour. The latter were good II(1) standard. D. H. Robertson, Professor of Political Economy in the University wrote:

> I consider that the class obtained by Mr. J E Bolton in Economics Tripos Part II was satisfactory, especially in view of the number of social and organizational activities which he managed to combine with his reading for the Tripos. I also consider that his previous experience, both in accountancy and in the Navy, and his energetic and enterprising temperament, render him peculiarly well fitted to take up the place which has been reserved for him at the Harvard School of Business Administration and I hope that it will be made possible for him to do so.

MARRIAGE

By the time he reached maturity John had become a handsome man at some 5' 11" in height and some 11 stones 11 lbs in weight at the time of his Cambridge 'bumps'. He was highly intelligent and good at sports, had shown considerable leadership skills, was a useful pianist, and smoked a pipe (later it was to be large cigars). No wonder then that he was attractive to the opposite sex. Thus it is not surprising that before John set off for Harvard there was another major development in his life when on August 21, 1948, he married Gabrielle (Gay) Healey Hall, the daughter of Joseph Hall, a company director, and his wife Minnie. Hall Brothers (West Bromwich) Ltd were iron and steel stockholders at the Eagle Works, Greets Green, West Bromwich, and the company was run by the two brothers, her father Joseph and her uncle William, who employed Gay, then aged 19, after her father died in 1945. Together with her elder sister Una, Gay was a significant shareholder in the company under a deed of trust from her father, and was therefore able to bring a not insubstantial amount of money into the marriage once she had reached the age of 25. However, neither her uncle nor her sister were very good to her and she came into the marriage without strong family connections, although she remained devoted to Una.

Gay and John had met at the Wolverhampton Tennis Club and the marriage took place at St Bartholomew's Church in Penn on 21 August 1948, with John's brother Nigel as best man. Gay accompanied John to Harvard, and indeed they had their honeymoon en route to the US. Their first child, Nicholas, was conceived there in 1949, although Gay went back to her family home to give birth. A second child, Athalie, followed in 1951 after their return to Britain. John and Gay had an extremely happy marriage, mostly spent at their elegant country house, Brook Place, in Chobham in Surrey, where they lived for the next 35 years and proved themselves gracious hosts at numerous social engagements. They had wanted to live near London and planned it out on maps—not too far from central London, the airport, the coast—and chose the Guildford area, finding a substantial Carolean house at Chobham, Brook Place, of which much more in the final chapter. In spite of buying Brook Place with funds from Gay's trust, there is a note in John's handwriting of the detailed expenses of setting up home, from big items such as a refrigerator, a cooker, and carpets down to pots and pans, a torch, Christmas lights, and plugs, an indication that they had not been at all well off until Gay's trust came through.

HARVARD BUSINESS SCHOOL

Going to Harvard Business School (HBS) was to be the making of John Bolton. It was an extremely unusual thing to do at that time when managerial abilities were seen as inherited rather than learned or developed, when British industry saw little benefit in management education, and when management in industry was hardly a popular career choice at the ancient universities. There was only one other British student in Bolton's MBA class, Christopher Saunders, an Oxford graduate with whom John was to keep in contact when they both returned to Britain, and only nine in any of Harvard's programmes during John's time there. Harvard was expensive to attend; indeed John had great difficulty raising the money to go to HBS, writing to a wide range of possible funding sources and receiving negative replies before conjuring money from a Cassel Travelling Fellowship in 1948. These fellowships usually supported foreign language study, but John managed to persuade the sponsors that business management was a foreign language in Britain at that time! In other words, getting to HBS required considerable initiative and ingenuity. He went there because his Cambridge friend, Harry Newman, had been there, and Sir Noel Hall, then Principal of the Administrative Staff College at Henley, agreed that it was the best place to train for business.

Harvard Business School hardly requires an explanation. It is unquestionably the most famous business school in the world, even if 'league tables' sometimes rank others higher. It operates, as it always has, with the case method of teaching, which many regard as the best way of bringing reality and experience into the classroom. It provides a huge network of key people across the world for its graduates to relate to. And it does things on a scale for which other institutions can only sigh in envy. Thus much later JEB ruefully compared the 20 or so staff in the HBS fundraising office with the minimal personnel resources which Surrey University could devote to fundraising.

The case study approach was described in an article in the *Sunday Times* in 1963:

There are on the School's books some 25,000 cases, each a problem which actually occurred in some American—or foreign—company. Each has been fully documented by a member of the faculty, after several weeks' discussion with the firm concerned, and each year 300 new ones are added and 200 others brought up to date.

A class of anything up to 90 students is presented with the case by its professor. The members study its full details, go away and discuss it in groups of about eight, and come back to offer—in a classroom designed like a small amphitheatre—their ideas on how the company should have solved its difficulties.

They may be arguing over whether a certain man should have been sacked; whether capital should have been invested in a certain way; whether a certain method of advertising is desirable or not. There is no answer book. 'The most fascinating thing' said one graduate, 'is that you can find a class emerging with eight possible decisions, all of which could have worked'.

In their two years, students are presented with about 1000 cases. 'It means' says the Dean, 'that we force each man to face up to a thousand decisions, logically and relatively unemotionally, using the tools, figures and concepts available to him. We teach him how to make a decision and defend it—and how to deal with human beings'.

JEB found Harvard to be tough: 'We worked eighty hours seven days a week. I found that American educational standards were no lower than ours'. Bolton found himself studying every kind of organization 'from Joe's Snack Bar to United States Steel'. He performed brilliantly at HBS, being elected as a Baker Scholar in 1949, which is the highest academic honour at the School, elected by the faculty from amongst those in the top five per cent of the class according to end-of-first-year grades. (Christopher Saunders was also elected a Baker Scholar at the same time, quite an achievement for them as the only two Brits on the course and perhaps not too bad a comment on Oxbridge academic standards.) John was also elected to the HBS Century Club for achieving first year honours; the Century Club was founded in 1933 to enable second year students to meet with key figures outside the world of business and has an alumni group for later support and networking. These achievements were all the more meritorious when it is remembered that John had a wife and small baby during his time there, although Gay helped considerably by doing the typing. As well as being a family man and living off campus, another feature that differentiated John and was remembered by Christopher Saunders was his ownership of a Cadillac, the most expensive of American cars at the time and not one normally driven by students, even at Harvard. It was a large black car and although admittedly second hand was very smart and gave the impression to the other students that John was wealthier than he was in reality. John and Gay also managed to have a good social life and were good hosts; Christopher also remembered that they were happy to host a girl-friend of his who had come up from New York for the weekend. He also noted: 'an abiding memory is John's mild and even gentle manner—at the same time one would be aware that he was a powerful and able personality'.

HBS students were expected to obtain some work experience in the summer recess between their two years. So, as well as his business school work, in the summer of 1949 he contacted manufacturers in Britain, and having formed a firm of Manufacturers' Agents, undertook several market research assignments, subsequently arranging distribution in the New England area. Moreover, he formed an antiques importing firm and exhibited at Boston Antique Shows. In addition, during 1949–50, he did research into British export problems in the Dollar area. These showed a great deal of initiative, entrepreneurship, and self-confidence, as well as helping with the costs.

An interesting and important episode at HBS was his membership of a group set up to examine the way in which students used their time. It was set up at the suggestion of the Student Association and with the support of the Dean's Office, and its eight members were chosen from the higher grade bracket of the 1950 class; four of them, including John, were Baker Scholars. Clearly, it was something of an honour to be selected, and it appears from the amount of handwritten material (much of it in red pencil) in John's handwriting and written comments by others in the group on 'Bolton's Notes' as though he played an important part in the preparation of the ultimate report. It had 12 discussion meetings, each lasting about two hours during March, April, and May 1950, apart from any preparatory or writing-up work, so a considerable effort was put into it. The range of topics discussed was quite wide and challenging: the growth of extra-curricular clubs and activities; poor preparation for classes; apparent frustration about the value of the second year; the impact of job worries on students' work; the limitations of the case methods; the workload imbalance between different courses; and other issues of a similar nature. The report was quite aggressive, blaming both the professoriate for excessive workloads, lack of awareness of the content of other courses and therefore overlap, and ignorance of what motivates students, and also students for cutting classes, not shaving and not being prepared for classes, and going on to challenge issues of the School's philosophy on assessment policies, an 'academic' versus a 'business' approach, and what the group saw as an often inverse relationship between research and teaching abilities. It certainly would have given food for thought to the School's administration, and if, as seems likely, John did indeed play a large leadership role in its preparation, it would have marked him out and contributed to the respect he was accorded by successive Deans. Coming near the end of his second year, it was a culmination of a hugely successful stay at Harvard.

John certainly seems to have made an impact on his peer group. One of his old classmates, Ed Anderson from Georgia wrote to him in the 1980s saying that he was coming to London: 'Years ago I was a classmate of yours at Harvard Business School (1948–50). You may not remember but I sat next to you in Section D and listened to your brilliant and erudite comments on business cases'. Needless to say, he was invited to Brook Place and a car sent to meet him at Heathrow.

In Bolton's HBS first-year final grades, he received a distinction in Administrative Practices and Finance and a Higher Pass in the other five papers, sufficient for him to qualify as a Baker Scholar. In the second year he received four higher passes and one pass, in Investment Management II. As he noted in a letter he wrote to a lecturer at Bristol Polytechnic in 1981, he took the 'Management of New Enterprises' course at HBS and 'this not only changed my outlook, but helped to guide my way into the Solartron Electronic Group at its formative stage'. Harvard also gave him a valuable network both in the US and Britain. Membership in London of the Harvard Club and the separate Harvard Business School Club (of which Christopher Saunders was secretary in the 1960s) were two of his most cherished links.

RESEARCH IN BRITAIN

After Harvard JEB spent a year in Britain doing research for HBS on British industry, which also enabled him to look for a suitable job for himself, of which more in the following chapter. Just how this year came about and was activated is not entirely clear. A letter from the President and Fellows of Harvard College noted that at their meeting on June 21, 1950, John was appointed as 'Research Assistant in Business Administration, to serve from September 1, 1950 through June 30, 1951'. However, a further letter noted that at their meeting of September 18, 1950, the President and Fellows voted to rescind this appointment. Yet the research went ahead and with the cooperation of Harvard.

It appears that what happened was that there had been discussion of a possible higher degree for which the research would have been the fieldwork basis, and that the assistantship was tied to the degree. This would have meant residence at Harvard. But the Boltons, and particularly Gay, felt that they wanted to settle down back in Britain, and this was incompatible with the assistantship, so John had to withdraw from it.

The basis of the research was to collect case study material in British industry for use at HBS, with a view to helping students 'obtain a better understanding of the industrial situation as it affects business decisions and administrative problems in Britain', to quote the memo proposing the setting up the project, which went on: 'In particular, it is hoped to highlight some of the essential differences between administrative problems in Britain and the U.S. and to indicate some of the underlying reasons behind these differences'. It then suggested some areas that might be looked at, and noted that JEB would hold discussions with interested members of the Institute of Industrial Administration (not the BIM!) and various other organizations. But perhaps the key sentence was:

> Mr. Bolton is convinced that America seriously lacks detailed information about, and understanding of, foreign business conditions; this shortcoming is leading to much misunderstanding and also retards the progress of and reduces the effectiveness of efforts to exchange information between countries.

The report was entitled: 'Preliminary Report on the Possibility of Conducting Case Research in Britain', but in reality it was much wider in scope, no less than a suggestion, in fact almost a demand, that America and especially HBS should change its attitude to foreign economies and business contexts, 'that proposed solutions to foreign social and business problems were most unlikely to be applicable, in the foreign countries, if the analyses and recommendations for action were drawn from an essentially "American" base of thinking'. Indeed, he went on 'I feel that Harvard Business School has a signal responsibility in *giving the lead* in promoting studies which will lead to greater understanding'. What he did was to spend a month and parts of the two succeeding months in Joseph Lucas, the electrical parts manufacturers, talking with directors and managers, foremen and workers, before widening out to talk to a range of other British organizations, governmental, institutional and industrial, large and small. He then identified differences in operation and differences in attitude, and saw the opportunity to devise case studies to help to elicit the differences, and ultimately saw the goal as being to internationalize the operation of management, with HBS playing a lead role and America's historic mission in the world being a lever.

Having sent the report back to HBS, he had a very positive response to it from Andrew Towl, the School's Assistant Director of Research, who wrote on July 31, 1951:

> Considering the merits of your report, I am not at all satisfied that these brief comments begin to let you know how effective your report is. It really has been quite timely in helping to move forward our thinking about this whole area of enlarging our understanding of foreign problems. We do look forward to carrying on with you the next steps which will surely emerge from this effort.

JEB replied on August 12 with a long letter which began:

> Very many thanks for your kind words about my report. Though I realize that my recommendations imply a major change in the educational policy of the School. . . . Nevertheless I firmly believe that immense value would result if some way could be found of investigating them further.

He went on to note that he expected to move to Surrey shortly and to take a financial interest in a small electronics company near London. Towl replied again on August 20 welcoming John's move to Surrey and continuing:

> Among the steps that we have taken regarding your report is to call it to the attention of the editors of the Harvard Business Review . . . They do agree that you are talking about something of great importance and something which should be of great interest to American business. You have the seed of a tremendously important idea, and I am concerned that we get it planted in the most fertile field.

JEB was not being arrogant in making such suggestions, and HBS clearly took them very seriously. The later case studies of Solartron were part of the ideas for making contact with foreign institutions and cultures. And many years later in 1963, when John was a member of the Visiting Committee of Harvard Business School, there was a meeting at which the main theme was 'The Role of Harvard Business School in the Business Community in the Free World'. It would be pleasant to surmise that there would be some connection between JEB's report and the theme of this meeting.

His research report was crystallized in 'Report from Britain', an article which he wrote for the Harvard Business School Bulletin (not the Review) in the Spring 1952 issue. In it, he noted that he had concentrated on the differences between situations in Britain and the United States, especially differences which prevented the standard of living in Britain rising to that in the US. Recognizing that he was generalizing from the typical British situation, he put forward the following distinctions:

- Greater complexity of the average administrative situation arising principally from a smaller degree of standardization and a smaller total market for most industries
- Less effective production organizations because of relatively uneconomic product specification, less efficient use of labour and machinery and less conscious planning of workflow
- Less planned coordination of the tasks facing management, based partly on the above factors, but also on education and training courses being too specialized, a wider division between the workshop and the office, less planning ahead from the retailer to the foreman, less attention paid to the efficiency of the purchasing function, and less reliability in many raw materials and components
- Overfull employment with shortages of various grades of labour
- More government controls, operated remotely by civil servants
- Higher taxation, both of profits and incomes
- A widespread lack of competition
- Less aspiration to a high material standard of life, with many negative attitudes toward change
- Less productivity consciousness in industry
- Relationships at industry, company, and personal levels are more formal than in the US, stemming from the Victorian master–servant relationship
- An elaborate system of highly specialized craft guilds, professional bodies, and manufacturers' associations, together with a relative remoteness of the Universities from the world of industry has resulted in a different attitude toward management education. Moreover social attitudes toward business have affected individuals' choice of education and career, with the Diplomatic Service, the Church, the Armed Forces and the 'professions' ranking higher in social desirability than industry.
- Attitudes toward competition suggest that it is not quite respectable, with that in America being seen as a ruthless, soulless thing which Britain should not copy
- Attitudes toward foreigners are more guarded and suspicious than in the US, with a defensive reaction toward recent decline.

He accepted that attitudes and practices were changing, but were 'likely to be far too gradual for the compelling needs of the situation. . . . greater understanding of the economic realities of the British situation has yet to be brought to a large number of businessmen, as well as to the population as a whole'. And:

Lastly, the remoteness of the older and more influential universities from the educational needs of industry towards the development of management skills and industrial efficiency . . . paradoxically reacts back on lower future incomes for the seats of learning, since, in an increasing degree, their future source of income must come, directly or indirectly, from industry—whose problems are not considered suitable for the best men of the next generation to study. The gulf is being breached, but far, far, too slowly for the pressing needs of industry.

These perceptive and highly critical views were to be echoed by other writers over the following years as the British economy fell further behind not just the US, but European countries including former adversaries. He was in effect creating a challenge to America and Harvard Business School more specifically to recognize the differences with the rest of the world, and to provide leadership in ameliorating them. The editorial prologue to the report made this point:

> . . . when Mr. Bolton got back home, he started digging. In the back of his head was the realization that America's role had changed in a decade from a relatively passive position to one demanding dynamic world leadership. And the change demanded a deeper understanding of foreign economic situations and their associated causes. But so suddenly has it happened that Americans have had no time to acquire the 'tools' for such understanding. Thus generously conceived foreign policies have been ineffective, and there has been frustration at home and distrust abroad.
>
> Hence Mr. Bolton's main thesis: there must be greater understanding both in America and abroad of the complex and individual factors in the economic lives of older countries. Else there cannot develop the essential nucleus of informed and dynamic opinion from which alone the most fruitful policies can arise.

At the end of the article in the Bulletin, there was an amusing justification for the Bolton thesis and challenge to HBS. The Research Directorate at HBS sent a draft to JEB for the author's OK. To hurry it back they enclosed their airmail-stamped envelope. But of course this was quite unhelpful, because American stamps were no earthly use in Britain!

It seems very likely that this year made him think very deeply about Britain in relation to America, and created the framework of beliefs and the need for action which were to drive him for much of the rest of his life. Even so, it is impressive for an MBA student to both see the need for and to have the confidence to urge it in such positive terms. Another example of the confidence which his Harvard experience gave him was in a letter he wrote to Winston Churchill, at that time leader of the opposition, about steel nationalization.

Moreover, it also seems likely that the report which he wrote emerging out of this year, in conjunction with his work on the review committee, impressed the senior echelons of Harvard Business School, and also created friendships on a personal level. He was to have extremely good contacts with successive Deans of HBS over the years, especially Deans Baker and Fouraker, extending to staying with each other when in the other's country. He also wrote to Donald K. David, the Dean in his MBA days, at a time when David had gone on to become President of the Ford Foundation, expressing gratitude for inspiring him during his period at Harvard. The fact that he was not afraid of telling Harvard Business School what it ought to do, in a courteous way of course, was probably the reason he became greatly esteemed by the faculty and especially the Deans at HBS, leading them to provide him with support in pursuit of his causes and to invite him to be a member of the HBS Visiting Committee, which he did from 1962–68. The Visiting Committee, which reports to the Board of Overseers of Harvard University on the state of the Business School, is comprised of the good and the great in American industry and commerce, and it was a major honour for a foreigner to be invited to sit on it. His own designation was as 'British business statesman and a prime mover of professional management education to meet the economic challenges of today'.

The year also gave him an opportunity to look for work for himself, and to this end he created a CV and defined his interests as follows:

> I am interested in the financial side of business, if possible with a concern having English interests, and offering an opportunity to use wide background. Slight preference for a manufacturing company or import/export company, of medium size, connected with a relatively new industry, e.g. electronics, alloys, or their industrial applications. Alternatively, a management consultancy firm.

He looked for a growth industry because he felt that it would be easier to make a mark in a growth industry, and considered aircraft, plastics, and alloys, but decided against them all because 'the big boys call the tune'. The organization which he chose fitted fairly well with these specifications, and we now turn to the company in which he made his name and fortune, Solartron.

2   Solartron

INTRODUCTION

The story of Solartron is a fascinating story in its own right as well as being an important part of John Bolton's career. Solartron was a significant part of the new growth of the electronics industry in the 1950s and was a very exciting place to work at a time of new opportunities and heady expansion in the industry. The danger was of growing too fast and not linking the financial results with the rate of growth, and this is what happened. This chapter initially looks at various aspects of the company's operations up to 1958, and then takes the story beyond 1958 to 1965 when John left, covering the period when the strains were becoming apparent.

ORIGINS AND PEOPLE

Two young electronic engineers called Eddie Ponsford and Leslie Copestick started Solartron in an old stable behind the local Odeon Cinema in Kingston in 1948, having scraped together a few hundred pounds and set up as makers of electronic test instruments. Both had been apprenticed in the electronics industry and had worked on the development of radar, and were aware of the shortcomings of existing equipment. They started with only one employee and took on Government repair, development, and manufacture contracts. Their company was initially called The Electronic Construction Co., then six months later, in July 1948, it became Solartron Laboratory Instruments Ltd. The name Solartron came from a mixture of solar and 'tron' from electronic. At the beginning of 1949 the sum of £5000 was introduced, a move was made to a small factory of 3000 square feet at Kingston and the firm began to grow in numbers. Two years later came the introduction of their first proprietary instrument which the company was invited to exhibit at the Physical Society's Exhibition, regarded as a mark of acceptance in the sphere of electronics. Many of the founders' old associates were interested in joining, even at lower rates of pay, for the sake of what they could see as the potential to come, and were duly rewarded by executive positions and becoming employee-shareholders. The first year's trading turnover was £5000 and this amount was to double itself every year for a decade or so to come. There were many reasons for this auspicious start, but a key one was the enlightened policy of the two founders in terms of a strong teamwork ethic and uncompromising maintenance of the highest standards of performance for all Solartron products. As a consequence the name Solartron was from the start synonymous with quality and reliability throughout the world. However ploughing back the inevitably small profits was never going to be sufficient to finance the rapidly growing production and development, so new sources of funding were very welcome.

John Bolton must have been a dream come true when he became known to the founders of Solartron. Not only did he bring an unrivalled promise of industrial expertise to what was still a very small company, but he was also able to introduce £50,000 in additional capital, money which Gay had inherited from her father's business, which immediately made them the main shareholders. But it was also an excellent opportunity for John Bolton. When he joined in 1951, Solartron had some 20 employees, factory space of under 5000 square feet and assets of about £5000. As Peter Gorb said in introducing him at the Royal Society of Arts some 30 years later: 'he joined a small shaky business and what is more a business in the field of high technology. That was quite a remarkable thing for a business school graduate to do in 1951'. (He should have added 'especially for one of the top graduates of Harvard Business School who could have picked from a range of jobs in finance or multinationals, and in America rather than Britain'.) Bolton became financial director and then quite rapidly chairman and managing director of the Solartron Electronic Group when it was formed in 1954 to plan and coordinate the growing Solartron Group of companies.

If Bolton was the major catch at this time, he was not the only one to see the opportunities. John Crosse joined in 1952 and also provided valuable extra finance; indeed Bolton had introduced him to Solartron, having first met him at Wolverhampton's tennis club. Bolton was also later to put money into Crosse's own new company, Plasmec, which was founded with the aid of four Solartron foremen. Another Wolverhampton friend was Dennis Burton, who was to be a long-time director and to be the key to maintaining the spirit of the old Solartron well after Bolton had left. And there were others over the next few years: Eric Jones became commercial director in 1954 and was also to later found his own company into which JEB put money, although he was not such a satisfactory business partner as Crosse. Bowman Scott, who became personnel director, had been a wartime Army colonel at the age of 26 who was awarded an MBE for organizing signals for D-Day and was also a Harvard Business School graduate as well as having a first in engineering from Imperial College. He was to stay with John for a long time after Solartron through his role in Riverview Investments, the Bolton family venture capital fund. Christopher Bailey, another HBS graduate, the developer of the electronic reading machine for Solartron, was very creative on the technical side. And there were at least a couple of other Harvard MBAs in Peter Curry and Peter Hamilton; the former was introduced by Scott, while the latter was hired through Peter Curry. To have at least five HBS graduates, at a time when there were probably well less than 100 in the whole country, was quite exceptional for a company of its size. Arthur Middleton was sufficiently promising to be sent on the Harvard Middle Management Programme, while Laurie Malec ('a breath of fresh air') and R.B. Catherall from the research side were both impressive enough to be promoted onto the Solartron Board in the early 1960s. These were all energetic and go-getting managers, creating a team at the top well worthy of a much bigger business, and there were also other very talented people further down. Solartron was very far from being a one-man business, and indeed John Bolton would not have had it so, even if he was to become the well-recognized figurehead. And perhaps above all they were young, at a time when British industry was largely dominated by the elderly.

By the end of June 1953, five years after its foundation, Solartron had become well established with 110 personnel, 7,500 square feet of floor space, and a turnover of some £100,000 pa. There were then two companies, Solartron Laboratory Instruments Ltd (SLI) with a growing product line of electronic test instruments, and Solartron Engineering Ltd (SE), responsible for the precision engineering and metalwork aspect of Solartron products as well as doing some external contracting. In 1956 the average age of the Solartron directors was 38, that of departmental heads 31, and all personnel 32, while by 1960 there were some 120 in the management team, with an average age of 35, and the average for the total 1400 workforce was still 32. If the targets were ambitious, so were the people, and the sky was the limit in those heady days. Others thought so too, and in the *Electronic Journal* of December 1955, under the heading of 'Success Story', an article finished by saying that the achievements to date seen from the origins of eight years previously 'would have seemed beyond the bounds of all possibility'.

SOLARTRON IN THE ELECTRONICS INDUSTRY

To go back a little, as JEB did when he gave a talk at the London School of
Economics in 1958 on the growth of Solartron within the electronics industry,
the industry had grown out of the discovery by J.J. Thomson in 1898 of the
electron as a fundamental constituent of matter far smaller than the atom. In
1901 Marconi received the first transatlantic radio signal, in 1904 Fleming
invented the radio valve, and two years later Forest added a third element or
'grid' inside the valve, thus increasing the capacity for amplifying very small
currents. Baird added his work on television in the interwar period, and then
in World War II there was a rapid growth in applications of radio-related
techniques, especially radar and sonar. The electrical equipment, radio and
communications companies became involved in the birth of electronics, but
were joined by a number of smaller independent companies, often under the
stimulus of Government contracts. Solartron was one of these. It was a very
exciting industry, requiring intellectual vision and ingenuity as well as practical
skills and engineering inventiveness. As the journalist Harry Miller wrote in
'Triumphs of Enterprise No. 33', 'electronics has kindled the imagination and
ambitions of young men in industry. As an essential element in the automation of factory and office routines they see it as a frontier worth conquering'.

The electronic engineer converts all classes of natural phenomena such
as sound, movement, heat, light, and weight into electrical signals and with
the aid of valves develops equipment with which these phenomena can be
measured, analysed, and controlled very accurately. The thermistor bolom-
eter, for example, is so sensitive to heat radiation that it can detect a change
in temperature of one millionth of a degree and will register the heat from
the human body a quarter of a mile away. A number of product groups had
emerged by 1950:

- Radio and television
- Telecommunications
- Industrial control equipment
- Instrumentation for measurement
- Computing and data processing equipment
- Military equipment
- Radar and navigational aids

Within these groups, Solartron concentrated on that dealing with instrumentation. As the *New Scientist* put Solartron's position in the market

> From their firm base, the manufacture of electronics instruments of spe-
> cial accuracy, Solartron are free to manoeuvre in an intensely exciting
> area where bright ideas, elegant design, and bold anticipation pay divi-
> dends. Automation in its many forms—whether in digital computers,
> industrial control, or the new, surprisingly large business in radar simu-
> lation for tactical planning—require flexibility of thought from Bolton

and his colleagues, to produce equipment of sufficient flexibility to meet the very specialized needs of each customer.

("Profile: John Bolton," 1985: 24)

The potential field of operations was vast, so large, Solartron argued, that no two producers need overlap. Their policy was to supply industry's unfulfilled needs. By 1960 the electronics industry in Britain had expanded to some £400m a year, a 50 per cent growth from the time that JEB had joined Solartron.

In 'Achievement' for March 1962 Bolton was asked to talk about what was happening in the electronics industry, and concentrated on the acceleration of the trend toward using the computer 'for gathering and digesting the many facts vital in production planning; and in conjunction with data-processing, for trying out variations toward the optimum organization of a plant. We in the electronics industry are matching the need with available equipment'. In a draft for this article he had stressed rather different dimensions, notably the industry's export achievements in expanding sales some 45 per cent higher than in 1958, but also that 'It is certain that margins in the electronic equipment market throughout the world must increase if the heavy burden of development expenditure is to continue to be met in the future'.

A few years further on, JEB reported in a talk to Oxford Business Summer School in July 1965 that the electronics industry in the UK employed some 300,000 people and in the scientific and industrial instrument section, on which he concentrated in his talk, some 100,000. At that time Solartron employed some 1500, which gives an indication of the relative position of Solartron in the industry. He also noted that the main characteristics of the instrumentation field were: small and medium sized companies, where competition was largely based on technical design improvements; batch production; relatively high margins; and a rapidly advancing technological frontier. There was not a large requirement for capital equipment to make instruments and it was therefore relatively easy for engineers to start a small business of their own; at the same time however it was difficult to become large because few product lines offered significant volumes, and companies therefore tended to have a sizeable number of product lines each with a small sales volume. The rapidly changing technology also meant a high rate of product obsolescence. High development costs for new products and a relatively small British market meant that exports were vital and that competition with other countries was inevitable. With all these different factors, it was by no means an easy industry to work in.

The American industry dominated the world market and held about two-thirds of free world production, with other countries such as Britain, Germany, France, and Japan having about 5–6 per cent each. The British industry probably comprised over 1000 firms, ranging from those with only a handful of workers to a very few with up to 3000, and probably around a half employed less than 100 workers. There was a concentration of companies around London, extending to Oxford and Cambridge. Individual companies spent relatively large sums on research and development, with some, including Solartron, spending as much as 10 per cent of turnover. The industry also had a joint research organization, the British Scientific Instrument Research association, with laboratories at Bromley, Kent, giving technical assistance and information to member firms and its main research projects involved thin films, detecting elements, glass phosphors, and optical receiving systems. In addition, two Government research bodies, the Royal Aircraft Establishment and the National Physical Laboratory, were also of importance in the development of instruments.

THE SOLARTRON PRODUCT LINE, RESEARCH, AND DEVELOPMENT

Solartron's first proprietary instrument was a laboratory amplifier, and from this grew a range of laboratory and other precision test instruments such as oscilloscopes, amplifiers, and testing equipment. By 1958 there were some 80 products in this range and at this time they represented some two-thirds of total company sales. The oscilloscope made by Solartron was the only one that made use of modular construction so that the modules could be inter-changed when required. Two Solartron instruments were made standard equipment for the British Armed Forces. The first of the Solartron range of digital instruments and data processing amplifiers was developed as the start of Solartron equipment in the digital data recording field. Production also commenced of unbonded strain gauge pressure transducers.

The second main group of products was the 'systems' group, covering electronic systems designed to perform a specific function, often specific to the customer. Nevertheless each was chosen and designed so that it could become the base for a wider field of activity for the Solartron group. In this category were: an electronic reading machine; a radar simulator for defence training; an X-ray spectrometer; a cybernetic teaching machine; computer building blocks; and a high-speed check-weigher for industry. These products had much higher unit sales values than the instruments, which usually cost between £60 and £500. Solartron also performed design and development work on a contract basis, and sold other electronic equipment, produced by other companies, through its sales outlets.

Solartron saw itself as setting a fast pace in electronics. In a pamphlet entitled 'Solartron have given the world some of the most significant advances in electronics', the following categories, all developed within Solartron, were identified:

- Precision instruments
  - Dynamic analysis equipment
  - Communications test instruments
  - Metering and pulse equipment
  - Power supplies

- Radar simulators
- Electronic reading automaton (ERA)
- Oscilloscopes
- Computers
- Data handling
- Cybernetics.

As 'Triumphs of Enterprise' noted:

> Measurement to very fine limits . . . is provided by the Ignition Delay Meter, which is a new and quicker method of measuring the interval between the injection of fuel and its combustion in a running diesel engine. Originally designed in conjunction with British Petroleum for determining the most suitable fuels for different types of diesel engines, it has now been accepted as the new world standard by petroleum companies . . . Another remarkable instrument is the Transfer Function Analyser, used to test servo systems and to analyse the distribution of vibration along mechanical structures. For the latter purpose it is being supplied to aircraft manufacturers and constructional engineers as an aid in designing metal structures with greatly improved fatigue factors. It is said to reduce the time taken on these tests by as much as four-fifths.

Some of the instruments achieved previously unheard-of refinements of measurement: the Square Wave Generator enabled changes to be made in electrical voltage to within one fortieth part of one millionth of a second, while the Voltage Standing Wave Ratio Indicator could detect power levels as low as one hundred thousand millionth of a watt.

Underpinning these products was a separate company, Solartron Research and Development (SR&D). Its emphasis was on product planning, with a focus on exports, i.e. designing for the market, and this was where the research and development effort was focussed. Bolton noted in 1958 that

> we have established a prime objective of achieving entirely new developments which show substantial improvements in contemporary design practice. As a rough rule of thumb we have endeavoured to produce new designs which will be some three to five years ahead of the existing 'state of the art' in other countries, and in this way we hope to achieve a breathing space in which our new products can become fully established before the pressure of competition can catch up with them. We aim to equate the conflicting demands of performance, quality, and price in order to offer a wide-application instrument at an economical price. We regard reliability as an absolutely essential design requirement and it is perhaps significant that repair costs under our 12 months guarantee have never exceeded £2 per £1000 of sales. Our research budget totals about 10 per cent of our sales volume and about one fifth of our total

personnel. Suffice it to say that out of every 100 projects which we would like to tackle at the beginning of each year, we have to choose the top ten or so which our resources will permit us to develop. In practice we therefore aim those new projects into those future fields which we believe may have maximum scope for expansion.

The *New Scientist* noted:

There cannot be many businesses built around the scientists quite as carefully as Solartron . . . The research teams are required to be pioneers. Anyone can make a digital computer, but what comes next? Why, says Bolton's team, the deductive logic computer which can profit by its own experience, and its partner, the teaching machine.

("Profile: John Bolton," 1958:25)

Similarly, in 1966, Wainwright's article noted:

John Bolton backs his research teams liberally and so organized the company that new inventions could be put swiftly into production. He claims it was mainly due to the research and development staffs. They say that, but for him, not much of it would have got off the ground. Thanks to him, the most complicated and refined electronic devices in science and industry throughout the world are now 'Made in Britain'.

Solartron, unlike many companies, had a very open culture of research; encouraging research from the outside was exemplified in several ways, including being willing to be picked apart in the very influential Harvard Business School case study. In addition Tom Burns, the eminent Edinburgh sociologist, was encouraged to write about the company, while Allan Williams was allowed to carry out his own graduate research at Solartron, even to the extent of Solartron paying for the last year of his PhD after his grant had expired. In his research, Williams worked on SAKI (Solartron automatic keyboard instructor) which was the brain child of Gordon Pask, a brilliant cybernetician and psychologist, who Williams described as a genius operating at a different cognitive level than most people, while Peter Curry noted that Pask was impossible to work with. But then Solartron was an ideal place for eccentric boffins.

To give some idea of the scale of development that was going on, the following products were recorded as being in development in the 1961 Report, some being new, others developments from previous products:

Electronic Instruments

LM 1010 Digital voltmeter
VF 1040 AC voltmeter
CD 1012, CD 1212, XT 484, CD1016, CD1015 New oscilloscopes

GO 1101 Pulse generator
AS 952, AS955, AS956, AS1200, AS1211, AS1164, AS1165 Power supplies
PZ1128 Automatic noise spectrum analyzer
Digitohm
DO1001 Signal generator

Analogue Computers

Beam Riding Simulator for the Royal Radar Establishment at Malvern
SCD60 for the Vertical Flight Research Institute at Stuttgart
Blind Landing Simulator for the Royal Aircraft Establishment at Bedford

Digital Computers

AMDEC computer for computing share dividends
LP1115 Conversion equipment to translate the language of digital into
    analogue
Digital computing and data handling equipment for the Royal Aircraft
    Establishment at Aberporth

Data Logging and Recording

LP1132 Commutator
LU1103 Capacitance transfer unit
LP1131 Fast punch encoder
LX1018, LX1110, and Controller LX1079 Thermocouple reference ovens
LW1080 Instrumentation tape system

Radar Simulators

Ground control approach
Height finding
Permanent echoes
Moving weather
Aerial coverage patterns

Transducers

NT1171 Scanning valve
NT1224, NT1225 Vibrating cylinder transducers
Platinum resistance thermometer bulbs

X-Ray Spectrometers

Improving reliability

Reading Machine

Reader/marker/sorter for Littlewoods Football Pools
Reader for cash register tally rolls

New low cost system of character recognition for which a patent was applied

Tangential Fan Division

2KW fan heater units ready for production

Development of   60mm high pressure blowers
                         Fixed wall fan heaters
                         3KW wall fan heaters

As well as these developments linked to the product line, there was some exciting pure research looking into an unknown future, such as Gordon Pask's experiments with growing electronic 'trees'. All this was a huge range of development for a company of its size, and inevitably, there was a cost to the focus on research and development. The challenge of funding major developments such as Optical Character Recognition (OCR), of which it was announced in the 1959 Annual Report that £120,000 had already been spent and a further £50,000 would be required before the first production model was delivered, meant that the company, even though showing remarkable rates of growth, nevertheless incurred significant financial losses. And inevitably, quite a lot of the developments, of which OCR was the most conspicuous, did not reach, or if they did reach, did not succeed in the market, although OCR came close. Indeed one manager of the period, 'Mike' Parson, felt that many of the development products were 20 years ahead of their time and that the costs of establishing a product in the market over and above the development costs had been underestimated. Moreover, as Peter Curry pointed out, there was always the danger that by the time the necessary development work had been carried out, new technology elsewhere had by-passed it. Yet Solartron continued starting up new activities, as the list above indicates.

GROUP ORGANIZATION, FACILITIES, AND PREMISES

Some of the other significant dimensions of growth in the 1950s were expansions in the number of companies in the group, in staff facilities, and in the group's premises. By November 1958 Solartron included Solartron Electronic Group, the parent company, eight domestic companies each given its date of incorporation, its personnel strength in November 1958, and its chairman:

- Solartron Laboratory Instruments (SLI)—1948—375 employees. Chairman Eddie Ponsford—Production of instruments

- Solartron Engineering—1951—194 employees—Chairman John Crosse—Provision of mechanical engineering requirements of group companies and some outside work
- Solartron Electronic Group—1954—280 employees—Chairman John Bolton—General management and staff services and merchanting
- Solartron Research and Development (SR&D)—1954—144 employees—Chairman Leslie Copestick—Internal research and development and some external contract work
- Solartron Electronic Business Machines—1955—20 employees—Managing Director—Bowman Scott—A development company for business machines, including the reading machine
- Industrial Automation Developments—1956—jointly owned with Scribbans-Kemp—A development company for a hydraulic programmed actuator, with work carried out by Scribbans-Kemp
- Solartron Industrial Controls—1956—29 employees—Chairman John Bolton—Also a development company for industrial controls
- Solartron Radar Simulators—1957—58 employees—Chairman John Bolton—Development of radar simulation for defence training purposes, especially an aircraft simulator for NATO
- Solartron-Rheem—1958—jointly owned with Rheem Co.—Managing Director Eric Jones—Development of products of joint interest to the two companies

There were two main groupings: the laboratory instruments side, and the systems companies, while the Solartron Electronic Group Ltd was created in June 1954 as a holding company for overall policy, planning, personnel, commercial, accounting, and financial functions. During 1957 two more UK companies were created, Solartron Industrial Controls Ltd (SIC) and Solartron Radar Simulators Ltd (SRS); both were soon moved to Dorking because they were primarily involved in development engineering rather than manufacturing and thus had to work closely with SR&D. The next phase of SR&D, covering the years 1957–61, saw the introduction of magnetic tape machines and transducers under licence from the USA, the growth of DC amplifiers to an analogue computer range, the digital voltmeter leading to digital data handling systems, and the emergence of special purpose digital computers. By mid-1960, SR&D was about equally active in instruments and systems.

By this time there were also three overseas subsidiaries:

Solartron Inc (USA)—1956—6 employees and with JEB as president
Solartron SRL (Italy)—1957—3 employees
Solartron GmbH (Germany)—1958—12 employees
In addition, plans were advanced in 1958 to convert the sales offices in France, Holland, India, and Italy into subsidiary companies.

The rationale for these developments was expressed in 'Triumphs of Enterprise':

> Departmentalization along functional lines is being consolidated with two aims in view. First, the directors believe that work on electronic equipment involving a high degree of skill and personal initiative requires comparatively small teams, and that a group of compact companies will work better than a single and increasingly unwieldy organization. Second, they recognize fundamental differences between each line of activity. For instance, instrument manufacture resolves itself into quantity batch production and the assemblies can be handled by semi-skilled girls. Industrial control equipment and business machines, on the other hand, need much higher specialization. On the sales side, too, requirements differ. Electronic engineers are needed to sell instruments, but the business machine salesman must be more of an accountant than an engineer.

Thus by the end of 1958, Solartron had developed into a multiple company structure consisting of six wholly owned subsidiaries in the UK and a number of partly owned companies operating at four locations in Surrey and Hampshire. The policy had been to develop a number of independent company units within the group, each concentrating on either a specialism such as research or a sales and production activity such as test instrumentation or radar simulators. The goal had been to allow each company to grow to an ultimate size of about 500–700 employees. The rationale for this was explained in the 1955 Annual Report:

(i)   to maintain an atmosphere of work where men would be able to grow with their jobs and the benefits of close teamwork would be maximized;

(ii) to permit a flexibility of operation where each activity could progress at its own best rate;

(iii) to attract key men to the company when entering new areas of activity by offering directorship posts;

(iv) to segregate the new 'system-oriented' activities from the instrument company's dominant influence and at the same time to ensure that the instrument company, the 'cornerstone' of Solartron's growth plans, should not be hampered.

Agents were appointed in 14 foreign countries in 1953, but later commercial policy was based on setting up sales outlets throughout the world, cooperating wherever possible with the company's former agents. What was learned was that export sales bear a direct relation to the actual sales effort applied and that to do an intensive selling job abroad the company had to carry the ultimate responsibility itself (Paper 228, 1958). In the UK there were some 20 qualified sales engineers in 14 geographical areas. Internally, there was a development of support units which were not usual in companies of that size at that time, such as an O&M (Organization and Methods) team and an OR (Operations Research) Department; the latter established, for instance, that there was a direct relation between orders received and sales calls made. In another area of innovation Solartron was the first company in the UK to develop a marketing organization for industrial products—later Hewlett Packard were to build their sales organization in the UK by attracting Solartron staff.

Also listed in the 1955 Annual Review was expansion in the direction of employee facilities, including a considerable range of activities on the welfare side. The outside catering contract had been terminated and the Company's own restaurant manager and staff had improved the quality of service. The Sports and Social Club covered a variety of activities and had the following sub-committees—cricket club, theatre group, football club, photographic club, table tennis club, dance committee, and dramatic society (with chess, debating, and musical appreciation added by 1959). The company was also negotiating to buy 25 acres of land adjoining the Thames Ditton factory, scheduled for sports ground use. There was also a health centre under the supervision of an industrial nursing sister, which was handling some 175 attendances per month; it also distributed vitamin capsules. A monthly news sheet 'Solartron News' helped to keep employees informed about what was going on in the various parts of the company; it started with a picture of 'Miss Solartron 1958', and with the news of various clubs and lists of new employees. There was also a Works Council, whose suggestions contributed to morale and good relations. There was a growing Company library of technical and management books. And not least, staff were encouraged to increase their potential by having their fees paid for suitable courses, while 'Training within Industry' classes were run internally. Moreover in 1956 the Solartron Pension Scheme was started, and revised to take account of a new Act in 1958; this was at a time when very few companies of its size would have had a pension scheme. All this was welfare capitalism, rather like Lever Brothers and the Quaker chocolate companies of an earlier generation.

Premises, too, was an area of considerable growth. Toward the end of 1953, the company expanded to an additional factory at Thames Ditton, with three times the area of Kingston. In 1956 SR&D was moved as a result of overcrowding to Dorking, 14 miles from Thames Ditton. By 1958 the first phase of 50,000 sq feet in building a modern factory had been completed on a 15 acre site in Farnborough, Hampshire, some 25 miles from Kingston. These were high standard facilities compared with the converted buildings used by SLI at Kingston and Thames Ditton and the systems companies were moved there together with the mechanical engineering facilities. Starting with 50,000 sq feet of factory space and 200 people in August 1958, the Farnborough factory grew to 175,000 sq feet in a modern five-story block for factory, laboratory, and office space, with 1100 people by August 1961. For some time two free buses were run to Farnborough from Kingston, and the firm gave assistance with housing transfers. SR&D was also moved to Farnborough from Dorking in August 1961. The new Solartron plant and headquarters at Farnborough were opened by the President of the Board of Trade, Reginald Maudling, on 17 July 1961. It was a big day for the company with lots of Press and guests. In the speeches, Bolton introduced Maudling, while Charles Hayward, chairman of Firth Cleveland and by this time also Solartron, thanked him after Maudling had officially opened the new headquarters. This was followed by demonstrations of various pieces of equipment.

In SLI moves were also made to provide more and better factory facilities and during 1959 a five-acre site was acquired at Chessington, about three miles away from Thames Ditton and Kingston, as a centre on which to establish all SLI activities. Existing modern buildings providing 20,000 sq feet of office and laboratory accommodation were increased by building a 50,000 sq feet factory which was occupied in October 1961. The new location was convenient for most of the existing personnel and was believed to be a better centre than Thames Ditton for further recruitment of production personnel. Thus by 1961 Solartron had become concentrated on Farnborough and Chessington; however, the cost of these two factories must inevitably have been considerable at a time when financial strains were beginning to show. Farnborough alone was projected in the 1957 Annual Review to cost £1.25 million to build and equip, or more than the annual turnover at that time.

MANAGING IN SOLARTRON

In 1958 there were eight board members of the main board of Solartron Electronic Group, and together with a further eight directors who were directors of the subsidiary company boards, there was therefore a group of 16 which developed policy and was responsible for its implementation. The average age of these top men was 38, and the main board consisted of:

- J. E. Bolton, Chairman and Managing Director, Solartron Electronic Group
- L. B. Copestick, Chairman and Managing Director, Solartron Research and Development
- J. E. Crosse, Chairman and Managing Director, Solartron Engineering
- R. A. Henderson, merchant banker
- E. E. Jones, Group Marketing Director, Managing Director, Solartron-Rheem
- ERT Ponsford, Chairman and Managing Director, Solartron Laboratory Instruments

- B. Scott, Group Personnel Director and Managing Director of Solartron Electronic Business Machines
- JLE Smith, merchant banker and Chairman of Solartron Industrial Automation Developments

It is worth noting that by the early 1960s, two internal career managers, R.B. Catherall and L. Malec, had been promoted to the main board, an indication of the potential for promotion. In addition to the general management functions performed by the board, the parent company SEG also provided a number of services to the Solartron companies, including purchasing, personnel, commercial activity, publicity, secretarial, accounting, and internal consulting through the group productivity services department.

In terms of ownership, on the formation of Solartron Electronic Group the original allotment of the 100,000 shares as of 22 October 1954 was: the Boltons 53,900 Ordinary and 25,050 Preference shares; Eddie Ponsford, Leslie Copestick, and John Crosse 7,700 Ordinary shares each, with Crosse also having 5000 Preference shares, and another 10 shareholders each holding small numbers of mostly Preference shares. Clearly the Boltons were outstandingly the dominant shareholders. From 1951 until December 1958 a majority of the common shares were held by John Bolton. After that the holdings were distributed: John Bolton 40 per cent, other managers and employees 40 per cent, outside shareholders 20 per cent.

In 1960 Bolton summed up the Solartron management outlook:

> We are endeavouring to help people—managers in particular—to move into a correct approach to life in business. We must therefore place a prime emphasis on the philosophy side of management education.
>
> What is management trying to do? My experience suggests that too much emphasis is put on techniques, and not enough, perhaps, on this constructive approach to life. This requirement suggests to me a wider use of case studies and role playing—of finding really effective 'carriers' which will help people to learn—technical knowledge then follows automatically.

Heavens (2006: 19) wrote of Solartron's attitudes toward people: 'Integral to successful, *productive* innovation is the synergy between individuals in groups and the relations that subsist between groups, their company and the wider business environment'. The company recognized this, stating in its objectives with respect to people:

> the essential need to devise a permissive system in which individual initiative is nurtured and encouraged to make its maximum possible contribution to the whole . . . We recognize that in selecting a team of potentially outstanding young men and women at all levels and in training them to carry increasing responsibility, the natural corollary is that

they should want to make a personal contribution to decisions affecting their particular working group or company's future, in an atmosphere which is as free as possible of status barriers and prejudice.

Central to these concepts was the principle of delegation, although this changed over time. In his talk to the Oxford Business Summer School in July 1965, Bolton admitted that certain lessons had been recognized:

- During the period of growth 'we were too non-directive in approach and a better result could have been achieved with more positive direction without swinging too far toward an autocratic organization'.
- In the early days all members of the management team were well briefed on the whole range of activities and we felt that they could and should participate in making decisions. However, as the complexity increases, so it becomes necessary for individuals to specialize, and also to develop routines by which a whole host of minor decisions are automatically made.
- Although decentralization into separate product groups was of value in getting new activities started, it did increase the difficulty of keeping an overall sense of unity and 'Solartron purpose' amongst the separate units.
- When development of a new product runs behind schedule the effect on profits is multiplied beyond the cost of development by incurring expense with production and sales facilities, and also that the departments concerned with delays have to handle an increasing proportion of problem items and complexity.
- The company had been too ready to take on more people to resolve issues of complexity.

Asked his main managerial goals, he replied better human relations, more effective planning ahead, and more creative selling. Forward planning was indeed the subject of the first sentence in the Solartron case study: '"I do not think we could have expanded as we have if it had not been for forward planning" said Mr John Bolton . . . in November 1958'.

We have seen in an earlier section the provision of excellent facilities; but this does not necessarily lead to high morale. However in the case of Solartron there certainly was high morale, partly due to the facilities but arguably even more so to top management leadership and attitudes, and especially that of John Bolton himself. Bolton was very approachable on a personal level at Solartron, and several people noted that nobody ever said a bad word about him. The workers would even ask for his advice on an intimate level such as personal finances, according to Gordon Pasley, a shop floor worker. It was, he said, a big family concept. And there was a strong sense of camaraderie, for John was good at keeping spirits up and engendering enthusiasm. This created a great atmosphere, in which every win was celebrated in the pub across the road from the factory. Peter Curry said that Solartron was an incredibly exciting company to work for, suggesting that Solartron and Racal were neck and neck in the 1950s as the two industrial companies to belong to. Even Dennis Burton's daughter, who had been a girl of five when her father joined Solartron, later remembered with fond memories that it was a very social place to work—launch rides on the river, car rallies, and so on—along with the creativity and innovation. John was indeed a great risk-taker and innovator and this also made Solartron very enjoyable to work for. He threw people in the deep end and gave them their head, although arguably his weakness was that he was too soft with people—quite a lot of people let him down over the years and he was willing to give them two, three, or even four chances.

There were other management weaknesses in Solartron. Cost control systems was one, over-optimistic sales forecasting another, but taken overall the biggest weakness was R&D costs outstripping market development and the financial losses that this caused. Nevertheless optimism was the order of the day; the company was quoted in the Evening News in November 1956 as aiming for a turnover of £15 million in five years. As we will see, this did not happen.

PUBLICITY AND COMMUNICATION

Bolton was very conscious of the value of publicity, both for Solartron as a company, and for himself as its head, even though his natural instincts were toward modesty and even reticence. Open Days, with a focus on public relations, obtained a very good range of acceptances, especially from the Press, as at Dorking in 1956. The Farnborough Air Show was another major occasion for publicity, with a big stand and a hospitality tent. Indeed Solartron arguably became one of the best-known small/medium businesses in the country, certainly in the electronics industry attracting a quite remarkable amount of attention for its size. As well as the obligatory Annual Report and Accounts, featuring the Chairman's Statement, Solartron also published an annual Review of some 30 pages, giving a much broader range of information about the company, with frequent use of optimistic words like 'horizons' and 'opportunity' rather than negative words like 'barriers'. Indeed the 1957 Annual Review noted that while progress was often measured in terms of breaking barriers: 'At Solartron it has become an annual practice to measure our advancement more in terms of horizons—because it is in the nature of horizons that each step forward progressively discloses a further horizon'. Returning to the issue of publicity, the same review also noted: 'In addition to many specially commissioned articles on technical subjects, over 300 newspapers and magazines featured us editorially as new'.

John himself did a great deal on the publicity front. The following list illustrates the number and range of John's speaking and writing activities while at Solartron.

- Gave a short talk at the Royal Society of Arts on 'Capital for Scientific Development', 27 June 1957
- Interview on the BBC in October 1957 in the series 'Men of Industry'— he was into the media very early on indicating that Solartron had already achieved recognition
- Chaired a panel of the SIMA—Scientific Instrument Manufacturers Association Annual Convention in October 1959
- Organization for European Economic Cooperation—European Productivity Agency—Committee on Management Techniques, which John chaired in 1958, comprised of six people including two management consultants, and which included specific consideration of small business
- Henley talk at the start of a new session 1965
- Article 'Industry and the Inventor' in The Listener in May 1958, based on Jewkes et al.'s 'The Sources of Invention' first heard on the Third Programme
- Chosen by 'Achievement' to write on 'Trends in the Electronics Industry' in 1962 and 1963
- 25 min programme on 'Management in Action' for Grenada in February 1965—seen as a speaker for the electronics industry
- Article in *New Scientist* 22 May 1958 on 'It Is the Team That Matters' about Bolton and Solartron
- BBC 26 April 1958 Programme *The World of Industry* 'The Organization Scientist under Fire'
- BBC programme Feb 1964 on the 'brain drain' to the US Woman's Hour, with an audience of three million
- BBC 10 pm news 21 July 1961 commenting on the emergency Budget
- BBC 'At Home and Abroad' on 5 March 1957 about emigration

Of all the articles, however, none was as extensive or reached such an audience as Bolton's four pieces in the Christian Science Monitor in May-June 1958. How did he obtain such an opportunity? Probably through old friends from his Harvard days; although the heading to the series does say 'The Christian Science Monitor has invited John E. Bolton to explain the ideas that have made this growth possible', so perhaps Solartron's fame had indeed reached the United States sufficiently to justify an invitation. They wanted ideas, and it was in linking ideas together that JEB constructed the major piece that he wrote himself, and in four separate articles, he used some fairly purple prose to describe 'this twentieth century exploration into the unknowns of our natural physical world, every bit as exciting as were the explorations into the geographical world in the Middle Ages':

There is something perhaps symbolic in the fact that our main plant is within sight of historic Hampton Court Palace where unfolded

Cardinal Wolsey's hopes and struggles against that 16th century law of nature, King Henry VIII. At that time mankind was finding a new horizon in the discovery of unknown lands. Even today we are exploring new horizons of technology, automation and power—new horizons of learning and communication—new horizons of space and opportunity.

Or, in his final piece on June 5, 1958:

Thinking ahead, this internationalizing of people's outlook—individual people's outlook—this shrinking of the world, must inevitably lead to the ultimate revolution in communication—to one universal language. . . . Already our 'code' languages are common ones—to the international language of art, of music, of literature, we at Solartron are playing our part in developing the use of new symbolic languages of scientific meaning of figures, of the digital phraseology of computers, through the medium of punched cards and punched tape and magnetic tape.

Or in his final paragraphs:

In this era of education for individual responsibility the harshness of totalitarian forms of government and of management must mellow. We can already see them mellowing about us. Forms of leadership must evolve which are catalytic, making it much easier for people to work effectively together. The catalyst is information. The process is the linking of peoples' understandings thus making a broader base of thinking from which a chain reaction of better individual decisions is born.

The times are with us. We at Solartron, valuing the heritage which lies behind, press on together towards these new and brighter horizons.

In all this is the power—and the danger—of ultimate optimism and self-confidence. 'Horizons' was a word which JEB used a lot in the series.

In 'Triumphs of Enterprise' Bolton listed four policies without which the company's progress could not have been achieved:

- Complete originality in design and development
- Uncompromising standards of performance
- A habit of forecasting which makes long-term planning possible
- A team conception of work which starts at Board level and carries inspiration down the line

As an example of JEB's unusual mode of managing, he distributed to all the managers and supervisors the Radio Programme 'Lift up Your Hearts' for 27 February 1953. This was by the Rev. Wilfred Garland and was entitled 'Honour All Men' in which he advocated respect for all workers. At the heart of the message was the point 'nearly everyone does better if dignity is conferred on him by those who he serves'. He saw the talk 'as an indication of the type of attitude which I believed to be essential for the creation of an effective, human, organization'.

Communications is always an issue in any organization, and Bolton was asked to write about it for 'Communication 64'. As always, he showed himself to be very modern in his thinking:

> When we get down to the purpose of communications we are aiming to achieve the specific objectives of the company concerned—so company policy must be clearly defined. Then the individuals must be able to identify themselves with the company—so they must be involved. . . . The answer lies in a combination of advanced communications practice and leadership skills.

He went on to review the techniques for vertical communications in Solartron, but admitted that lateral communications were often the most difficult, involving demarcation problems and decisions as to how many people should be concerned with any one activity. Another big difficulty lay in defining the objectives of the company at any one time, because the situation was always changing; 'perhaps this is why you can often detect a kind of pendulum law of centralization and decentralization'.

A *New Scientist* profile of Bolton noted:

> There cannot be many businesses built around the scientists quite as carefully as Solartron. Bolton's aim is always to get the most he can out of them, by giving them their head. Out of a staff of 750, almost one quarter is engaged on research and development, a ratio that few manufacturing companies could challenge, and the direct labour content in the cost of Solartron instruments has fallen from 28 per cent of sales price in 1951 to 7 per cent today [1958].
>
> ("Profile: John Bolton," 1958: 25)

A two-page survey in the Daily Mail on 16–9–59 featured Solartron as 'Britain's Space Age Industry'.

In 'Good Business', 1960, Robert McKinnon profiled Bolton, starting from the axiom that

> Solartron enjoys a leading reputation for electronic equipment not only in Britain but throughout the world. What, specifically, is the philosophy of management on which this reputation has been built. It is actually composed of many beliefs and practices, but linking them all is the underlying concept that the working atmosphere of the firm should be as permissive and attractive as possible. . . . In accordance with this

outlook, there has developed at Solartron a form of personnel management which they call 'catalytic leadership'. In simple terms, this involves telling employees what is going on and encouraging them to think about it. . . . The importance the Group attaches to the individual is also manifest in its structure. Every effort has been made to keep the average size of each unit at between 500 and 700 people, a size at which the management believes everyone can get to know the others.

JEB could take a very patriotic view. Thus he finished a talk at the London School of Economics on May 27, 1958 with the following:

When one reflects on Britain's future role in the economic world, it must surely be essential to the well-being of the country that the younger generation of businessmen show a new standard of success by their skill and enterprise and we feel a growing sense of destiny and responsibility in the small contributory part we ourselves can play. A young team such as we find in Solartron with a wide range of experience, freedom to control our own affairs and the open field of a healthy and growing industry before, has the opportunity to show that these higher achievements are well within reach. We at Solartron intend to venture on to new and brighter horizons, proud of our heritage, as part of truly Great Britain.

Also to be included in the publicity of this period are the public roles that John was involved in at this time, notably various committees in the British Institute of Management and from 1960–1962 membership of the Economic Committee of the Department of Scientific and Industrial Research (DSIR), the predecessor of the research councils of the present day and a very important body in the interaction between government and industry on the policy front.

But perhaps the most important piece of publicity was the business school case study 'The Solartron Electronic Group Ltd (A)'. This was prepared by the Swiss business school IMEDE in 1959, and used at Harvard and many other business schools over many years, as well as being incorporated in a major case study text produced by four eminent Harvard Business School professors, *Business Policy: Text and Cases* (Learned et al. 1969); naturally, only particularly important or interesting cases were used in a text of this kind. Many thousands of MBA students read and discussed it and would have remembered its thrust and details for many years. Indeed this was arguably the best publicity that a company could get, since those MBA students would not only have learned about Solartron but would have applied its lessons in their own managerial careers. John's son Nicholas actually did the case as a student at London Business School in the 1970s, and remembers that the view of the class was that Solartron was over-committed and would go bust!

EMERGING STRAINS

The third five-year period started with great expectations and bold predictions. In the *New Scientist* of 22 May 1958, there is a final comment: 'Bolton and his colleagues intend to increase the Solartron output fivefold by 1961–62, and a substantial part of that will come from exports' ("Profile: John Bolton," 25). Similarly, in the 1958 Chairman's statement the mood was bullish:

> With substantially enlarged production facilities, a growing order book and successful new products with an international market, we look forward in the current year to a further expansion of approximately 50% in both deliveries and orders received. Translated in profit terms, this will mean that with maintained gross margins and better use of our overhead organization, the expansion of profits should more than keep pace with the expansion of turnover. I think you are aware that our programme for 1958/59 is part of an overall plan which aims at achieving a carefully controlled expansion to several times our present size during the next five years.

Nor did the 1958 Annual Review recognize any problems. Indeed, its theme can be summed up in a single sentence, 'The times are with us'.

It is now time to put these descriptions of growth into some figures, and Table 2.1 illustrates this in three key areas. There is no denying the impressive progress of all these dimensions, but equally there is no denying either that the target turnover of £15m which we saw projected within five years in 1956 had nowhere near been achieved. Yet much of the expenditure,

Table 2.1   Leading statistical indicators, Solartron 1950–1961

Year	Deliveries £000s	Personnel	Floor space (000 sq ft)
1950 (July)	15	18	3.5
1951	25	22	3.5
1952	35	66	6.0
1953	130	110	7.5
1954	210	237	30
1955	398	400	35
1956	758	550	65
1957	1,005	600	70
1958	1,430	830	85
1959	2,107	1,330	118
1960	2,633	1,550	150
1961 (December)	4,891	1,953	250

Source: Solartron Annual Reports

especially on development, was predicated on this faster rate of growth, and moreover, even if it had been achieved, the company would still have been seriously under-capitalized. Clearly something needed to be done.

As a result, in 1959 the mood in the Chairman's statement was much more cautious:

> This was a year, however, when we also experienced the normal problems of rapid growth and, for the first time, I have to report a lower profit than I expected a year ago. By a relatively small margin we fell short of our delivery target for the year and . . . substantial increases in overheads following the expansion in our factory space were coupled with initial losses in our overseas operations. The task of moving personnel from various locations to our new factory and reorganizing the space and facilities they vacated at the old locations, together with the need for absorbing and training a large number of people, meant that we lagged behind both in production and in completing the development of new products . . . In retrospect it is clear that we undertook more development and expansion than was compatible with showing good trading results for the year.

A pattern of early losses due to development costs is, of course, not uncommon in start-up situations, but the issue soon becomes one of when can the growth produce financial success. Money had to come from the outside, and the initial investments by John Bolton and John Crosse only lasted so long. There was an ongoing need for more capital for growth. The Group raised £150,000 by issuing a 7.5 per cent Unsecured Loan Stock to the General Accident Fire and Life Assurance Co in 1956 and was reported as intending to raise another £150.000 the following year. But this method of raising funds was not sufficient and could not continue indefinitely. The R&D programme, together with working capital demands of sustaining an annual growth rate of around 100 per cent, meant that the business was eating more cash than it could possibly generate from trading and to make matters worse, sales targets were falling well short of projections. There was only one answer; a larger funding partner was required, even if it meant selling out much of the equity.

Initially, however, growth was still the watchword, with ambitious financial targets, and this required new premises, as we have seen. SLI also continued to expand, its sales reaching £2 million in 1961. Solartron's sales of own products were now 83 per cent of total sales and export sales 27 per cent of the total. A further 20 new instruments had been developed in 1961 and additions were made to the range of analogue computers, digital data logging equipment, and high speed printers. The first models of an automatic X-ray spectrometer for automatically analysing certain metals and chemicals were developed.

During the years 1959–61 an excellent job was done at Farnborough in building the foundation of an important and expanding unit in the 'systems' field. It was clear that this area of activity had a major role to play in

Solartron's future. Solartron were now the largest suppliers of laboratory instruments to the Armed Forces, while the proprietary range of Solatron instruments totalled 160. Moreover the systems side had grown to about the same size as the instrument side.

FIRTH CLEVELAND

All these issues inevitably had financial implications, and Bolton had to look outside the company for help. In January 1960, a major financial move was made involving the sale of 53.125 per cent, a majority interest, in Solartron Electronic Group's ordinary share capital to Firth Cleveland, an industrial holding company with engineering, metals, and retail electrical trades and with adequate financial resources to back Solartron's growth programme. Much was made of this at the time as a means of providing new opportunities for Solartron, with the rationale being explained as follows: In an article of June 1960, Bolton noted:

> Solartron are now engaged on their third ambitious five-year programme which calls for an increase in the volume of sales to £7.5 million by 1964/65, including over £3 million in exports. Total personnel employed are expected to rise to over 3000 by that date. Such a programme requires substantial additional capital and in order to ensure that this is available, Solartron merged in January 1960 with the expanding Firth Cleveland Group, which now owns 53 per cent of their equity capital. By this association, Solartron have access not only to a substantial source of new capital, but also to a wide range of other engineering techniques, which give further assurance that the ambitious expansion plans will be fulfilled. At the same time Solartron retains its technical and management independence to develop the business according to its own philosophy. The link with Firth Cleveland provides even greater opportunities for cooperation in the export field through the medium of Firth Cleveland's international network of manufacturing and selling subsidiaries abroad.

At this stage the shareholding of John and Gay Bolton had grown to 154,000 shares, worth some £675,000, an excellent return for the original input of £50,000. After the deal Firth Cleveland's shares rocketed from 30s to 47s.9d at one time, so clearly the markets saw the deal as being a very good one for Firth Cleveland as well as Solartron. Indeed in 1961 Firth Cleveland attempted to purchase the remaining shares in Solartron, but this bid was not successful, implying that Bolton, as the largest remaining shareholder, was not in favour of a complete takeover.

Nevertheless, there was also an important personal dimension involved. Charles Hayward, who controlled Firth Cleveland, was himself a Wolverhampton man, born in 1893, and we have seen him in the previous chapter advising JEB to go to Cambridge after his demobilization (and probably also to Harvard Business School). He had started a successful business in Wolverhampton making sidecars for the motorcycle company AJS in the early 1920s, but then in 1928 went to London to exploit his idea of financing new inventions and processes. He formed the Electric and General Industrial Trusts which then led in 1953 to the formation of Firth Cleveland, and he was its chairman from its inception until his retirement in 1973. The Firth Cleveland Group of companies became a substantial organization, with a turnover of £47 million, some 9000 employees and 23 factories in the UK by 1970, when it was taken over by GKN. Hayward was knighted in 1974 and before his death in 1983 created two charitable trusts, the Hayward Foundation and the Charles Hayward Trust, which were combined into the Charles Hayward Foundation in 2000. He was a generous benefactor to Wolverhampton and is buried there. He was something of a father figure to Bolton, and so when additional funds were needed, he was a logical person to approach. In John's personal appointments diary, there is a note of Hayward and his wife coming to lunch in September 1959, four months before the takeover, almost certainly for John to talk about funding with his mentor. After the merger, really a takeover, Hayward became Chairman of Solartron Electronic Group and John Deputy Chairman and Managing Director.

Hayward began the 1960 Chairman's Report with his own bullish outlook:

> A first class team of brilliant technicians and administrators, so ably led by Mr. John Bolton, has been created. Your Group's products are among the leaders in their respective fields and the Solartron Electronic Group has an international reputation. Not least, your Group has achieved a firm footing in a pioneer field capable of almost limitless expansion.

However, he also noted:

> The paucity of profits are mainly attributable to the bold and consistent policy of heavy investment for the future. Continually, current production has had to bear the initial losses that almost invariably are associated with the introduction of new products and the setting-up of overseas subsidiaries and also the costs of recruiting and training personnel and providing accommodation and other facilities for economic use in future, rather than current years. Furthermore a large part of the Group's assets and, not least, its personnel have been engaged in difficult long-term projects, such as our reading machines, which from the short-term aspect, reduce profits. Indeed, but for your Group's success in constantly adding to its growing deliveries of proprietary products, the effort of the above expansion would have been far more marked.

Hayward also noted that the next reporting period would be for 18 months to bring the date in line with the rest of Firth Cleveland. On the accounts themselves, the most notable features were a substantial rise between 1959 and 1960 in stocks and work in progress from £810.041 to £1,174,567 and in development expenditure from £207,947 to £478, 906.

SCHLUMBERGER

However, the Firth Cleveland involvement was to be short-lived. A second, and totally unsolicited, major financial development came on November 9, 1961, involving the sale of Firth Cleveland's majority interest in Solartron Electronic Group to Schlumberger. Schlumberger was an international company with a dominant world position in the instrumentation of oil well drilling, founded by two French brothers in 1926 and about to be listed on the New York Stock Exchange in 1962; it was in the business of measurement and wanted to broaden its interest in this field with its substantial cash resources. The offer for Solartron, effectively to Charles Hayward, was an out of the blue approach through the Schlumberger bankers. According to someone who was present at the negotiations, Jean Riboud of Schlumberger put a figure on the table, and the Solartron team asked to move to another room to discuss the offer. Charles Hayward was keen to accept, but his colleagues Gordon Harries and Peter Hamilton advised him to ask for more. After a lot of discussion Charles Hayward agreed. They returned and as soon as they sat down Jean Riboud said that he realized that Solartron was a great company and if Schlumberger wanted it they would have to pay a premium, and immediately increased the price. Once again the team left the room and the same discussion took place. This time Charles Hayward said the price was extremely attractive and he was going to accept.

What this episode illustrates is that the key figure in Solartron had become Charles Hayward; John Bolton was not directly concerned with these negotiations, although of course his remaining shares were worth much more. The second takeover must, nevertheless, have been one of the factors, if not the main one, which led to him leaving the company some four years later. In addition to the attractive price, Hayward was probably concerned about the way in which the Solartron needs for cash were imposing on his own financial resources; the fact that he was apparently willing to accept the first offer suggests that he was happy to be bought out. From his point of view it was probably a fortuitous outcome, overriding his personal relationship with Bolton. Indeed, from a personal financial perspective, the arrival of Schlumberger was beyond both of their wildest dreams.

If Hayward had become the most important figure at Solartron, Jean Riboud was a massively more important figure still in the wider world, a legendary and iconic leader who made Schlumberger one of the best managed companies in the world, with a 44-fold increase in earnings during his

20-year tenure. Over those years, he expanded the company from its base as the world leader in testing oil wells into a diversified enterprise with a focus on technology, including electronic instruments, semiconductors, and computer-aided design systems. Wall Street regarded the company and its chief executive with a degree of awe, and the story led to a book by Ken Auletta (1984) entitled *The Art of Corporate Success: The Story of Schlumberger*. From one of the most influential families in France, he had a heroic record in the French Resistance which culminated in escaping from Buchenwald, and later developed close relations with Francois Mitterand in the post-War period; indeed Mitterand during his presidency offered him the prime ministership of France, which he declined. He also had a fascinating wife, the Indian Krishna Tagore, and between them they became major figures in the modern art world. As Krishna's obituary noted: 'their fingers were firmly placed on the cultural pulse of three continents—America, Europe and Asia'—and they had vast private collections of art and ancient textiles. Like the Boltons, their hospitality was legion.

To return to the main story, in November 1961 Schlumberger Well Surveying Corporation bought the majority holding in the Company from Firth Cleveland and later that month made an offer for the remaining shares, raising their holding to 67.3 per cent of the Ordinary shares and all the Preference shares. In the 1961 Accounts published in June 1962, the Group loss was £317,876 and it was also decided to write off £974,219 of development expenditure; after taxation recoverable the Group loss was £983,557. Moreover in order to provide the Company with additional working capital it had been agreed at the end of December 1961 that the parent company would make the Company a loan of £892,857, repayable in dollars in 1967. Clearly, the financial situation at this time urgently necessitated further action, probably far more than Hayward was willing to give, while Schlumberger was a much bigger company and in a period of rapid growth itself.

Riboud became chairman but based in Paris although coming to dinner at Brook Place at least a couple of times in 1962. Schlumberger did not immediately provide hands-on management for Solartron other than putting in a financial controller. John was the Deputy Chairman and Managing Director, making the day-to-day managerial decisions, although now as a manager rather than an entrepreneur. However the business structure used previously, with subsidiary companies, was consolidated into a single business with common marketing and R&D. Solartron was able to access technology platforms owned by other Schlumberger companies as well as benefit from its established sales and distribution facilities. The Chairman's statement by Jean Riboud for the 18 months ended 31st December 1961 started:

> I was privileged to be elected Chairman of your Board of Directors a few weeks before the end of the 18 month period covered by the Accounts which are before you. From these it is clear that Solartron has faced some difficult problems. Major factory moves adversely affected

both production and the progress of development and the expansion of deliveries which was expected in the last six months was not achieved.

He went on to say that the underlying position of the company remained healthy, that he was impressed by the quality of the people, by the product range and by the factory facilities, and that there was a firm foundation for growth. Nevertheless although SLI at Chessington was expanding satisfactorily and profitably,

at Farnborough, where the bigger systems and associated industrial control products offer great prospect of future growth, a sound, profitable situation is more difficult to achieve. Not only must their relatively complex new developments be perfected, but at the same time world markets for them must be created. This is costly and takes time, but I am sure that the Farnborough field of activity is essential to our plan to create a very powerful organization in the electronic industry.

CONSOLIDATION

There were several stages of consolidation after 1958, when the alarm bells began ringing. At Farnborough, following a period when SE, SEBM, SRS, and SIC led separate lives, a unification of these companies was put into effect in 1959–60, combining into one company, Solartron (Farnborough) Ltd. The main reason for the centralization of the systems companies between 1959 and 1961 was the desire to make the operations more profitable by avoiding bottlenecks.

The next two years saw further simplification of Solartron's structure, especially after the Schlumberger takeover. In June 1962 Solartron Inc, which was out on a limb, was sold to Electro-Mechanical Research Inc, a US subsidiary of Schlumberger. Also, between October and December 1962, the UK side was reorganized to operate as one trading unit, Chessington becoming solely an instrument manufacturing plant and all sales and administration being centralized at Farnborough. In December 1962 the Solartron X-Ray Spectrometer activity was sold to Elliott Automation and development was concentrated on oscilloscopes, digital instrumentation, dynamic analysis equipment, radar simulators, analogue and digital computers, industrial data logging equipment, and transducers, as well as a 'bread and butter' line of tangential fan units for domestic heaters and other applications. Early in 1963 the remaining Solartron European subsidiaries were sold to Societie d'Instrumentation Schlumberger, a French subsidiary of Schlumberger Ltd., to permit better coordination of sales of all Schlumberger electronic products in Continental Europe. In March 1963 the reading machine activity was closed down as not being commercially viable.

Thus the years 1961–64 were ones of 'much needed' (John's words) consolidation with more emphasis on achieving a better return on capital employed rather than a quest for growth for its own sake. Something went substantially wrong in that sales remained at £4m rather than rising to the projected £7.5 million and certainly not the £15 million that had been cheerfully mentioned to the Evening News in 1956. But although consolidation did take place around the fringes, in structure and with some development projects, Schlumberger did not make any major redundancies. Indeed it would be wrong to overstate the difficulties, since revenues did not actually fall. Solartron entered 1965 with sales running at some £4 million, about the same as 1961, but nevertheless for lower than the optimistic projections of the 1950s. Exports had risen to 40 per cent of sales and the order book was at an all-time record. The organization was healthy with clearly defined responsibilities. Output per person employed had risen from £2000 in 1961 to almost £3000 by December 1964. R&D expenditure was about 10 per cent of sales and the range of new equipment coming into production was the best ever. Thus there was still a sizeable company with some good product lines, and still quite a lot of optimism in the February 1965 document.

On November 6, 1961, in association with the Schlumberger takeover, an Extraordinary General Meeting passed a resolution to increase the capital of the company to £1,400,000 by the creation of 1,600,000 shares of 10/- each, which were distributed in the proportion of two new shares to one old share held on October 19, 1961. In March 1962 the share register for the new shares showed more than 100 separate holders of shares. Of the 1,600,000 shares newly distributed, Schlumberger took 1,109,684 and John and Gay Bolton 276,186. Of other senior members of Solartron, Leslie Copestick and his wife took some 23,000, Eddie Ponsford and his wife some 16,000, Bowman Scott and his wife some 18,000, and John Crosse and his wife some 35,000. Most of the other holdings were quite small, many doubtless held by Solartron employees, but some also by outsiders: thus the Maharajah of Jaipur and the Master, Fellows and Scholars of Trinity College Cambridge each had 2272, while the Williams family of Leamington Spa appeared to be largest external holders with just over 80,000 shares. On October 31, 1964, Schlumberger converted all the Preference shares, which it owned, into Ordinary shares. Then on November 16 SEG passed a resolution to take the company private, with Eddie Ponsford chairing the meeting. This was the point at which Schlumberger bought out the other shareholders, including John, and was the marker for him to leave, which he did in 1965. JEB was no longer calling the shots, and by temperament he was an entrepreneur, not cut out to be an operational manager. He had been willing to stay on for a time to keep the staff on board and to maintain continuity, but that time was limited.

REVIEW

In the period after 1958, sales of new products were falling behind projections, while development costs were considerably higher than budgeted. Delays in new product development meant that sales and production operations set up for the new product were incurring expense without activity and that sales projections were too optimistic. Associated with these issues, cost controls were not good. And finally, the Company was too ready to take on more people to solve problems. Why were results not better? Management was competent and the engineers and production people well qualified. The answer, it was concluded in the re-evaluation of the period, must lie in management coordination of the unwieldy organization, especially coordinating R&D, resolving production priorities and the difficulty of providing common staff services while trying to maintain independent company structures. The system was also seen as being too non-directive, with a need for more rigorous routines for decision-making (for which probably read more centralized), and for an integrated Solartron sense of purpose.

But there were other and perhaps deeper problems, mainly to do with the interface between development and the market, and the way in which costs were handled. For many of the development activities, there were the twin dangers of not being able to make a product successful in the market of the time, and of having one's own development overtaken by developments elsewhere. What was required was for at least a few products to hit the jackpot but in Solartron's case none of the markets were large enough for this to be the case. Second was the question of costing and pricing. Take the costs of labour and materials and double it was the crude rule of thumb of pricing, with little relation to the market, while there was a mishmash of unallocated costs at Solartron, which created large overheads. Peter Curry pointed out that in Racal, which was in many ways similar to Solartron, there was a very strong accountant, Ernie Harrison, to complement its John Bolton equivalent, Ray Brown, and that Harrison was able to provide the controls that were absent in Solartron.

Solartron was undoubtedly a significant force in the development of British electronics. It was a company from which other companies poached and learned, it was a wonderful place to start a career or launch a spin-off, and it provided many technical breakthroughs. However in what happened to Solartron there was something symbolic of the way in which small businesses in Britain found it difficult to progress beyond a certain stage, usually due to financial issues and especially the lack of capital. The City of London may have something to answer for here, since other countries seemed to find it easier to find the capital for growth without entrepreneurs losing control. Nevertheless it must be admitted that Solartron was being too ambitious in trying to achieve what it did with the capital at its disposal, while, as noted, cost controls were not what they should have been. Overall Solartron was both a huge achievement and a considerable failure. On a personal basis was Bolton carried away by the ambition and optimism of the early days and the ideas and analogies expressed in his Christian Science Monitor articles to the extent of arguably developing something of an Icarus complex? Or was he too concerned with other activities such as management education and the BIM?

Nevertheless, John did well out of Solartron in his role as a shareholder. As Peter Butler wrote of examining Solartron as a case study:

> John sold the business to a big UK public company for a value 20 times greater than his original investment, with the consideration in shares that had to be held for a certain period of time. That time elapsed two years later when the UK company sold it on to an American company for twice the value it had arranged with John. The fascinating feature of this case, therefore, is to demonstrate how, even in the 1950s, it was possible rapidly to grow a company—and shareholder value—without achieving large profits.

John had decided to take two years' sabbatical holiday to plan a new career as a merchant banker but as we shall see in the succeeding chapters, this was not what happened. He had made sufficient money through the sale of his Solartron shares to establish himself and Gay comfortably for the rest of their lives and to enable him to take on a range of activities of a public service nature which were of great value to Britain as a country. Indeed even while still very busy at Solartron, he had become involved in such interests and was about to start up his own companies and a small family-based venture capital company in Riverview Investments. There does not appear to have been any rancour in his leaving, since he got on perfectly well with Jean Riboud, although after he had left he did not have much further contact with Solartron. He was already busy on other fronts, and we will shortly turn to the most important of these, his obsession with furthering management education in the UK. But before we move onto his new career, it may be interesting to recount briefly what happened to Solartron after John left.

EPILOGUE

By 1965 Solartron was consolidated and stabilized with a turnover of £4 million, employment of 1500, exports of some 50 per cent, operating as one company in a single location, and most importantly profitable and ready to move forward. Later Solartron annual reports show that Eddie Ponsford was to become the chairman of SEG, retiring at the end of 1973 in a period of steady growth. In 1977 Schlumberger Measurement Control (UK) was created as a new holding company, one of its subsidiaries being Solartron Electronic Group. The Solartron products were then reorganized into four separate product divisions:

Measurement Group:

Producing digital instruments, data loggers, digital voltmeters, and dynamic analysis systems, which were the forerunners of today's Frequency Response Analyzers.

Weapons Simulation Group:

Producing the Simfire devices for weapons training exercises.

Radar Simulation Group:

Producing radar systems for training air traffic controllers, etc.

Transducer Group:

Producing aerospace gas pressure and fuel density sensors for use in air data computers and engine management systems, industrial gas and liquid density sensors used in process and fiscal measurement of fossil fuels, and protective systems used for energy control in the electricity power production industry.

There was a good deal of buying and selling of divisions, both internally within Schlumberger and externally, but also with considerable growth of both turnover and employees. Thus in 1983 there was a turnover of £75 million, with a profit before tax of £14 million and with 2364 employees; there were however only two directors, the minimum necessary. Next, as of July 1, 1988 the company name was changed to Schlumberger Electronics (UK) Ltd. A big jump was in buying the Thorn-EMI gas metering division for £60 million in 1989, after which gas and electricity metering became an important part of the company's activities. By 1992 the turnover had grown to £145 million and the employees to 2449. Although the financial results are not sufficiently explicit to prove it, it seems likely that Schlumberger did eventually make a financial success out of Solartron, at least up to this point, because in the mid-1990s there was a decline in the market. In 1993 the Solartron transducer businesses were sold by Schlumberger to the Solartron Group Ltd (note the return to the old name) in a management buyout for £29.3 million which in turn in 1994 was acquired by the Roxboro Group Plc.

Roxboro was a holding company and over the following 10 years acquired and divested a number of other businesses. The former measurement group became Solartron Analytical, and concentrated on developing a range of frequency response analysers, supporting electrochemical interfaces, and digital voltmeters.

In July 2000 Solartron Analytical's head office function, including product development and marketing, was relocated to the current facility in Farnborough, while production moved to other Roxboro locations. (A nice coincidence is that when Peter Curry retired, long after leaving Solartron in 1960, he was asked to become a director of Roxboro, and found himself meeting at the same offices where he had worked some 40 years previously!) In September 2005 four of the Solartron group companies (Solartron Analytical, Solartron Metrology, Solartron ISA, and Arun Technology) were acquired by AMETEK, a leading global manufacturer of electronic instruments and electric motors. At the same time production and service of Solartron Analytical products was transferred to the current facility in Farnborough, so that once again all key business functions were located on the same site. AMETEK itself is an international company based in Paoli, Pennsylvania, which was founded in 1930 and in 2011 had a turnover of US$3.0 billion and some 11,600 employees. A separate successor company is Gemalto Terminals Ltd, based in Wimborne, Dorset, a company of some 150 employees making instruments to measure electricity. On a more social tack, into the 21st century there were still reunions to celebrate the 'golden age of Solartron', largely led by JEB's old friend Dennis Burton, with many people keeping in touch over a long period, JEB included.

3 The Foundation for Management Education

Introduction
Management Education in Britain
The British Commonwealth College of Administration
The Dining Group
Formation of the Foundation for Management Education
Robbins, Franks, and the Creation of London and Manchester Business Schools
The Council of Industry for Management Education
The Later Years of the FME

INTRODUCTION

The Foundation for Management Education (FME) was arguably the main organizational catalyst for creating management education in Britain as it is today. Even before its creation, John Bolton had attempted to create a business school through his own personal efforts. Then, within the FME Bolton was the main personal catalyst in bringing it into existence, as well as playing a key continuing role during many decades of valuable contribution, both financial and advisory. Without Bolton, events might well have turned out quite differently.

MANAGEMENT EDUCATION IN BRITAIN

Into the 1950s, the education and development of British managers had, to put it mildly, a chequered history. While Bolton was chairing Solartron's growth spurt in the middle 1950s, he was also concerned (evangelical might be a better word), about a totally different issue, that of management education in Britain. It was a subject into which he put a great deal of thought, time, and effort, and not a little financial pump-priming and other assistance over the rest of his life. Having appreciated Harvard and the American system, and being only too well aware of the deficiencies of the British system as a result of his research in the year after Harvard, it would not have been surprising to find Bolton feeling that something ought to be done in Britain. What is more surprising is that he was willing to do the something himself, entirely off his own bat, as the busy chair of what was still a relatively small company.

His concern was certainly understandable. There was widespread recognition in the post-war period that British industrial management was poor. The Anglo-American Council on Productivity teams which visited the USA in 1949–50 all came back with a common theme, that the greatest single factor in American industrial supremacy was the effectiveness of its management at all levels, something that the union delegates fully agreed with. But there was still widespread complacency, and as Barnett put it (2001: 276):

> Worst of all, managements in Britain still widely failed to perceive the need for leadership, in the sense of systematically fostering enthusiasm and team spirit as practised in a good British regiment or American industrial company. They still cleaved to their great-grandfathers' notion that they were 'the masters'.

It followed that they had very little interest in education for managers except in technical areas.

There had been limited attempts to initiate university-level management education in the interwar period, notably at the London School of Economics, Birmingham, and Edinburgh. But these had not been welcomed by industry and had not developed further. In the post-war period the main new development had been the 'Administrative Staff College for Industry' at Henley, but it, as Lyndall Urwick described the situation in a letter to Bolton, had had to make 'a virtue of its limitations'. The British Institute of Management was supporting the Certificate and Diploma programmes in the college system that had been recommended by the 1946 Urwick Committee to pull together the programmes of the various professional institutes; but it did so without much enthusiasm, and in any case industry did not feel that the colleges had the appropriate status. A not insignificant factor was that the two most prestigious universities, Oxford and Cambridge, had not shown any leadership or indeed much interest. But even beyond them the whole university system at that time was complacent and inward looking, with a cosy incestuous relationship with the University Grants Committee (UCG), which discouraged new developments.

The outcome of this context was the sort of vicious circle well described by Bolton in his important letter to John Marsh, the Director of the British Institute of Management, in November 1963, in which he reflected on his efforts in management education up to that date:

> no demand from industry, therefore no premium salaries payable to chaps who had spent a year or more at a business school, therefore no

students, therefore no teaching career opportunities in the field, therefore no teaching staff, therefore no research, therefore no status as an academic field at University level, therefore no demand from industry, ad infinitum.

Bolton was of course not the only one who was concerned with the education of British managers; Lyndall Urwick (Brech, Thomson, and Wilson 2010) for one had also been obsessed with the issue since the 1920s, but was committed to the Certificate and Diploma structure in spite of a great deal of knowledge about the American system of postgraduate MBAs. But there was not a clear-cut organization with the American approach as its primary focus in spite of a rising tide of recognition that something more was needed. So JEB decided to go it alone. To continue the letter to Marsh noted above: 'By April 1956, I had experienced five or six years of beating about the bush and discussing what should and could be done', and Nind (1985: 8) noted: 'His experience had convinced him that Britain needed to foster management education at the highest academic level (since 1949 he had been discussing his ideas with anyone who showed an interest)'.

It is also important to consider Bolton's philosophy of management; it was not, as might be expected, a mere replay of the Harvard approach. It would seem that while he wanted to use American systems and theory, he wanted to modify them to British conditions—he certainly realized from his year of research that there were considerable cultural differences—and he also wanted to incorporate the Commonwealth. He certainly wanted research to be done, with the assumption that this would create British theory. His perspective can be seen when he was appointed a representative of the European Business Community at the European Productivity Association Conference on management education and training at Baden-Baden in April 1958; his address started from the proposition that there are three stages of management which require a continuing relationship between training centres, their students, and industry. This two-way process of contact and cooperation should last throughout people's working lives. The three stages were: an awareness of technique areas about which each manager should know something; acquiring a facility in the use of these techniques; and achieving a sense of timing and deep skill in the use of the techniques. This concept of ongoing learning throughout people's lives was ahead of its time and was to lead to the more modern mantras of lifelong learning and Continuing Professional Development (CPD).

This first proposition was then enhanced by the importance of external courses in which managers can discuss their problems with men from other companies and the importance of liaison with other bodies on as wide a front as possible. Instancing such other bodies he identified local productivity associations (perhaps because of the audience he was addressing), management consultants, and other types of teaching such as apprentice training, accounting, technological courses, and even science. A further proposition was the importance of better public relations and advertising for management and management training, this in an era when the public image of the manager was still uncertain. Finally, he noted that as we are trying to help managers move into a correct approach to life in business, we must therefore place a prime emphasis on the philosophy side of management education, i.e. what is management trying to do? He suggested, somewhat in contradiction to his opening remarks, that perhaps too much emphasis is put on techniques and not enough on this constructive approach to life.

THE BRITISH COMMONWEALTH COLLEGE OF ADMINISTRATION

This was Bolton's boldest and most ambitious project. It has not been given much recognition in the history of management education, but it is important in understanding the sense of personal mission which underpinned Bolton's thinking. As he wrote to Marsh in the November 1963 letter: 'I could not stand the strain of waiting any longer'. This level of impatience was to repeat itself several times in the future, and without it, progress would have been less rapid. The College of Administration was something which he said in the letter he had been pushing for five or six years before, in 1956, he decided he had to do something. It was solely his brainchild, and a very ambitious one for someone who already had a very full-time job with Solartron and was still relatively young in the management world. Peter Parker said that he was struck with the scale of the thinking and argued that there was a lot more talking and consulting to be done, i.e. that it would not be possible to move as fast as suggested.

So what did this ambitious project consist of? In the 'Brief Outline of the Proposed Foundation to be Set up on 1st July 1956' he started by saying that the various developments in administrative education should have a focal point and

> It is therefore essential that a British Commonwealth College of Administration should be built. . . . It is because of my conviction that urgent action is necessary that I have decided to set up a Foundation to endow such a College *now* rather than wait for a more convenient time four or five years hence.

The initial composition of the Foundation was to be 10,000 Ordinary shares in Solartron, whose value he estimated to be £250,000 then and would appreciate to £1 million in five years. He set a minimum target of £10 million to be achieved by 1 July 1961. One way of raising funds would be for companies to donate £1 per annum per employee under a covenant for 7–10 years; Solartron was promised as the first of these subscribers. The funds were to finance buildings, chairs, scholarships, research, and the

interchange with other institutions abroad. He favoured an association with
an existing seat of learning, preferably Cambridge. There were to be a total
of 15 trustees and listed a dozen possibilities. In addition, there was to be
an Advisory Council, and again listed a number of possibilities, including
Sir Winston Churchill and Lord Nuffield. Cooperation with other organizations was to be expected, such as the BIM, the FBI, the Institute of Directors, the Harvard Business School Club of London, and, perhaps a little
surprisingly but not entirely out of keeping with his political perspectives,
the Trades Union Congress. He finished with a characteristic disavowal: 'I
wish to avoid any form of personal publicity in connection with this College
project'. This last, if the College had succeeded, was certainly naïve, and
indeed there was some naivety in the whole project, as he himself admitted
in his 1963 letter to John Marsh. There are several features of this—its sole
authorship, its vision, its impatience, its generosity (in terms of shares about
15 per cent of his net worth at the time), and the sheer amount of effort that
he was willing to put into it, when he was already very busy with Solartron.

When he wrote to various people he had seen as possible trustees, one well-
known figure offering very positive support was Lyndall Urwick, whom we
will later find described as 'the grand old doyen of British management'. Writing in longhand on New York hotel notepaper on 9 May 1956, Urwick said:

> The scheme for a British Commonwealth of Administration seems to
> me admirable in conception and, of course, urgently needed. Your own
> generous gesture in offering to 'set the ball rolling' does offer a chance
> of starting something practical and on a scale commensurate with the
> need. I should naturally be delighted to help you in any way I can'. He
> then went on to give some very practical advice about suitable contacts
> in the Commonwealth and warned against 'people who won't water
> the idea down in practice because they are not sincerely convinced
> that management can be taught' Urwick had had plenty of experience
> of such people in his own previous endeavours along these lines, and
> felt that Lord Heyworth, whom Bolton had proposed for his Advisory
> Council, 'while full of common sense and carrying great weight with the
> British business community, is always likely to underestimate the need
> for instruction and to water down the teaching of management to what
> British industrialists are prepared to 'take' immediately.

And he went on:

> Sir Charles Renold is a very old friend of mine. But I regard his leader-
> ship of the British Institute of Management (for which initially I was
> partly responsible) as disastrous. He can always be persuaded to take
> his feet off the ground and to hang up practical action by officials with
> purposes of their own (He had Lionel Russell in mind here). He is deaf
> to the 'grinding of axes'.

He then pointed Bolton to some suitable Cambridge figures, and with some prescience, continued

> I should have thought that a 'must' for this Advisory Council, if you can get him, is Sir Oliver Franks, now Chairman of Lloyd's Bank, formerly British Ambassador here in Washington. He knows what's needed and having been head of an Oxford college, is a bridge between the business and educational worlds. Macmillan, Chancellor of the Exchequer, is an Honorary Fellow of the Institute of Industrial Administration and would, I think, be sympathetic.

Finally, though, he warned:

> I would emphasise the danger of the essential conservatism of outlook in Great Britain. There are many individuals subconsciously sceptical about training for administration (or management) in Gt. Britain. They don't oppose openly. They tend to capture any institution that is set up and to slow down its progress. This has happened with the British Institute of Management. They force 'compromises' which are in fact completely restrictive. It's a tendency all the more difficult to combat because, with some exceptions, it is honest enough.

Another pointed comment in the letter was about the Administrative Staff College, Henley: 'while it has done some excellent work, it has gone too far in making a virtue of its limitations'. Henley had been Urwick's idea of a staff college for industry, based on the military staff colleges.

Bolton would have been aware of the dangers against which Urwick was warning from his own research, but nevertheless Urwick's views were valuable. JEB entertained Urwick for dinner at the Bath Club in mid-September 1956, and Urwick wrote again being very supportive and giving some data on ratios of management education as between the US and the UK. Urwick was not the only significant figure he persuaded to act as a trustee. Hugh Tett the Chairman of Esso, Geoffrey Crowther (then editor of *The Economist*, later Lord Crowther and high on anyone's list of the Good and the Great), John Smith of Coutts, and far from least, Dean Stanley Teale of Harvard Business School, also agreed. Other people to whom he wrote asking them to be trustees included Sir Walter Puckey, Philip Singleton of Warner-Lambert and its subsidiary the Pro-phy-lac-tic Brush Company and ex-Monsanto, Professor Hawthorne of the Cambridge University Engineering Dept., Colin Bagnall of British Nylon Spinners, and GPS Macpherson of Robert Benson, Lonsdale and Co. One of two turned down the proposal, such as Sir John Whitworth Jones on grounds that several colleges were needed, not just one.

Hugh Tett went out of his way to provide in confidence a list of contributions to the Industrial Fund for the Advancement of Scientific Education in

Schools as a means of indicating what level of funds might be raised—£3 million in a matter of weeks. Bowman Scott of Solartron also became involved, especially in trying to link the College to the Duke of Edinburgh's Study Conference on Human Relations in July 1956. John Smith of Coutts was particularly helpful, giving a long and detailed 16-point critique of the proposals in his letter in April 1956. In particular he said that it was a very stirring and imaginative idea which appealed to him enormously and that it was 'fantastically generous' of JEB, as well as offering to find a suitable 'house of distinction'. He also acted as an intermediary with several people, notably Jock Colville, Lord Altrincham, and David Wills.

Dean Stanley Teele of HBS wrote to say that 'your idea has really caught my imagination, and I do hope that it will be pressed'. JEB had written to him saying 'Moreover, Stan, it is very true to say that this idea would never have arisen but for the personal inspiration and encouragement which you have given to me and to other 'B' School people over here'. Clearly what he was trying to do really impressed Harvard and was almost certainly instrumental in his appointment as a Trustee. Moreover, it was not just the current Harvard contacts. Donald K. David, the ex-Dean of HBS but then in the extremely powerful role of Chairman of the Executive Committee of the Ford Foundation, a position at the very height of the American Establishment, wrote to JEB on June 11, 1956 (i.e. quite soon after he had broached the idea), saying:

> Philip Singleton [a close American friend of JEB] visited at our home on Cape Cod last week-end and told me of your most generous act in proposing to establish a foundation toward a fund to endow and build a British Commonwealth College of Administration. This is a splendid thing for you to do, and I believe as you must that this will encourage others to contribute toward it. . . . I merely want to congratulate you on what you have done and to wish you all success. I do hope that the plan is accepted by others and that it prospers.

This appears to be an unsolicited letter, although perhaps JEB had asked Singleton to brief David. But whether unsolicited or not, it must have been very heartening for Bolton to receive it, David was not of course offering money, but the letter could be read as implying that he would not be averse to an approach. Almost a year later, on March 8, 1957, Bolton wrote to David asking if he might meet him again and thanking him 'for the very kind interest which you have shown in the British Commonwealth College of Administration project and for your thoughtfulness in writing to me on this subject'. But of course in spite of this level of American support, he still had to sell the project in Britain.

JEB sent his draft trust deed to Slaughter and May on 26 July 1956 asking for comments. It starts: 'The Founder being desirous of advancing the cause of education and of promoting the study of the science of public administration within the British Commonwealth of Nations'. There were to be 15 trustees of whom five would constitute a quorum. The college was to be called 'The British Commonwealth College of Administration' and the purposes of the fund, once the college was created were:

- to establish scholarships,
- to finance chairs in administration and to train future teaching staff,
- to undertake research into administrative problems, and
- to provide for the interchange of teaching staff and students with those from management institutes abroad.

It can be assumed that this model was what Bolton had in mind as the later debates about management education within the FME developed. In other words, the college was to be very like what London and Manchester Business Schools turned out to be.

David Wills owned Ditchley Park on the South Downs which he was prepared to give to a suitable institution, preferably connected with the Commonwealth. Bolton went to Ditchley with John Smith (John Altrincham was also there) in August 1956 and wrote back to Wills on August 14, saying that 'the house surpasses all one's expectations and in my view would make an ideal Senate House-cum-inspirational focal point for a Commonwealth College of Administration'. Ditchley had Royal associations and had been used a lot by Churchill during the war and indeed lease-lend was negotiated there, which would have given it a great deal of cachet by the Americans and the Commonwealth.

Of particular significance, JEB also wrote to Jock Colville (Churchill's wartime private secretary), who was running the Churchill Technological Trust which was planned to start just in advance of the College—and who suggested 'a second scheme, on a much wider and more representative basis, to cover both the Churchill Scholarships and the Administrative College'. The Churchill Technological Trust had two main components: the building and equipping of a postgraduate technological institute attached to Birmingham University, and Churchill Scholarships to be awarded at the discretion of the trustees. Colville had already approached some 33 of Britain's largest companies and consulted over 20 key figures in British public life, including almost all the large newspaper publishers. In other words he was well ahead of Bolton.

Colville therefore wrote to his prospective subscribers for the Churchill Technological Trust:

> While the present proposals were under consideration, Mr John Bolton, Chairman of the Solartron Electronic Group, has quite separately produced a scheme for the establishment of a Managerial and Administrative College, possibly attached to one of the older universities, to which he was himself prepared to contribute a very large sum and for which

he has good reason to think he would obtain support from the Ford Foundation and from Harvard. This college would be intended to take up to 1000 students who would be trained on much the same lines as the present small but most successful administrative college at Henley. Mr Bolton has now suggested that, bearing in mind the related importance of training managerial staff and technologists, his college should be included in the proposed Churchill Trust, which should aim at raising a larger sum than originally proposed and which should also seek to tap American sources of finance.

Jock Colville, now a director of Philip Hill, Higginson, wrote to Bolton on October 3, 1956 about his meeting with some of the largest companies to discuss the two projects. He had found it rather disappointing, due to ICI's falling profits and the shadow of Suez over the oil companies. But privately one or two people had advised him not to be too discouraged. He was looking to have some £6 million underwritten, and felt that this would depend on what the Americans were willing to do. Alexander Hood of Schroders, who had himself been at HBS, joined Bolton in thinking that such funds might well be available, especially from American companies with subsidiaries in Britain. But more immediately Hood proposed to send documents about both schemes to a range of British companies.

A second letter on November 21, 1956 reflected the response of these companies and may have been the key to not pursuing the College. In it, Colville says that he had had a letter from the Chairman of Tube Investments, Sir Ivan Stedeford, who along with others was arguing that the Churchill Technological Trust and the Administrative College should be kept separate, and then goes on

> I am anxious that nothing we are doing should get in the way of your own most valuable proposal, but I do think that there might be advantage on a number of grounds in its postponement for two or three years, and I rather felt at our luncheon together that you yourself thought this might be advantageous.

So, in his November 1963 letter to Marsh, Bolton sadly reflected:

> It became clear that we were really way ahead of our time and, whatever the pressure applied, the measure of support forthcoming (and demand from industry for men with Business School training) was just not adequate to ensure success. The final decision to postpone the idea until a more opportune time, came when it was clear that the Churchill College Appeal was sufficiently far advanced to be certain of being launched before we could get anything going, the more especially so because it emerged that the Churchill technological education theme was more in line with what British industry felt it required at that time.

THE DINING GROUP

The first act in the creation of a dining group to discuss management education was a letter from Keith Joseph to John Bolton dated February 11, 1958, starting:

> I recently spent ten weeks in America as the guest of the Ford Foundation and have come back convinced that we should take management training more seriously. When I was at Harvard, I was told at the Business School of your enthusiasm and I would like very much to meet you for a general talk.

At the same time, he confessed to uncertainty about what was needed. JEB replied on March 4 (after a reminder from Joseph), apologising that he had been so long in replying, 'but my business affairs have been particularly overburdening'. He also noted that his own idea had been put on hold. Nevertheless, he agreed to meet Joseph in the House of Commons on March 11. Joseph followed up the meeting with a letter noting that he had booked a room at the House on May 28, so that they could begin to invite people. Sir Noel Hall of Henley was brought into the picture by Joseph, and Joseph and Bolton had a positive meeting with Sir Keith Murray, the chairman of the UGC and a key figure in the university world. Joseph also sent out a letter on May 22 to the prospective attendees together with an agenda and some notes for discussion.

Those attending in addition to Joseph and Bolton were: Peter Parker of Booker Engineering, John Rodgers MP, Neil Salmon of Lyons, John Smith of Coutts, Duncan Courtney-Taylor of the BIM, and Hugh Tett of Esso. Parker and Smith were contacts of Bolton, Salmon was a friend of Joseph, and the others were probably known to have interests in the area. The minutes indicate a majority in favour of immediate postgraduate students, support for a link with an old university, an academic emphasis with the need for research, and finally an agreement to meet regularly with chosen guests to define the ideas more closely. Over the period from February the initiative had been taken by Joseph; it is probably also important, especially for the academics, that he was an MP and junior minister and a Fellow of All Souls, thus adding both academic credibility and political clout. We argue later that without Bolton, management education could well have turned out differently in Britain; but it must also be recognized that without Joseph, Bolton could not have set up the dining group so successfully.

On June 5, Joseph followed up with a letter to Bolton setting out a further list of issues and suggesting that it would be desirable to have a clear plan of action for the next dinner on July 1. He also suggested a sub-committee of which Bolton and Hugh Tett should be part and that there should be a paid secretary 'to devil and to go around consulting experts'. The July 1 dinner had as its guest Sir Keith Murray, who suggested a small academically based unit and let it grow. The meeting also considered someone to help in the long vacation and quite separately, a 'man of stature, acceptable to both University and to Industry', as the nucleus. The names of Sir Oliver Franks and Sir Geoffrey Crowther were mentioned. After the August meeting Keith Joseph sent round another note to what he now called 'the Dining Group', accepting that there would not be a working paper until the New Year, and suggesting Duncan Courtney-Taylor for the paper. It is noteworthy that several times in this note, and indeed in others, he referred to 'Bolton and I', suggesting the two of them as co-equal key figures in the Group. At the October meeting Professors Edwards and Hunt challenged the Group to prove that a demand existed, while at the November meeting there were three Vice-Chancellors including the Morris brothers, Charles and Philip, V-Cs of Leeds and Bristol respectively, whose interests understandably were their own universities. All the dinners took place at the House of Commons, which was very pleasant for all concerned. But there was little that could be described as tangible progress.

The meetings went on into 1959 without achieving a breakthrough and a hoped-for contribution from Lord Heyworth of Unilever did not materialize; it appears that he told the Group that *they* were the ginger group of active youngsters, and that they should get on with it. It is easy to envisage that JEB became impatient. The main indication of this is a letter to Keith Joseph of April 28, 1959 in which he said in a three-page letter (inter alia) 'I feel strongly that now is the time for positive decisions and positive action, however preliminary in nature, if we are not to founder in a summer sea of indecision' and went on to make four points: first to set up an educational trust for which he already had an adequate set of articles (presumably from the Commonwealth College of Administration) prepared by Slaughter and May; second that he would supply £3000 under covenant for seven years (which after reclaiming tax this would yield £5000 pa), but an offer which would lapse if nothing was started within three months, i.e. by July 31. On fund-raising he also undertook to canvass several companies privately, such as AEI, Shell, Vickers, Rolls Royce, and Courtaulds; third to talk to the Vice-Chancellors who had met with the Dining Group and ask them to put up proposals which would provide a platform on which to raise the initial monies; and fourth to review the situation after a year. He finished: 'We have the vigour, experience and skill within our group to pull this off and I think the time is now appropriate to do something definite'. Joseph's reply, while saying 'I enormously admire your willingness to back your judgment in this impressive way', said 'I think we are underestimating the difficulty of getting good teachers', in a very short response. One gets the feeling that Joseph didn't really want to give full-hearted support to Bolton's proposal, and that without this fairly aggressive approach by Bolton, there could well not have been a next-stage development.

By August 1959 Bolton was drafting a trust deed, having had some experience with the College of Administration, although he obviously needed lawyers (Slaughter and May) to get the language right. He was also pursing industry, although unsuccessfully in the case of Vickers and AEI. These were two significant responsibilities. One has to be impressed by the way in which he pushed these developments forward, especially given the difficult situation at Solartron at this time. But having done these, he did not push himself forward and was willing to defer to Keith Joseph and then Jim Platt in terms of chairing the committee. At the meeting of December 2, 1959, members were asked to commit funds. JEB confirmed his willingness, in spite of the expiry of his three-month period, a gift of £5000 pa for seven years, which infuriated his wife Gay. Joseph reported that since he had had to resign all his business connections on becoming a minister, he would only be able to guarantee £500 pa for seven years rather than the originally intended £2000. Esso confirmed £2000 and Peter Parker guaranteed £500 but hoped for £1000. By this time the Group had focussed on Leeds and Bristol as first-stage projects and agreed a target of £20,000 for seven years. Joseph agreed to draft an appeal letter, while JEB introduced Mr. Belton of Slaughter and May to talk through a draft for a Management Education Foundation. The momentum generated by Bolton's vision and determination was thus sufficient to move to the development of an institution. However, by the end of 1959 John Smith and Neil Salmon had pulled out, the former due to other commitments and the latter through disagreements with the emerging plans and more particularly an unwillingness to contribute to fundraising. On the other hand at the beginning of January 1960, Jim Platt, newly retired from Shell, came on the scene, initially seen as the Secretary but quite soon to become the Chairman and a key figure in developments over the next few years. And although the Dining Group may not seem to have produced much in the way of tangible results to this point, it was in fact sowing seed in fertile ground with industry, the UGC, the universities and not least with the Government. As put more emphatically by Bolton, 'our particular group have visited, wined, dined, discussed with, cajoled, bullied, and we hope, influenced literally thousands of industrialists, educationalists and politicians'. A somewhat more cynical comment was by Peter Parker (1989: 116): 'we ate our way through two years' worth of vice-chancellors—pretty tough going as most of them were bored'. The Dining Group itself was to continue to have monthly meetings at least until Bolton's letter to Marsh of November 1963 and perhaps beyond. After the FME had been formally set up, the meetings moved from the House of Commons to the Shell Building.

FORMATION OF THE FOUNDATION FOR MANAGEMENT EDUCATION

To help with the raising of funds, in June 1960 the Group produced a substantial prospectus entitled 'Management Education in the Universities', laying out their views and intentions. It would be surprising if John Bolton did not play a large part in the writing of it. It essentially set out to justify the need for supplementing managerial experience with courses of instruction at University level, whilst pointing out the divisions of opinion which existed in both academia and industry. The essence of their argument was that: 'A high proportion of the country's best talent now enters Universities. The responsibilities of managers in the generation to come will grow constantly in weight and complexity and we must do our best to ensure that the Universities play their full part in preparing them for their careers'. They went on 'Nothing could be more important than the assurance of a sufficient quantity of high-grade teachers'—this was a particular hobby-horse of Keith Joseph. As for cost, while recognizing that the calculation was not easy, they suggested that a minimum programme of teaching and research could be started at a cost of about £15,000 a year. If this could be developed in, say, eight universities within the next few years, 'that may prove to be as far as it is possible to go without prejudice to quality'. They noted that they had received 'carefully considered schemes' from Bristol and Leeds Universities and a smaller appeal from Cambridge, amounting in total to a cost of about £30,000 a year. The gap between this figure and their own sources of £9000 was what they were seeking to fill. They pointed out that the UGC had expressed sympathetic views in its last quinquennial report, and ultimately sought to transfer financial responsibility to UGC funds. Moving to the types of courses, they argued that full-time undergraduate courses in management would not be desirable, but rather sought postgraduate courses of one or perhaps two years, providing 'a real intellectual test'. As an outcome, they believed that 'able men building on these additional post-graduate studies will reach a higher maturity at an earlier age, and it is not fanciful to anticipate that the best men may find themselves at least five years ahead of present normal expectations'. This was of course a very attractive prospect. In conclusion, they noted that they had kept the FBI and the BIM advised of their activities, and had also discussed their plans with the Ministry of Education, which had welcomed their initiative. Then there was a plea for remembering the needs of the Commonwealth—undoubtedly a Bolton input—followed by another such, a plea for urgency, 'since if we procrastinate, the ultimate effect can be serious, and the process of correction long and painful'.

Philip Nind, the Director of the FME between 1968 and 1983 has written its history in an 88-page booklet entitled 'A Firm Foundation: The Story of the Foundation for Management Education'. This tells the story of the FME in far more detail than is appropriate here, but it is now out of print, so what follows is largely a synopsis of the booklet, mainly in relation to Bolton's role. The booklet starts by introducing the founding fathers, essentially the members of the dining group, concluding,

and, in the light of the thought he has given to the subject since the late 1940s and of the time and effort he has devoted to British management education as Chairman of the FME since 1968 and in many other ways, the *primus inter pares*, John Bolton.

Nind is perfectly right in referring to Bolton as the *primus inter pares* for reasons we have seen above, but it also needs to be noted that John did not want to push himself forward to positions of authority. Rather he was happy to stay behind the stage unless he was needed, which he was frequently, and later as Chairman for many years. And of course we are talking of a period when he was very heavily involved in Solartron. So when the FME began operations, he was not the dominant figure. That role was taken by Jim Platt, who being retired had time on his hands, unlike the other founding fathers.

Allan Williams (2010), in his history of UK business and management education, emphasizes the dominant role played by industry in the creation of business schools. This is true, but the FME would not have got off the ground without the financial input and leadership significance of Bolton, who in turn was largely influenced by his experience at Harvard Business School and was indeed supported by HBS in his attempts to do something in Britain. Several others, such as Keith Joseph and Peter Parker, were also strongly influenced by the American business school model.

On September 19, 1960 the FME was officially incorporated under the Companies Act 1948. The first Board Meeting of the FME a week after incorporation on 26 September 1960 consisted of Keith Joseph, John Bolton, George Noble, Peter Parker, and Jim Platt. Keith Joseph and John Bolton were appointed Chairman and Vice-Chairman, respectively, and David Aylett of Slaughter and May was appointed Secretary. Jim Platt was appointed chairman of the Executive Committee, which was responsible to the Council for the day to day management of affairs. He noted that £25,000 pa for seven years had been promised, with the likelihood of a further £5000. At that point, Cambridge had requested £5,000 pa, Bristol £15,000 pa and Leeds £16,600 pa. The requirements of the FME were placed at £40,000 a year. Sir Keith Murray, Chairman of the UGC had said that if approached by the Foundation, he would be willing to put a request to the UGC for a contribution of £10,000 for the next quinquennium. It was also agreed to approach the Ford Foundation. Other points: agreed to thank Sir Noel Hall for his services to the Dining Group; not to forget the Commonwealth; to consider additional appointments to the Council, the Executive Committee and the formation of an Advisory Committee. As Nind eloquently put it: 'With its sails set and the wind in the right quarter, the ship had left harbour for the open sea'.

Ultimately the first grants went to Cambridge, Leeds, and Bristol, amounting to £35,000 a year. It is something of an irony that none of these leading universities went on to develop a business school of their own, at least for a considerable time, so that whether this initial FME funding was used to good long-term effect must be open to question. In July 1961, Keith Joseph, having been promoted in the Government to Minister of State, resigned the Chairmanship of the Council and resigned from the Foundation later in the year. He had in any case said that he was not in it for the long term, but wanted to help something get started. Jim Platt took over the Chairmanship of Council with Bolton continuing as Vice-Chairman.

At the first AGM on December 8, 1961 (whose minutes are surprisingly terse and procedurally focused) Peter Parker was invited to prepare a draft of objectives, which remained for the duration of the organization:

(a) To enlist the support and interest of industry and other organizations in the initiation of projects at university level in management education, in general agreement with the University Grants Committee;
(b) To co-ordinate the raising of funds for agreed projects, and in particular to support projects which have good prospects of being financed subsequently by universities in the usual way;
(c) To assist the universities in the development and recruitment of good staff capable of conducting courses at university level and of furthering research in management education;
(d) To encourage industry to nominate individuals as members of university courses in management education;
(e) To assist and promote the exchange of teaching staff and research information between universities in the United Kingdom and other countries.

1963 was the key year in which the vision of John Bolton and his fellow founding fathers became reality. From then on developments in the business school world mushroomed well beyond any previous expectations.

ROBBINS, FRANKS, AND THE CREATION OF LONDON AND MANCHESTER BUSINESS SCHOOLS

The academic world was still very uncertain about management education, indeed much more negative than positive. Events were moving in other dimensions of higher education, recognizing that it needed to be greatly expanded. On February 8, 1961 the Government set up the Robbins Committee 'to review the pattern of full-time higher education in Great Britain and in the light of national needs and resources to advise Her Majesty's Government on what principles its long-term development should be based'. The Robbins Report (Robbins 1963) was the most extensive review of higher education ever in Britain and responsible for major expansion. But on management education, which the report noted had been 'much to the fore in public discussion recently' thanks to the FME and rising interest in industry, it said

> education for management as such . . . is the subject of considerable perplexity and opinion is divided on what methods of training are proper. Nevertheless we agree that the present situation is not satisfactory . . . We therefore recommend that at least two major postgraduate schools should be built up.

This was hardly a ringing endorsement of the need for management education from the perspective of improving the British economy, but it was sufficient to start the ball rolling toward a system of business schools broadly along American lines. This is what the FME and Bolton in particular, had been fighting for.

On July 17, 1963, there was a meeting attended by the FBI, BIM, Platt on behalf of the FME, and the Savoy Group, a group of senior industrialists led by Lord Rootes, at which it was decided to invite Lord Franks, diplomat, academic, businessman, and ultimate pillar of the Establishment (whom Urwick had strongly recommended for Bolton's College of Business Administration) to 'give guidance and advice' on next steps, essentially to take up the Robbins recommendation of two postgraduate business schools and provide a more concrete framework to operationalize the proposal. The invitation to Franks was duly made on July 24, some two months before the Robbins Report was published, although it is impossible not to believe that Franks was privy to what the Robbins Report was going to say. Similarly, it is impossible not to believe that although the Government was not involved directly in setting up the Franks invitation that it did not promise to accept his recommendations. A wide range of individuals and organizations, including the FME, gave their views to Franks, and his report (Franks 1963) was published by the BIM on November 21, only four months after his appointment. Essentially he recommended two postgraduate business schools linked to London and Manchester Universities but enjoying considerable autonomy. He also suggested that these two new foundations should do nothing to discourage the development of management education in other universities. The mood of the country was ripe for such a development; in April of 1963 NEDO had suggested the same as part of its influential report 'Conditions favourable to faster growth', in which it argued that management education should be at the postgraduate rather than the undergraduate level, an important support for the FME view.

The Franks Report suggested that the capital cost of a residential business school of the suggested size of about 200 students, might approach £1 million, with running costs of some £400,000 pa, of which as much as reasonable should come from fees. On this key issue, the Government agreed to share equally with industry represented by the FBI, the BIM, and the FME, the costs of setting up London and Manchester, providing assistance to a number of other universities (Durham, Edinburgh, Glasgow, Liverpool, Aston, Strathclyde, and Regent Street Polytechnic), and setting up a development fund for other applications known to be in the pipeline. The National Appeal was led by Lord Nelson of Stafford with the support of a strong committee and the backing of the FME, FBI, and BIM. The target for these three sets of funds was just over £3 million but with spectacular success the total achieved was over £5 million, contributed by over 350 companies. This was a major achievement and duly noted not only in Britain but abroad in the United States and Europe. Some part of this success must be attributed to the assiduous way in which Bolton in particular and other members of the dining group had prepared the way with industry in the previous half dozen years.

The FBI and BIM (of which John Bolton was by this time Chairman of Council) agreed that the FME should administer the fund, and guidelines for the administration of it were agreed. Given this responsibility it was recognized that the Council of FME should be made more formally representative, and it was agreed that of the 15 members of Council, three should be proposed by the FBI, two by the BIM (of which Bolton became one), and one each by the Association of British Chambers of Commerce, the Bank of England, and the nationalized industries. It was also decided to appoint a chief executive officer, and J. F. Sinclair, until then a director of Shell, was appointed as the Foundation's first Director. The three sponsoring institutions, the FBI, the BIM, and the FME, remained collectively responsible for the determination of policy, although with Bolton wearing two critical hats as Chairman of Council of the BIM and Vice-Chairman of the Council of the FME, he must have wielded disproportionate influence. In June 1964 it was agreed that the Chairman of the FME should be agreed between the President of the FBI (which was shortly to be replaced by the CBI), the Chairman of the BIM and the outgoing Chairman of the FME. However the actual invitation to serve as FME Chair should be extended by the Council of the FME. This is the way in which JEB was appointed a few years later.

The management education system took off from this point, with the majority of funds going to the setting up of London and Manchester Business Schools but some funding also for the development of management education in a wide range of universities and also private institutions such as Henley, Ashridge, and Roffey Park, all of which were helped by the FME funds. Equally importantly, the UGC came into the picture with funding of its own, soon moving to play the dominant role in overall funding of management education. Indeed this was the point when the university system largely came on board what became the management education bandwagon, although not without some qualms about sullying academic purity, as the story of one of the most successful of the new universities exemplifies in *Warwick University Limited* (Thompson 1970).

Bolton himself continued to take an active role in FME affairs. For instance, when the Ditchley Foundation held a conference on Management Education to bring together people from Britain, the United States, and the Commonwealth, Bolton was one of the British representatives, while one of the Americans was George Schultz, then Dean of the University of Chicago Graduate School of Business but later to become successively US Secretary of Labor, Commerce, and finally Secretary of State. This was also the period when Bolton wrote the letter to John Marsh in November 1963 which has already been mentioned, in which he was very positive about the work of the FME. As well as being the key to understanding the link between the Commonwealth Institute and the FME, this letter was also arguably the key to JEB becoming the Chairman of Council of the BIM, as we will discover in Chapter 5. It is also very interesting that he sent a copy of this letter to Dean Baker of HBS as well as Jim Platt. On June 30, 1964 JEB gave an address on 'British Business Schools' to the Tuesday Club, an extremely distinguished group of industrialists organized by A. D. Bonham-Carter of Unilever. In it he saw himself talking 'in the role of the enthusiastic amateur—a somewhat persistent one I like to believe—but very much the amateur'. Nevertheless, this may have been his most important speech on business schools and the best statement of the period of the expectations of what they might do.

So what did Bolton propose? He set himself five questions, of which the fifth and final question, 'what answers do we expect the new business schools to produce, when once they are established' is the key for defining his expectations:

The main educational effort of the new schools must therefore and inevitably be centred round the immediate post-graduate man. In this category, of course, I include the lucky few who will be able to have a year or two of experience in business before taking their post-graduate training in business administration.

And we must also hope that room will be found for men at the advanced management level, because they are bound to require re-training in the newly available techniques—and in very short order too. When we look into a future, not only of increased complexity, but also of increased leisure, we are forced to think in terms of what has come to be known as 'a continuing voyage of education' throughout a man's working life. And then—a happy thought—will come education for retirement.

We expect the business schools to impart a basic knowledge of the specialized parts of a whole business and of the increasing range of techniques which are available in those areas. The obvious specialisms are in sales, production, research and development, finance, and control—and I think we must also include personnel management. Study must also embrace basic fields such as human relations, economics and government policy.

Finally, we shall require a summation of the specialisms, in the form of consideration of overall company policies and plans—indeed a study of the job of general manager, for it is upon him that the final responsibility for effective decision-making squarely rests.

We must also impart to the student a whole range of abilities and understandings. Harvard catalogues these as follows:

The ability to analyse business situations, to recognise problems and determine issues, to seek pertinent facts, develop alternatives and to reach reasoned decisions
The ability to organize and understand the basic ingredients of leadership
The ability to use oral and written communications

> The ability to deal with people
>
> The ability to train subordinates
>
> The ability to establish standards and to control and judge performances
>
> The ability to execute selected operating tasks, including those involving severe time pressures
>
> Considerable knowledge of business techniques, in one or more areas, is required
>
> Acquaintance with sources of business information is useful
>
> Our student of management requires a broad understanding of the useful generalizations of political economy, and the ability to develop at least the beginnings of an integrated social and economic philosophy
>
> An understanding of the businessman's social role in a democratic society
>
> And finally, perhaps the most difficult of all, a spirit of vigorous and courageous enterprise—an attitude of mind which accepts and welcomes the challenge of change which lies ahead.
>
> That's quite a list—but it represents the bare bones of the task which the new business schools can, and must, undertake.
>
> Behind these needs must lie research, and constant experimentation in teaching techniques. Lectures and reading will not satisfy so complex a requirement. Case studies, business games, syndicate discussions and role playing, must all make their contributions.
>
> We face the problems of training a new generation of teachers, in what, for us, is a comparatively new field of study. We face the problem of creating real cooperation between the academic world and industry. Finally, we face the task of really making management a profession—a profession having such prestige that the very best brains will be attracted by the challenge of making Britain economically great—for if we fail in this all-important challenge, the future that lies ahead will indeed be bleak.

How far the present-day business schools have lived up to these expectations might be a question for the reader of this book, as might the analogous question as to whether the expectations themselves were realistic and appropriate. This author's views are at the end of this chapter.

THE COUNCIL OF INDUSTRY FOR MANAGEMENT EDUCATION

Another important institutional development in management education was the setting up in 1967 of the Council of Industry for Management Education (CIME). By this time the FME Council, notwithstanding its industrial members, saw its main role as promoting the supply side of management education at university level, in terms of both quantity and quality, doing this mainly but by no means only through the funds available for dispersal through its hands. The CBI (having replaced the FBI as the main spokesman for industry) took the initiative to create a coordinating body able to express industry's needs in management education, hence the CIME. It was agreed that the Chairman of the BIM, the FME, and the CBI's Education and Training Committee would be ex-officio members, but that other members would be invited as individuals and not in a representative capacity. It was also agreed that the Director of the FME would act as Secretary of the CIME and that the FME's office would provide any necessary services. John Bolton, unsurprisingly, was selected as an individual member, although shortly to become an ex-officio member. In 1979 Bolton became chairman of CIME on an interim basis but nevertheless for over a year after Michael Pocock died suddenly until John Raisman was appointed in 1981.

The CIME took it upon itself to set up another appeal fund in 1970, with an ambitious target of £7.5 million. In the event £6.25 million was raised, still a very creditable performance. In the 1970s CIME made frequent representations to the UGC, and to ministers and senior officials on a wide range of topics concerned with management education. CIME also continued to raise money. In 1976 the FME noted that it would run out of funds in four or five years at the existing rate of expenditure. John Bolton did four drafts for such an appeal himself in 1978. But it was not until 1983 that the appeal was actually launched. Lord Ezra, in launching the appeal recognized that many companies now had direct links with individual business schools but nevertheless argued that there were some issues for which central funding was desirable. It made an appeal for £2 million, which was overtaken by the General Election, but only raised £481,000 by September 1983. The same appeal continued and had raised £893,000 by September 1990 when CIME seems to have been closed down. Nevertheless, this was not an insignificant amount of money to raise and was very valuable for the FME.

THE LATER YEARS OF THE FME

In 1968 important changes took place in the FME. Jim Platt decided to retire as Chairman and was replaced by, again unsurprisingly, John Bolton, who was to retain this role for 18 years. In addition, the FME's Director, Sinclair, decided to retire and was replaced early in 1969 by Philip Nind, who was to stay for 15 years until 1984. Nind was a very able administrator, a Balliol man who had served in Special Operations in Greece and Albania in WWII and then gone on to a career in Shell, and when he joined the FME, was also appointed to some key posts in management education, such as the UGC Management Studies Committee and the NEDO Management Education, Training and Development Committee, both from 1968–83. He also wrote his autobiography, *Never a Dull Moment*, in 1991. Between them Bolton and Nind formed a powerful partnership to take the FME forward and to help management education in Britain through its second stage of development. Between them, they were arguably two of the most important and influential people in British management education. There were many projects to be considered, universities to be visited, cases to be made to the Department of Education, and policies to be decided. Bolton did not get involved in all of these; his two vice-chairmen, Sir David Watherston until 1976 and then Ted Choppen, both did a great deal of the visiting. And there was a certain amount of acting as an intermediary between the forces of industry and academia, where both sides sometimes felt that the other did not understand them (something which holds true to this day). Bolton wrote in his Chairman's report of 1970:

> Management education is for the improvement of management performance and there can be no doubt in anyone's mind that the future of our country depends on raising the standards of our industrial performance—which in turn can only be done by an improvement in management skills and techniques. It is unlikely that there will ever be full agreement between industrialists and academics in any area of higher education, and in management education in particular there will always be the need for constant adjustment of views by both sides after inevitable differences of opinions. But at present there is some evidence of a communications problem which has left some industrialists feeling that some of the business schools are taking up too much time with subjects and sessions of little value to industry, and to some academics thinking that their programmes and intentions are misconstrued and misinterpreted by industrialists and businessmen.

Bolton must have spent quite a lot of time being lobbied by one side or the other about the deficiencies of the other and must have felt like a piggy-in-the-middle, which indeed he was. He also did some lobbying himself; a significant example of this was writing to the Chancellor of the Exchequer, Anthony Barber, in 1972 in his role as the Chairman of FME, to plead that management education should be permitted as an allowable expense under Section 133 of the Income and Corporation Taxes Act of 1970. This Section established that only technical education 'specially requisite' to the role of the payer should be allowable. John argued that management education was required to facilitate the effective management of business and was therefore 'specially requisite' under the Act.

The FME produced two useful 'accounts of stewardship', one from 1964–1969 and the other from 1969–1975. The first showed an expenditure of £5,336,000 to 23 separate institutions, still mainly London and Manchester but clearly also widening the field of disbursements, with 10 institutions receiving more than six figure sums. The second mainly covered the £6 million raised from the 1970 Fund. Teacher training took up a substantial slice of both accounts.

Philip Nind used to write briefs for Bolton on a wide range of issues of the moment, such as:

- whether research projects supported by FME should be reported directly by the instigator to the FME Executive Committee;
- suggesting the setting up of an Inquiry into Industrial Democracy should be discussed by FME with a view to providing programmes of common interest to unions, management and government officials;
- how a pension scheme for FME staff might be organized;
- the idea for FME to provide possible funding for a journalist from THES to attend a business school or at least visit one or several;
- the concern of business schools as to the recruitment and calibre of faculty. In particular Nind reflects that in the first decade or so of the business schools the first priority had to be teaching, but now there should be an equivalent focus on research. He notes that there isn't much to be done about it other than be aware of the issue, but it does illustrate Nind's broad perspective over business school issues;
- whether JEB could have a word with Keith Joseph—Jan 1982—about the announcement of further cuts in the SSRC budget with the danger of cuts in management studentship grants. Nind suggests: 'Perhaps a quiet talk with yourself, whom he knows well, and myself would be appropriate'. JEB wrote to Joseph three days later suggesting this;
- whether the setting up of Robinson College Cambridge might be a means for introducing management sciences to Cambridge in a more formal way than hitherto;
- issues to do with London Business School such as relationships with the University and relationships with the LBS Board of Governors, asking JEB to have a word with Jim Ball (the Principal) on these matters, presumably on the assumption that he (JEB) could use his influence to LBS' advantage;
- on a particularly contentious and on-going issue, the independence of business schools within the university complex, Nind wrote 'I am sure it is healthy that we should have controversy about this but FME needs to resist pressures being brought on it by university authorities'.

What all these points indicate is that the FME was involved in aspects of management education well beyond funding. Indeed during this period the FME managed to be a pretty effective organization. Nancy Foy, in carrying out a research project for the Foundation to review management education over the forthcoming decade ('The Missing Links—British Management Education in the Eighties') found as a by-product that the FME was held in high regard by the business schools for its non-bureaucratic approach and quick decision-making and administration of funds. It also acted as a catalyst for discussions on various topics such as business history, leadership in management, production management, computer applications in management, corporate social responsibility, and others. The Chairmanship was in fact an ongoing important role at the centre of British management education. In February 1976 the number of members of the FME Council was raised from 20 to 25, which does not indicate a declining role. The 21st AGM of FME was an excuse for a nostalgic reunion of the surviving members of the House of Commons Dining Group; it was suggested by JEB and supported by Keith Joseph in March 1982.

On his retirement as Chairman, Bolton offered a prize for a student at Cambridge who showed practical evidence of entrepreneurship, while on John's death the FME offered the Judge Institute at Cambridge the John Bolton MBA Memorial Prize for five years at £400 per year and also two Management Studies Tripos prizes of £100, also for five years. When John stepped down from the Chairmanship he became President of FME in January 1986, a role which he only relinquished with his death in 2003. He still occasionally attended Council meetings when he was President. What sort of role was it?

> Any person for the time being holding the title of President of the Foundation. . . . may attend all general meetings of the Foundation but shall not have any further powers or be entitled, in such capacity, to vote at any such meeting or to any remuneration.

Eventually, with a declining income, FME moved to Oxford in 1983 to cut administrative costs, using surplus accommodation unused by UBI and then a few years later to Witney, where it existed until very recently, having done its duty nobly. It closed on June 30, 2013 after a last AGM on April 23, 2013 had decided that there were not enough funds to continue. CIME had closed some 25 years earlier.

The FME was not without influence even up to the time of its closure, as one way in which industry could make its views felt about the state of management education. A quotation from the Epilogue of Nind's history reflects on the role of the FME:

> No other country boasts a body quite like the FME because no other country possesses the kind of cultural traditions and educational patterns which require a privately bred bee to sting the official administrative system into essential action—but action, let it be said, which was quickly and effectively implemented once the stimulus had been imparted . . . Through FME, university management education in Britain grew from a sapling sown in soil that was rich for tillage and nurtured by a small group of far-sighted men until it was strong enough to stand on its own in the academic and industrial forests around it.

John Bolton, that *primus inter pares* of those far-sighted men, had good reason to be proud of his offspring. Overall, his influence on the activities of the FME was immeasurable. A counter-factual view of the history of management education and the FME might argue that if JEB had not been there, industry would not have got its act together, the academics would not have acted by themselves, and even his colleagues on the Dining Group wouldn't have contributed their funding if John hadn't embarrassed them into it. In fact events could have turned out quite differently.

Looking from a longer time perspective than the setting up period, how far can we say that management education has achieved what Bolton wanted from it? Certainly the views of both British industry and British education that management was not a subject worth teaching has changed completely. Management is now the most popular subject in the university system and industry is very conscious of the need for developing managers. It is nevertheless the view of this author that the main driving force in the widespread growth of management education was neither industry nor academia, but rather the managers who saw their own need for development and were either willing to pay for it themselves or cajole their employers into doing so. Bolton would have celebrated this change in attitudes by all three parties. However, whether management education in Britain has achieved the professionalization of management that he saw Harvard, Chicago, Stanford, Wharton, and their peers achieving in America is a more open and doubtful question.

4   The Harvard Programme in Britain and Other Management Education

Introduction
Advanced Management Programmes International
The Business Graduates Association
Sub-committee on Business Management Studies, University Grants
   Committee
Others

INTRODUCTION

The FME was arguably the most influential organization John Bolton was associated with in the management education field, but it was far from the only one. Almost any organization in the early days of management education had JEB attached somewhere and this chapter examines these while focussing on one for which he had a particular fondness.

ADVANCED MANAGEMENT PROGRAMMES INTERNATIONAL

The Harvard Advanced Management Programme was first devised in 1943 with the very practical aim of 'converting businessmen into vitally needed war production managers'. Held twice a year on campus from 1945, the 13-week course

> has attempted much more than merely giving new faces to old tires. It now aims to change a man's whole way of work. It tries to free him from the confines of his specialty and start him thinking about problems of broad policy and strategy of long-range significance to business. (Wingo 1967: 4)

How it came to Britain is the subject of a monograph by Sally Heavens (2006), and the account that follows is very largely taken from this source.

Sir Adrian Cadbury (Heavens 2006: 5), in writing the foreword to the history of the AMP in Britain, reflected:

> It is right that we should be reminded that the concept of courses of learning which would strengthen the ability of British managers to succeed in an increasingly competitive world owed nothing to the formal institutions established for the purpose and everything to three very different and remarkable individuals.

The three people he had in mind were Denys Scott, Harry Hansen, and John Bolton.

Denys Scott was the managing director of Lexington International, the PR subsidiary of J. Walter Thompson when in the summer of 1963, before the Franks Report was published, he took a flight to America and went to the Harvard Business School to discuss a proposal. He did this with no prior connection to the School and no form of introduction, based on one of his favourite sayings: 'Be brave, be bold—don't wait, innovate!' On his arrival, Dean Baker referred him to Professor Harry Hansen, to whom he said:

> As you know, there has been during the last year great discussion about management training. Lord Franks will be producing a report this coming autumn. Also there has been much argument on the Harvard case approach. The debate is strong. Couldn't Harvard come to England to do a programme to show what it does? I might say that I am here only as an interested citizen representing nobody but myself.

Hansen responded that any official programme must be held at the Harvard Business School, but that it might be possible for a team of faculty to do it unofficially and that he could organize such a team with the Dean's permission. This was the synopsis of a discussion which took no more than 20 minutes and it was agreed that the two would meet again when Hansen was passing through London in September. In parting, Hansen said: 'You must bring John Bolton into this. He is a graduate of this School, a member of its Visiting Committee, familiar with management education developments in Britain, and we value his judgements'. This was the origin of the British AMP.

Scott was later to say of Hansen: 'Harry was a marketing man, a salesman, a missionary . . . he wanted to change the world'. At that time, Hansen was a full professor of 14 years standing, the Program Director of the Advanced Management Program in the Far East, a position he had held since 1956, and was about to take up the Directorship of the Business School's Division of International Activities.

Marketing was Hansen's passion and specialty; in 1965 he would be appointed Malcolm P. McNair Professor of Marketing at Harvard

Business School, and it is undoubtedly the case that his approach to the wider issues of international business education was informed by his marketing philosophy.

John Bolton responded as enthusiastically as Hansen had to Scott's proposal and contacted Hansen to ask him to address the British alumni of HBS in London on the possibilities at their September 1963 meeting. The actual process of 'contacting' is worth quoting (Heavens 2006: 22):

> Late in August, Professor Hansen was in Sidu Sharif, some 1500 miles north of Karachi at the Swat Hotel, when one of the bearers came running saying 'Sahib, telephone London'. This was indeed a surprise because although some try to reach Rawalpindi several hundred miles away by telephone and Karachi was known as a long-shot chance, London was unheard of. At the telephone a small group of the hotel staff was gathered to witness the prodigious feat of talking to London. But all failed despite many shouted 'hullo's'. Once in the static distance a faint female voice said 'Mr Bolton' but that was all. Two days later a cable came: 'Can you speak at the Harvard Business School Club meeting September?' The answer was 'Yes'. What about the subject? Hansen assumed it would have to do with a summer programme.

Hansen's presentation to the HBS Club in London was in the nature of a case; should the programme be presented. This was just as well because club members had invited guests, some of whom 'were sceptical of formal management education, of case study teaching, and of American professors'. The response ranged from qualified support to very negative comments, some of which included:

- Britain was far ahead of the US in the study of administrative theory
- Britain needed no help from the colonies
- Cases would not work in Britain
- Senior British managers would not attend.

The dinner ended with no clear conclusions, and after it a group sat around to review the meeting, and in spite of the obvious challenges, the decision was made to go ahead. Hansen's wife later reflected on how this decision was reached: John looked at Harry and said: 'So much for progress, that does it, let's do it'. This was typical Bolton decision-making, always optimistic, always wanting to push ahead.

But there were still issues of sponsorship and venue, because quite understandably Hansen made it clear that the British side must resolve these dimensions in a formal invitation. In the event the North East Development Corporation became the sponsor, with the support of the BIM and the

Harvard Business School Club of London, and unsurprisingly but critically, John Bolton stood as financial guarantor for the programme. The venue was to be Bede College Conference Centre at Durham University, the fee was set at £400, which included all tuition, materials, accommodation, and meals, and the timing was 27 June to 4 August 1964, a six-week programme as opposed to the 13 weeks of the Harvard-based AMP. The administration of the programme, including the recruitment of participants, was handled as an account within Scott's Lexington company. The programme was announced as being for executives between 37 and 55 years old, and

> an applicant must have demonstrated in his business career unusual qualities of ability, leadership and adaptability. Candidates should have had about 15 to 20 years of business or organization experience and should now be in top-level management, policy-making positions or expected to be in such positions within the foreseeable future.

There were however no formal academic requirements. The size of the course was set at 62, with a mix designed to reflect a wide cross-section of industry. The content was composed of: administrative practice, business policy, cost and financial administration, and marketing administration, and they were taught with an emphasis on integration. Integration was not only in the classroom, though; meals were taken together and with the four Harvard professors staying on-site, there was plenty of opportunity for individual advice and social interaction. One of the case studies was, again unsurprisingly, Solartron, and as Peter Butler put it: 'The fascinating feature of this case, therefore, is to demonstrate how, even in the 1950s, it was possible rapidly to grow a company—and shareholder value—without achieving large profits!!'

It should also be noted that Harry Hansen at least of the four Harvard professors gave up his summer vacation to organize and help teach the course, and he continued to give up a big slice of his annual holiday for the rest of his 19-year involvement with it. His wife, Carolyn, for her part, acted as unpaid house-matron/nurse/nanny to the 50 or 60 participants on each course, which always included an inevitable few who took most unkindly to being away from home comforts.

Durham was undoubtedly a success, both as an enjoyable and fulfilling learning process, in terms of its conception and marketing, and gratifyingly in producing a financial surplus, but inevitably the participants still had a lot of suggestions as to further improvements. The Durham programme had been planned and promoted as a one-off exercise, but its success raised the obvious question of what happened next. Hansen, Scott, and Bolton got together to work this through. The need for a more formalized infrastructure to organize and promote the programme was obvious, and initially it was hoped that the BIM would take on this role (JEB was at this time Chairman of the BIM Council), and in December 1964 Katharine Northridge, the BIM courses organizer, wrote to the BIM solicitors, Corbin, Greener and Cook, to initiate the legal processes for establishing Advanced Management Programmes International as a charitable trust for educational purposes. The Harvard Business School Club of London was to be a co-promoter together with the BIM. The Trust was to be intended as an ongoing entity, offering an annual programme, and a draft deed would be submitted to the Ministry of Education for vetting and then filed with the Inland Revenue. However the BIM solicitor at Corbin, Greener, and Cook, Mr. H. J. Killick, cast doubt on the sponsors, the BIM because as a sponsor, it would be precluded from remuneration as the manager of the course, and the Harvard Business School of London Club because of its indefinite constitution. Killick had talked with John Bolton and they felt that it would be better if the sponsors were named as individuals. So Denys Scott and John Bolton became the named sponsors and also trustees, together with Frank Morgan and James Whitaker who were members of the Durham programme, and on July 1, 1965, approval of the Draft Deed was received from the Department of Education, enabling the Trust to be registered as a charity under the Charities Act 1960. For operational purposes, there was also a committee of management composed of the Trustees, which John Bolton chaired from its inception in 1965 to 1981. The number of Trustees was expanded over time to incorporate more participants of the programmes.

The main purposes of the Trust were (Heavens 2006: 48):

> the promotion in the United Kingdom of studies in advanced management (in so far as such studies are charitable) and may with a view thereto but not by way of restriction or limitation the trustees may
>
> i.   Institute establish and promote conferences and training courses in advanced management for persons who have reached or are closely approaching the level of general policy-making whether in business industry national or local government or trade unions
> ii. Provide or endow or assist in providing or endowing scholarships for teachers of advanced management studies
> iii. Award certificates to those who graduate through the training courses referred to above Provided that no such certificate shall be issued which does not clearly state on its face that it is not issued by or under the authority of any Government Department but is issued by the authority of the Trustees or the Sponsors only
> iv. . . .

So John Bolton had taken on another substantial commitment, and one with which he was long to be associated. Coincidentally, it was not a million miles removed from what he had wanted his British Commonwealth College of Business Administration to become just under a decade earlier. The Trustees had quite a lot to do, as Harry Hansen noted in 1985:

> Not enough can be said of the efforts of the British trustees in keeping the programme on a proper course. While the American contribution came in determining the objectives and content of the programme, its manning and approval of its site, the trustees oversaw admissions, the administration of funds, and relations with the outside world—no small contributions over two decades.

And in its administration there was enough work to justify an EC2 address and a separate phone number.

While all this was happening, a second programme was being organized at the University College of North Wales at Bangor for the period June 19 to July 30, 1965. The model was the same as at Durham with a few modifications suggested by the Durham participants, such as additions of specific relevance to British conditions in the areas of accounting, economics, and industrial relations. John Bolton wrote the introduction to the programme guide in which he provided an insight into the thinking behind the programme. Again, the programme was a resounding success, and a key figure for the rest of the AMPI programmes emerged in Chrissie Napier as the administrator. Carolyn Hansen was later to say that they would have been lost without her. In 1966 the programme was held at Strathclyde, and then for the 16 years between 1967 and 1982, it was held at Clyne Castle, a self-contained hall of residence just over a mile from the main campus of the University College of Swansea. As the 1967 brochure explained (Heavens 2006: 59):

> The hall is situated in wood and parkland overlooking Swansea Bay. It occupies an ideal position at the eastern end of the lovely Gower peninsula and is only three miles from Swansea town centre. The castle is of baronial style, but has been extensively modernised and adapted to the requirements of a university hall of residence. The main rooms constitute a spacious and comfortable common room, quiet room, library and refectory. There are bar facilities.

As the long tenure suggests, it was a very popular location. The model remained largely the same: the age limit was lowered in 1968; the fee inevitably went up from £400 to £3200 in the last year at Swansea. But the Harvard professors continued to be top-quality senior people, with Harry Hansen an ever-present programme director for 20 years until the handover to the Oxford Centre for Management Studies (later Templeton College) in 1983. Many of the participants went on to head their companies, benefitting from what was felt by impartial observers as well as the participants to be an outstanding programme. And the programme was financially successful, creating a capital of £100,000, with which, as Harry Hansen put it: 'we managed the programme, gave scholarships to members of university and polytechnic faculties, and provided grants to ease its transfer into the Oxford Centre for Management Studies'. It was also important that AMPI gave awards to academics and trade union officials to attend, recognizing their roles in the development of management. It may well have been Bolton who suggested access for unionists, since he had also included them in his proposals for a Commonwealth College of Administration. And there was even a refresher course of a single week attached to the 1970 programme, but it was not repeated due to the strain it put on the organization.

The 1979 programme guide is illustrative of the Swansea period. It is based on a series of questions, starting with 'Are Managers Born?' (still something to be considered in Britain at that time), following it with 'What is Unique about this Programme?', and later 'What?', 'For Whom?', 'Why?', 'How?' and 'Where?' before providing the CVs of the seriously distinguished Harvard faculty members and administrative information, including about the AMPI Club. Interspersed in all these questions is a piece by John Bolton in his role as Chairman of the AMPI Trust, 'Management Education—AMP's Contribution', in which he parades the success of the programme, for which he notes that there are

> a number of reasons . . . but there are three that stand out to me above others: the pragmatic approach to live business problems that characterises its content, the careful screening of applicants to the Programme, and the teaching skills of the Faculty.

After 1983 the programme continued to flourish at Templeton College Oxford, evolving into two four-week sessions a year with a maximum of 30 places on each. As Harry Hansen noted in his 1985 memorandum, it was always the intention that the programme would be transferred to an established British institution and that control by the Trust and the Americans would be ended. It took longer than expected to find a new home but the opportunity came with the Oxford centre, where the case study approach continued to be used.

The Advanced Management Programmes International Trust remained in existence with its funds intact and decided to focus its future thrust on promoting entrepreneurial management and the management of technological change in Britain. One element of this was creating the Hansen Research fellowship at Cambridge University and another has been an association with the Centre for Tomorrow's Company, founded by Mark Goyder at the Royal Society of Arts. Another significant development was research funding, such as a survey of AMP graduates by Harry Hansen entitled 'British Managers in the Mirror'.

There were various other developments, the most important being the creation of an AMPI Club shortly after the Durham programme, of which

James Whitaker was the first chair. Its objective was to continue the networking opportunities through a newsletter, a club tie, an annual lecture and especially through the annual reunions at University College Oxford each spring. The list of speakers at the annual lecture event was outstanding and guaranteed an excellent attendance, indeed the good and the great of British industry with a sprinkling of top politicians and a few outliers, such as Jack Dash, the London dockers' leader, and Arianna Stassinopoulos, author and celebrity (and more recently blogger). A particular highlight was the address given by Prince Philip at a luncheon held at the Grocers' Hall in March 1978, at which all three of the original founders were able to be present. To be graced with a royal presence and especially with a speech written from a very personal perspective on the nature of society, is a mark of substantial recognition by the British establishment, and the founders must have felt suitably honoured. In his talk, Prince Philip reflected on his own experience in the Navy, likened the AMP to the Staff College principle, advocated an ongoing sandwich course framework for learning, noted the cynical phrase of Juvenal, 'sed quis custodiet custodies?' and finished by praising the consumer as the ultimate and only guardian of a free society. The final meeting was held without a speaker when the club set aside the evening to pay tribute to Harry Hansen after his death in 1992. The Trustees subsequently decided to rename the Trust 'The Harry Hansen Research Fellowship'.

Hansen was not only a professor of marketing; he took a wider view of the social responsibilities of business and business schools, as he articulated in 'The Aims of Business Education', published in the Harvard Business School Bulletin in 1970, and he tried to inculcate these in the AMPI programme, views with which Bolton would certainly have been in accord. One important dimension was: 'Business schools should impart more than technical competence; they should begin the education of architects of a new better economic order'. AMPI was not just about case teaching; it was about how managers should view the world, including a commitment to customers and the involvement of people in companies. Hansen as might be expected took a strong line about the importance of marketing: 'Marketing is the measure of a free society. I'm in favour of what the consumer wants. In a controlled economy marketing is merely distribution by the State. In a democracy, marketing is a socially desirable function, necessary to democracy'.

JEB's commitment to the AMPI and to Harry Hansen is nowhere better illustrated than in the episode in which in 1982 and again in 1984 he nominated Hansen for the Benjamin Franklin Medal at the Royal Society of Arts. The Royal Society for the Encouragement of Arts, Manufactures and Commerce, to give it its full title, or the better known acronym RSA, is a distinguished British organization dating from 1754 committed to finding practical solutions to today's social problems. The Benjamin Franklin Medal is awarded in alternate years to British and American citizens who have carried out important activities in promoting Anglo-American understanding and more broadly have shifted public debate in an innovative way and are deemed by the RSA 'to be significant to our core enlightenment values of developing human progress'. Those who have been awarded the medal are an extremely illustrious list, including on the British side such eminent people as Alistair Cooke, Harold Macmillan, Margot Fonteyn, David Attenborough, and Peter Ustinov, and on the American side Senators William Fulbright and George Mitchell, Secretary of State Colin Powell, Lewis Mumford the writer on urban design, and John Hay Whitney the publisher and philanthropist. So to be thought of in this category is an honour in itself. John, who was himself a life fellow of the RSA, put Harry forward 'for his uniquely valuable contribution to management education at senior level in Britain over the previous twenty years', using his own perspective as a member of the Visiting Committee at HBS and his FME role in Britain to 'say with conviction that the course is still uniquely important in the education of our top managers in the future' and finishing 'it would be most appropriate to crown his most distinguished career by awarding him the Benjamin Franklin Medal for his unique contribution to Anglo-American relations and understanding in the field of management education'. However Harry was not awarded the Medal in 1983, so John had to try again for the 1985 Medal and this time he sent copies of the recommendation to various key people. He also commented acerbically to one friend:

> I confess that if we again award the Benjamin Franklin Medal to someone like Professor Henry Russell-Hitchcock (who had been given the award in 1979) who discovered that American Georgian buildings built by British architects, or their pupils, are remarkably similar to British Georgian buildings of the same period I shall feel like giving up in despair.

The 1985 application was however successful, and it was a great honour for Harry.

Harry Hansen wrote an interesting paper in 1985 about the programme, after its handover to Oxford, 'A Summary of the Advanced Management Programme Emphasising the Anglo-American Collaboration', in which he reflected on its origins and its legacy. His take on the decision to go ahead was illustrative of his wider approach to life; after the difficult evening with the Harvard Business School Club 'we few enthusiasts retired to a pub to have a few whiskies and to decide what, if anything, to do. We decided to use Rule One of the experienced marketing practitioner; if market research contradicts your opinion, ignore it'. Of its origins, he talked of three men, 'Denys Scott, who first proposed the programme, John Bolton who swept it up in his strong arms, and myself, an American, who directed the programme for twenty years'. Using the phrase 'swept it up in his strong arms' is an evocative and appropriate way of describing John Bolton's way of getting involved. It is also worth noting that Bolton, in commenting on the draft of Hansen's piece, added that he did not consider that 'the emerging British schools of London and Manchester had the expertise to embrace the tuition of senior managers', hence the need for a programme like AMPI. Harry Hansen later became involved in 'The Foundation for Management in Asia' and proposed John as an International Director, to which John said he was flattered and time permitting would be 'absolutely thrilled'.

There was in AMPI a sense of belonging and togetherness, which John played a considerable part in creating. As the course's administrator, Christine Napier, put it after John's death: 'As well as having tremendous respect for [John] and all that he had achieved, I will always remember him for his great sense of fun and how he gathered around him the whole AMPI extended "family"'. Carolyn [Hansen] wrote that her sanity was saved often by a phone call from John with his latest dirty joke, delivered in his beautiful distinctive voice—how he loved a good joke!!

Perhaps not now given the attention it deserves, this programme was nevertheless massively influential in the careers of those who undertook it. And as Harry Hansen noted in his 1985 memorandum on the programme, it was a unique example of Anglo-American collaboration and particularly an attempt to bring the Harvard experience to the UK. Over 1000 senior managers participated in the programmes, from some 470 companies and representing over 30 countries other than the UK. Harvard played its part too, with 24 full professors teaching on at least one programme and many of them quite a lot more.

THE BUSINESS GRADUATES ASSOCIATION

The Business Graduates Association was founded June 1967 by eight MBAs from American universities and two graduates from the very new London Business School. John Bolton was the Founder Chairman of the Advisory Council of the BGA and thereafter remained on the very distinguished Council, which also included Bowman Scott from Solartron days. Recognizing that despite the value of the MBA, there was a distinct lack of knowledge about the qualification in the UK and Europe, the BGA's intention was to promote the benefits of business education through five key objectives: help the development of existing business schools, support the founding of new business schools, encourage employers to take on MBAs, help increase the number and quality of students attending business school, and advocate the importance of professional business education in general. By the end of their first decade the BGA had grown to a membership of 1,900 as well as 175 corporate members, together with a robust organizational structure. It also had an office in Jermyn Street and a substantial quarterly magazine, on occasion running to 50 or so pages, while its administrative director, Sir David Clutterbuck, was himself to become a well-known management author.

In 1983, in response to the growing number of polytechnic business schools offering an MBA programme, the BGA established an accreditation programme to champion the MBA as a brand and to ensure standards were maintained. It soon became clear that there was considerable demand for this kind of quality assurance in the MBA market. This somewhat unintentional development was to become its major role in business education and arose out of bank loans for the still relatively new MBA programmes. The banks, looking for some dimension of credibility by which to justify the loans, took to issuing guidelines by which only those MBAs at business schools associated with the BGA were eligible for loans, thus making it desirable for all MBA schools to want such an association and accreditation. There is a letter in 1983 from the Polytechnic of Central London lobbying John to help them obtain membership.

Thus by 1987 the BGA's stakeholder group had evolved into graduate members, accredited business schools and MBA employers. To reflect this change the BGA became the Association of MBAs. Throughout the 1990s, the Association of MBAs continued to grow, adding members and accrediting programmes, including many outside the UK. The Association, until then staffed by volunteers, also adopted a more professional structure, adopting a full-time head and management team.

Bolton wrote an article in the Summer 1978 Edition of *The Business Graduate*, which was an issue on the small firm. This was the first special edition the BGA had done, and it was an interesting and somewhat unexpected topic given the corporate career patterns of most business graduates. Other notable contributors were Harold Lever, who had the primary focus on small firms in the Cabinet, Anne Mueller, Deputy Secretary in the Department of Industry with primary responsibility for small firms, and Graham Bannock, the research director of the Committee on Small Firms, in an attack on the banks. Christopher Saunders, the other Brit on the Harvard MBA programme of 1950 also contributed a piece, having spent much of his time with McKinsey before developing his own engineering firm. It seems quite likely that JEB would have suggested the topic and some of the contributors, and possibly nobbled them himself to write for the magazine. John's own piece was a review of a Fabian Society tract (No 455) by Nicholas Falk entitled 'Think Small: Enterprise and the Economy' which was a summary of the factors forcing changes in the industrial structure and the measures needed to respond to these. One of Falk's suggestions was a comprehensive programme to reduce the barriers to small business, with which John was easily able to agree.

In 1978 the BGA through its research committee decided to set up a programme of research based on topics which had been indicated to be of interest to its membership. It therefore wrote to its membership asking for indications of interest in participating, giving a list of 10 broad areas, in which it is interesting to note that causes of failure in small firms was the first. JEB wrote back endorsing all of them but suggesting that priority should be given to those in which the membership's specialist knowledge would have most leverage, such as MBA careers, business school curricula, and comparisons between UK and foreign business schools. On the first of these, he added a telling comment:

> As you know, the Prime Minister and other Cabinet Ministers have implied that the advent of the MBAs makes no perceivable difference to the problems of British industry (which is a pretty daft expectation at this early stage in the development of business schools in the UK) and it would be most helpful if we could produce a series of case studies showing not only how an MBA has helped an individual to progress, but also indicating how it helped him to make a significant impact on his company.

SUB-COMMITTEE ON BUSINESS MANAGEMENT STUDIES, UNIVERSITY GRANTS COMMITTEE

John Bolton and Philip Nind were both on the Business and Management Studies Sub-Committee of the UGC, the main mechanism through which the Government funded universities and therefore of great importance for all concerned. The creation of the UGC was first proposed in 1904 and eventually created in 1918, to address a need for a mechanism to channel funds to universities, which had suffered from neglect and lack of funding during the First World War (Shattock 1994). The UGC's role at this time was to examine the financial needs of the universities and to advise on grants, but it did not have a remit to plan for the development of universities. This situation changed after the Second World War, when the Barlow Report of 1946 recommended that the UGC take on a planning role for the university sector, to ensure that universities were adequate for national needs during post-war reconstruction. The 1944 Education Act had also aimed to increase the number of school leavers qualified to enter higher education, necessitating a period of expansion for the universities that needed planning by the UGC.

During the post-war years the UGC continued to have a strategic role in the development of the university sector, acting as a buffer between government and the interests of the universities. In 1964 responsibility for the UGC was transferred from the Treasury to the newly constituted Department of Education and Science. Also in 1964, the UGC Chairman, Sir John Wolfenden, set up a series of committees which he described as his 'eyes and ears' into the university system. There were eventually 11 sub-committees split on a 7:4 basis between science and the arts, each chaired by a member of the main committee. Each sub-committee was given a broad remit of responsibility, including the maintenance of standards, and was expected to develop their own programme of visits and other consultations. In practice however their operation was variable, especially in following up the subject-based advice contained in the main committee report, the memoranda of guidance to universities to accompany statements of recurrent grant. There was an interesting anomaly in that accountancy, which might be thought of as a key subject within management, was part of the Social Studies Sub-Committee, probably because its existence in the university system long pre-dated management. The Business and Management Studies Sub-Committee was nevertheless an extremely influential body given that the main committee had little experience of management as a subject, and it was an area which required very considerable and rapid growth. The UGC was very aware that it needed the support of industry in these developments and therefore wanted high level industry representation to give advice from that perspective. Norman Hunt of the University of Edinburgh was the sub-committee's chair for several years. He had attended the Dining Group meetings and would have been very aware of Bolton's knowledge, initiative, and standing in industry. Thus John was a logical choice for an informed industrial perspective, as indeed was Philip Nind from the FME. And the Sub-Committee was treated well in the distribution of financial resources; even in the major cutback year of 1981, which we will meet again in relation to Surrey University, one of the basic criteria was to increase the science, technology, and management studies component.

OTHERS

John never liked to say no, especially when it came to his favourite topic. So he became involved with various other organizations, less significant than those above, but nevertheless not insubstantial commitments. Amongst them were:

- Oxford Centre for Management Studies, Founder Member of Council, 1964–72
- Oxford University Business Summer School, member of committee
- Advisory Committee on Industry, Committee of Vice-Chancellors, 1984–88
- Business Education Forum, 1969–74
- He also had good links with individual business schools, not least London Business School. He was a guest of honour at the 10th Anniversary Dinner for LBS in October 1975, sitting almost opposite Harold Wilson. Margaret Thatcher was there too.

5 The British Institute of Management

INTRODUCTION

The British Institute of Management (BIM) was founded in 1947 with wide support from industry and Government with the intention of becoming a strong national institute, capable of improving Britain's weak (and becoming weaker in the post-war period) managerial and economic position. This chapter deals with its fortunes in the 1960s and particularly the two years during which John Bolton was its Chairman of Council. Fortunately there is a magnificently comprehensive history of the Institute by Edward Brech (2002), to which this chapter is much indebted.

THE BACKGROUND OF THE INSTITUTE

In the 1950s things did not go according to the initial high hopes for the BIM, with internal disagreements, the innate conservatism of much of the membership in believing that managers were born as such, and poor leadership at both Chairman and Director level, making it slow to have any impact. Specifically, the first Director, Leo Russell, preferred to focus on large companies and the 'great and the good', while Sir Charles Renold, the first Chairman, resigned all contact with the BIM over its amalgamation with the Institute of Industrial Administration (IIA), which at least had a

local structure and was based around individual managers pursuing professionalism. As a result, at least until the amalgamation in 1958 there was
little if any move toward the professionalization of managers, disillusioning
key progressives such as Lyndall Urwick. More generally in the economy,
there was still a lack of recognition of management as a key factor if Britain's
declining competitiveness was to be addressed. The 1950s was not a good
decade for the Institute, although things began to brighten up somewhat
toward the end after the merger with the IIA, which brought not only a
much-needed branch structure but also a more progressive attitude to the
marriage. Lord Verulam also inspired the Institute like no previous Chairman, so his very premature death in October 1960 was a sad loss.

The problems of the Institute were not just the view of this author. John
Marsh, on taking over the Directorship in 1962, commented on the Institute's contemporary role in his first review (Brech 2002: 375):

> Unfortunately I have to say that the Institute's general reputation is
> one of disappointment in industry at large. After 14 years or so of
> work, the Institute's reputation and public image are not high and it is
> disturbing to be confronted on all sides, in Government offices, com-
> panies, educational circles, the Press and certainly among other orga-
> nizations, with the fact that the Institute has not lived up to its earlier
> expectations.

Clearly there was much to be done. But at least by the early 1960s there
was a lot of local activity. The 50 branches and their committees became the
main basis of the Institute's activities, based on the branches taken over from
the IIA after the amalgamation in 1958 and in keeping with the changes
made by Lord Verulam after the initial years had been dominated by centrist
London-based policies.

BOLTON'S APPOINTMENT AS CHAIRMAN OF COUNCIL

John Bolton was a member of the BIM from soon after joining Solartron, as
might be expected of someone with such progressive attitudes toward management, and he played a full part from his joining, becoming involved with
various national committees: the Education Committee 1957; the Finance
and Administrative Committee 1958; the General Management Committee;
and also the Activities Committee. There is a letter from the administrator
of the Education Committee that suggests John was a very active member of
it, unsurprisingly given his views.

John became Chairman of Council in a surprising way. It had been traditional for the Chairman to come from one of the four vice-chairmen in
a form of planned management succession. But while John had been on
various committees, he had not been a member of Council, never mind a

vice-chairman. Suddenly, however, at the Council meeting of June 1964, he was appointed as vice-chairman to succeed Sir Cecil Mead in October, and this is what duly happened. Such an unusual development requires explanation and since there is no written record of why it happened, some speculation. A plausible view is that it arose out of the letter John wrote to John Marsh, the Director of the BIM, on November 15, 1963, which has already been partly raised and discussed in Chapter 3. Marsh replied to the letter on November 20 as follows:

Dear John,

May I say what a tremendous help it was to have your letter of 15 November. I much appreciate the trouble you have taken to put me so fully in the picture about the work of the Foundation. This is what I have needed to have for a very long time. As you know, I have been backing the Foundation for all I am worth lately and now I am even more convinced of the job it has to do and the way in which it should be linked with BIM, FBI and other bodies concerned with the same subject.

I would like to show your letter in confidence to Cecil Mead, our Chairman, Mr. A C Durie, Chairman of our Executive Committee, and Mr. T J Roberts, Director of Education, as it would help them to be in the picture.

I do admire your tenacity over the years in getting things moving. It only goes to show how tough today is for men with creative ideas.

With regards
John Marsh

Marsh's response noted that he had taken the liberty of passing it on to the Chairman and one or two others and it might be speculated that he attached a note or perhaps said verbally words to the effect that 'here is a letter from an outstandingly dynamic man who is already part of our system and could be worth considering for the next chairmanship'. The minute of the Council meeting of June 3, 1964, is bureaucratically bland and tells nothing of the background:

The Chairman said that after consulting with the President of the Institute, Mr. H. C. Barker, his predecessor, other Vice-Presidents, the Vice-Chairmen of Council and the Director he wished to propose that Mr. J. E. Bolton should be elected Chairman-Designate of Council. This proposal was seconded by Mr. J. C. Blair-Conynghame and carried unanimously.

Nevertheless, it was a massive vote of confidence in someone who did not come from one of Britain's leading companies and was considerably too young to be part of the industrial establishment. That the Institute was willing to take what must have been seen as a risk was testimony to the impact that Bolton had clearly made on a still cautious and conservative leadership. Thus John succeeded Cecil Mead as Chairman at the AGM on October 7, following the Council meeting of that date. Mead introduced Bolton as his successor and welcomed him to the Chair as the penultimate piece of business. The final piece of business, with John in the Chair, was to appoint Mead as a Vice-President for life of the Institute. There was then a further meeting of Council following the AGM, which JEB chaired.

His introduction in *The Manager* was expectant:

> The man who succeeds Mr. Cecil Mead as chairman of BIM on the seventh of this month is one of a new breed of British managers. The term 'whizz kid' has been consistently overused ever since it was first applied to the dynamic representatives of the early Kennedy administration, but there are aspects of the career of MR JOHN BOLTON which bring it leaping to mind. First there is his youth: at 43 he is the youngest chairman of Council in the history of the Institute. Secondly, there is professionalism, and what might be described as breadth of competence. . . . The dynamism, however, is well concealed behind a composed, pipe-smoking exterior. Mr Bolton is a quiet, thoughtful speaker who gives a strong impression of conviction and very good sense.

CHAIRMANSHIP OF COUNCIL

He succeeded Cecil Mead as Chairman of Council, which had four vice-chairmen and a wider Council of some 60, comprising many of the key figures in British industry, probably more so than its contemporary equivalent. In his first Council meeting as Chairman, JEB laid out his objectives for his term in office (Brech 2002: 388): closer relationships with industry; upgrading the Institute's public image; developing relations with Members of Parliament; extending activities in management education; and considering the need to move to more prestigious premises. This last was a reflection of the greatly improved financial position that the Institute had achieved through the expansion of membership and higher subscription levels; there was also looming a considerable problem of accommodation at the Fetter Lane premises.

Being Chairman of Council meant controlling a substantially sized committee and covering a wide range of topics, most of which were spoken to by officials, but all nevertheless required some knowledge from the Chairman and indeed some were led from the chair. For the meeting on February 3, 1965, for instance, there were 33 members of Council present (with 23 apologies) with seven members of staff in attendance. The topics covered were:

- Change of name for 'The Manager'
- Role of the BIM in management development, education, and training

- Relations between BIM, FME, and FBI
- BIM named lectures—the Baillieu and Elbourne lectures
- BIM Parliamentary Panel
- BIM Five Year Plan Interim Report
- BIM relations with HM Government Departments
- Report of the Executive Committee
- Report of the Finance Committee
- Advanced Management Programmes International
- BIM accommodation
- BIM public relations
- Director's Report on Contemporary Matters

  - Dinner for Cecil Mead
  - Discussion of 'Professionalism in Management'
  - BIM and Exports
  - Joint Statement of Intent on Productivity, Prices, and Incomes
  - Focus on Automation Conference
  - BIM Conference March 16–18
  - Relations with Irish Management Institute
  - CIOS
  - Nigerian Institute of Management
  - Management Development Working Party
  - Visitors from the USA
  - Overseas Visits
  - OECD Management Education Conference December 1964
  - FBI, BEC, NABM Conference
  - Membership Assessors
  - Management Education Information Unit
  - National Industrial Conference Board Publications

Other big issues which came up under his watch and would at the very least have been influenced by his views were: a review of the BIM Standing Committee Structure and especially a review of the BIM's individual membership structure, which was to require a modification of the Institute's Articles of Association. The change in the membership structure, which was confirmed at an Extraordinary General Meeting in June 1966, was a very significant move toward managerial professionalism as a key focus of the Institute and was very much in line with Bolton's own views. The intention was to provide a means of progressive advancement from the point of entry as a Management Student, through the grade of Associate Member, which would be open to those with acceptable academic qualifications in management subjects and with knowledge and experience of management in action, to membership for those with wider experience and holding greater responsibilities. Entry into Fellowship, the Institute's senior grade, would continue to be by invitation to those who had achieved eminence in their management careers. At the same time an effort was made to increase the rate of application for admission or transfer to a higher grade, and this doubled in 1965–6 to nearly 100 a week, with a particular increase of those applying for admission to the full grade of MBIM, reflecting its standing as 'one personally committed to achieving and maintaining the highest professional standards in the practice of management regulated by his continuous and systematic study of its art and science and by collaboration with other managers'.

The Chairman was expected to attend a lot of functions outside the Council, both internally in visiting regions, branches, and activities, especially of course the annual Conference, and externally in being the representative of the BIM at other meetings—of those mentioned above in the February 1965 Council agenda John attended the joint FBI, BEC, and NABM Conference of leading industrialists and had a meeting with CIOS (Conseil Internationale de l'Organization Scientifique, the leading international management body). The Chairman would also have been present at many meetings with Government Departments and play a leading role at the National Conference in March. Indeed National Conference themes would often be influenced by the Chairman of Council. In 1965 it was 'Management Education and Development' and in January 1966 the same in the light of contemporary progress; these sound very much like topics that Bolton would have suggested, or at the very least supported.

This was a period when a new Labour government came into office with high expectations, but soon ran into trouble on the currency front, having to devalue the pound whilst making the famous claim that 'the pound in your pocket . . . has not been devalued'. It was also a period of the corporate state, with planning and interventionism being seen as a way forward, spawning a range of new bodies such as the National Board for Prices and Incomes to control prices and incomes, the upgrading of the 'little Neddies' at industry level, the Industrial Reorganization Commission (IRC) to encourage mergers and economies of scale, and a strengthened Monopolies Commission to prevent cartelization, all helping to lead to a National Plan. It was also a period when the quality of management was strongly suspected of being a major contributor to industrial inefficiency, and thus a body like the BIM was expected to play an active part in remedying this. However, and not unsurprisingly, many in the BIM did not accept this role that was expected of them.

A key issue of being Chairman of Council was of course his relationship with the Director, John Marsh. As argued above, it may well have been Marsh who suggested Bolton for the Chairmanship. Brech (2002: 364) is somewhat ambivalent about the appointment of Marsh in 1961:

> For the first time in its 15 years of life, the BIM had in office a Director with extensive links among industrial and commercial circles, and with personal prestige in the managerial environment, though he had no personal background of industrial managerial experience. Nor had he any extent of knowledge in management, either as a subject or as practice, confirmed by his own overt admission in later years.

Indeed he took personal pride in the claim that he had never read a management book (Brech 2002: 776). He had however shown in his previous role a competence in industrial administration as well as a sense of innovation for the development of services, and his early years in BIM were very successful when judged by the standards of institutional growth in several dimensions. Council also upgraded the title of John Marsh as Director to Director-General in June 1966. This was clearly a mark of confidence in Marsh himself and quite possibly at the behest of Bolton; at the least it would not have happened without his support.

The main day-to-day work carried out by the Institute, as Bolton noted in his 1965 Chairman's report, 'lies in its role as the national clearing-house for information and advice on management policies, practices and techniques', while through its regional and branch activities 'it provides over fifty regular meeting points in Britain for the study of management matters'. Also in his 1965 report he emphasized the significance of spreading the understanding of management development schemes, whilst showing himself to be way ahead of his time in 'the need for regarding management education as a continuous and planned process during the whole of a manager's career'. He also noted that top management meetings were another area of significant interest for the BIM at this time.

His 1966 Chairman's Report was even more bullish, starting with the claim that 'The British Institute of Management is now playing a crucial role in our national affairs', and continuing

> It is clear that there is a veritable managerial revolution under way in Britain. . . . It is also evident in the continuing expansion of the Institute. BIM is able to report that its wide range of activities is being supported on an ever-growing scale; large numbers of companies and individuals are joining in membership and we are constantly striving to ascertain members' wishes and to meet their requirements with first-rate services. New initiatives such as general management presentations, European study groups and management development seminars are well supported. All the 300 conferences and courses held during the past year were over-subscribed and this is a clear measure of the support given to the demonstration and discussion of new managerial policies, systems and techniques. Finally demands on the BIM information and advisory services during the year reflect a 60 per cent increase over the previous year.

He was also able to report the attendance of the Prime Minister, Harold Wilson, at the 1966 National Conference, and use his words to underline the move toward professionalism (a dirty word in the previous decade) in management. The Prime Minister noted:

> I am very happy to be able to pay my tribute to the work that you, Mr Chairman, and your colleagues, including in particular, Mr John Marsh, have been doing over these years. It did take some time for

you to sell yourselves to British industry but I can see that you have made a great breakthrough in British industry. There has been a certain amount of suspicion, even ridicule, about the basis of management being professional, but I have said a number of times that we cannot in this highly competitive world afford to treat this vital profession of management as something that should depend purely on birth, family background, school connections or anything else that goes with the former amateur status. We cannot in British industry afford to keep the professionals out.

Having the Prime Minister at the Conference was of course recognition of the status that BIM had recently achieved, and the recognition that Harold Wilson gave to the management issue. This was the first time that a Prime Minister had attended the BIM. Wilson's opening address was 'Managing in a Competitive Britain', while the after-dinner speaker was the Chairman of the National Board for Prices and Incomes (NBPI), Aubrey Jones, two instances of trying to introduce macro-economic issues to the Institute.

POLICY ISSUES OF THE PERIOD

There were a number of substantial policy issues during Bolton's tenure of office, several of them as result of Bolton's own initiatives. One, that of creating a Development Fund, was close to his heart. As he proposed it to the Council in October 1965, it would appeal for £50,000 a year for seven years, the money to be spent on the following purposes:

£100,000 for a Development division
£100,000 for new premises and facilities
£50,000 for international activities
£50,000 for repayment of the outstanding loan
£50,000 for a new project

There was a further discussion of this topic at the following Council meeting on February 2, 1966, at which it was argued that the £50,000 per annum would be raised if the 200–300 Collective Subscribers with more than 5000 employees were to pay according to the BIM Standard Scale, which was linked to a per employee basis. At that time, apparently, only five companies were paying the full rate: Unilever, ICI, Reed Paper, Esso, and Beecham Group. So it was suggested that the Executive Committee should see what could be done along these lines before going ahead with a scheme of covenanted gifts.

Another key issue was the Council asking the Director to prepare a 'five-year development plan' to be discussed at the October 1965 Council meeting. This was duly done and the primary objective was based around membership expansion. When the plan was presented there were some 4600 Collective Subscriber companies, 9000 qualified individual members and 2500 affiliates, while additionally the Collective Subscribers had nominated 'representative members' to a total of some 8000 (Brech 2002: 391). It was agreed that the category of 'representative member' should be abolished, with the incumbents being transferred to appropriate individual member categories according to assessment of their qualifications. This enabled the growth target for individual membership to be set at an ambitious 35,000 at the end of the five-year period in 1970.

One result of the BIM's new outreach to Government, together with a sympathetic Minister at the Board of Trade, Lord Wilfred Brown who had been one of the appointed members of the first BIM Council, was funding for three years from 1966–67, to be provided via the Board of Trade (Brech 2002: 393). The Prime Minister, Harold Wilson, announced this at the 1966 Conference; they amounted to a grant of £38,500 for the first year and up to £50,000 for the second and third years to permit rapid expansion of BIM services in the regions and in the field of management education. The grant for the regions was to enable the provision of activities such as seminars, top management meetings, and company presentations in areas of the country which not have been considered viable for the standard BIM activity programme. Non-member companies would also be encouraged to attend these activities to a greater extent than had been the practice before.

An interesting policy issue put to the October 1965 Council was the possible creation of a code of managerial ethics, prompted by the Government's National Plan. The Director provided a short paper, appending the 1951 Code created by the IIA, and the matter was remitted to a small group of members to review, but nothing was forthcoming. One dimension might have been the still controversial issue of management as a profession, something which the CBI had recently declared against.

A major policy issue led by Bolton was about the BIM monthly house journal. 'The Manager' had a circulation approaching 30,000 by the mid-1960s, but was costing the Institute some £20,000 net per year. There had been various discussions about reducing this figure, especially through greater advertising revenues to capitalize on the increasing interest in management, but to attract more advertising meant having a more commercially oriented publication than was easy to attain with a house journal. As Chairman, John Bolton took the initiative in initiating negotiations with external parties, and at its October 1965 meeting the Council approved in principle a new consortium, with Bolton announcing: (Brech 2002: 406)

> As you may know, we have formed a partnership with the Financial Times, the Economist and the Haymarket Press and last month (Feb 1966) a brand new management publication called 'Management Today' was launched, which . . . reaches an altogether higher level of authority in industrial journalism.

The new journal was certainly sizeable in its proportions, looking almost like a coffee-table book, with 176 pages and, at least in its first issue, well over 100 advertisers. It was to be slimmed down later, but in the first issue, a joint article by John Bolton and John Marsh, the Director-General, made the most of its size in an article called 'Tomorrow's Managers Need Management Today', as well as heralding its new editor, Robert Heller, as 'among the foremost economic and industrial journalists in Britain today'. Certainly Heller, only 33 when he was appointed, and previously business editor of *The Observer*, did very well for the new journal. They noted that it was not just aimed at the BIM membership but at managers everywhere. They claimed, justifiably, that the first issue of *Management Today* was a landmark in the progress of the BIM, although their finishing statement: 'We believe that together, this great new journal and the still young and enterprising Institute will become the dominant force in raising standards in British management in the years ahead' was a good deal more speculative.

The following month Bolton, this time alone, had a further message, emphasizing the changes that were taking place, calling for

> a well presented and authoritative journal which can reach even beyond the rapidly growing number of BIM's membership. . . . Management Today will continue to serve BIM and its members. It is also intended that the additional readers that the new journal will attract will provide a pool of potential members from which the Institute can steadily be strengthened and enlarged. To that extent it will constitute a valuable recruiting medium.

Although there was some criticism of the American style of the new journal, it was generally well received, and certainly there was a significant increase in the advertising revenues, while the circulation went up to over 50,000 by the end of the decade and to 80,000 by 1986, as compared to the 27,000 of *The Manager*. The cessation of *The Manager* as the BIM house journal in March 1966 necessitated launching BIM Bulletin as an alternative means of intra-institutional communication.

INSTITUTIONAL GROWTH

Financially, the BIM achieved a surplus in both years of Bolton's chairmanship, something not common in the past, with past deficits and loans still outstanding. In 1964–65, on a turnover of £392,000, the surplus was £28,000, while in 1965–66, with a turnover of £418,000, it was £1,500. While these were good compared with past deficits, more needed to be done, and hence Bolton looked forward to the creation of his Development Fund.

Membership grew significantly in the 1960s and especially in the second half, with the momentum of the five-year plan. For collective subscribers the numbers went from 4,650 in 1965 to 11,600 in 1969, while the subscription income associated with them grew from £114,000 to £228,700, while for individual members, although somewhat distorted by the changes in grade structure and the absorption of the previous category of representative member in 1967, numbers grew from 14,400 to 24,600 and income from £68,500 to £158,500. It will be noted that while the importance of the professional members was growing, the collective subscribers still contributed considerably more income, even in 1969. There was also a growth of a third in companies to 6,223 under John's leadership.

The BIM grew considerably during Bolton's period in office. On the income side, subscriptions went up from £162,365 to £207,225 (27.6 per cent) and income from conferences meetings and courses, indicating the level of activity went from £76335 to £122,952 (61.0 per cent), while on the expenditure side expenditure on salaries, indicating numbers of permanent staff rising to 160 at HQ and the five regions, went from £126,644 to £178,963 (41.3 per cent). There were 190 staff by end of 1966 and well over 200 by the end of the decade.

On another dimension there was a considerable increase in the demand for services, with an increase in library loans of 20 per cent over the previous year to 22,500 in 1965–6; a similar number of information notes and summaries were sent out, up from 5000 in 1962–3, as well as over 3000 visitors to the library. Organizationally a Management Information department was formed to create a more closely integrated information and library service, freeing the specialist advisers from having to handle day to day enquiries, while a Management Education Information Unit was formed in December 1964 as enquiries in that area rose to over 350 a month. The numbers of events provided by the BIM virtually doubled during the decade, from a starting point of some 400 in 1960–61 (Brech 2002: 398).

There were also some high profile lectures during John's period of office, named after key people from the past such as the Baillieu, Urwick, and Elbourne lectures, and with significant speakers in 1964–5 such as Sir Robert Menzies, Prime Minister of Australia, Sir William Haley, Editor of *The Times*, and Sir Ronald Edwards, Chairman of the Electricity Council.

All in all, the period saw a considerable increase in the momentum of the Institute; as the Annual Report for 1966 said: 'the BIM has advanced further as the national clearinghouse for information on management policies, practices and techniques, and in the vital and expanding field of management development, education and training'. It was a period of increasing interest in management generally, supported by the Government, but Bolton's fresh and vigorous approach would have added to the momentum. The BIM finally had a substantial status in the community after the squabbles and financial problems of the previous decade.

In his final speech as Chairman at the National Conference in 1966, Bolton said:

A positive managerial revolution is under way and the British Institute of Management is very much at the centre of these events. It is supported by some 5,000 companies including over 80% of the top 300. Individual membership exceeds 20,000 and the number of members is growing fast in all sectors. BIM has strong national and regional councils and some 50 active branch organizations throughout the country. With a permanent staff of 160 and an annual budget approaching £0.5m, it is the largest self-supporting management institution outside the USA and after the CBI it is the largest industrial and commercial voluntary body in this country.

(British Institute of Management, *Annual Report*, 1964–66)

The accommodation shortage already mentioned was to lead in 1967 to the purchase of Donald House (soon renamed Management House) in Hill Street. While this appeared to be an excellent development at the time, problems soon arose, with higher upkeep costs than anticipated and lower income from rental of unused space, and it became part of worries about managerial control systems which will be taken up shortly. In the mid-1980s Management House was to cause severe financial problems for the Institute before it was sold and a move was made to Corby for most of its activities.

Also on services, the library, which had developed out of Lyndall Urwick's personal library, continued to grow; by mid-decade it had reached 40,000 books and made 22,500 loans and had answered 5,000 enquiries about reading materials. The new Parker Street premises in March 1968 enabled much superior ground-floor facilities to be given to the library for ease of personal visiting.

The decade of the 1960s also saw an increase in international activities, which had been given little attention in the 1950s. The area was specifically identified in the Five-Year Plan and became an area of interest for the Director, who made numerous international visits, with a primary focus on assistance to the developing world and the Commonwealth (Bolton's interest in the Commonwealth will be remembered from Chapter 3). As well, there were perhaps 40 visiting delegations a year by the mid to late 1960s. Some in the Institute felt that too much attention was being paid to this area by the end of the 1960s. However with a typically British attitude the BIM remained outside CIOS as the main international management body.

At the Council Meeting on June 7, 1966, John noted 'one of the difficult duties of an outgoing Chairman of Council is to arrange for the election of his successor'. After consultation with his two predecessors and the Director, he proposed David Ducat of Metal Box, one of the vice-chairmen. After the Council meeting, there was an Extraordinary General Meeting of BIM to deal with the changes to the Articles of Association as a result of the new membership structure. JEB, 13 members of Council and 21 other voting members attended and the changes were duly accepted, although not unanimously. Then at the AGM on October 5, 1966, John gave up the Chairmanship in the same way as he had acceded to it, and in accordance with Article 54 was appointed a Vice-President for life. He also remained on Council.

REFLECTIONS ON THE BIM DURING BOLTON'S CHAIRMANSHIP

Things went 'extremely well' under his leadership according to his successor, David Ducat, taking a long look at the aims and objectives of the BIM and producing the Mead Report. By the end of Bolton's time in the chair the BIM had become a very substantial body, the largest management body in the world outside the USA. Its Council had 63 members, and with 5,000 corporate and 15,000 individual members. It had grown rapidly but also stabilized considerably and become more harmonious since the difficult days of the 1950s, when there were various serious policy disagreements. While Bolton had not been directly responsible for the origins of growth and stabilisation, he was in keeping with the policies which initiated these, including a willingness to champion management education and the business schools, which had been one of the sources of divisions in the 1950s. Moreover during his time there were no serious issues of dissent in spite of substantial changes.

Taking the decade of the 1960s as a whole, because it is difficult to isolate the years 1964–66 alone, the BIM moved a long way to becoming the central professional institute that the Baillieu Committee had foreshadowed. The initial period had emphasized the Collective Subscribers, but the merger with the IIA in 1958 had moved the BIM toward individual professional membership, and this was enhanced in the 1960s not only in numbers, but in objectives and activities. The BIM's growth in the decade was significant, even if helped by external circumstances and attitudes which were much more positive to management. Financially, too, the situation had changed from stringency to a stability which permitted expansion, although there was still an accumulated deficit of £41,770 in April 1965. In these changes, John Bolton was not only somebody who strongly supported these changes, but probably also owed his appointment to the recognition that a leader like him was desirable to achieve them. As such, he was the very model of what the BIM tried to become in the period.

Yet all was not entirely well. In spite of Bolton's claim for the BIM to be at the centre of events in his 1966 address to the National Conference, this is debatable. BIM gave up its national system of professional examinations, which had been a significant cost to the Institute but of great benefit to the managerial community. Early in 1963 the Director proposed to the Council that the Institute should discontinue the graduate examinations entirely, justifying this on the changing situation nationally, but irrespective of the original hopes and objectives of developing management as a profession and the tradition of professions in Britain to have their own systems of preparation and qualification. The date of eventual cessation was set as July 1966. By the later 1960s the BIM had been relegated to the fringes of the management education system, in spite of having representation on various key bodies, while its direct input was limited to the provision of information by the Management Education Information Unit.

> As the BIM Council had relinquished the role of professional focus for managerial education, there was no institutional provision for ensurance of relevance, of quality, of coherence, or of coordination. The Institute's Annual Report for the year ending March 1966 had already described that scene as confused and confusing, but neither then nor later was any consideration given by the Council to the possibility of exercising any role of guidance or any attempt at coherence, a role that could have been seen as natural for the central professional institute in the field. (Brech 2002: 495–6)

In 1966 the internal Education and Training Committee was remodelled to serve as the advisory committee for the Management Education Information Unit, having lost its earlier role of supervising the BIM Certificate and Diploma professional qualifications. The BIM's contributions to policy implementation were made indirectly through the FME and CIME, while in terms of power and influence it was overshadowed by the CBI, the Central Training Council, and the NEDC, with the universities and business schools also becoming more important. In addition, there were problems of internal management which were to become apparent soon after Bolton gave up the Chairmanship.

Moreover the BIM did not get involved in the conduct or promotion of research, something that Bolton would have supported, and this hampered the production of policy-oriented monographs at a time when policy leadership in the burgeoning management and management education fields would have been influential. Indeed such pioneering in management practice and technique as was happening at this time was coming from the management consultants, since the business schools were only in the process of getting off the ground. The BIM did however issue some helpful documents for its members. *Management Abstracts* was an extremely popular service to members on a bi-monthly and then from 1964 quarterly basis, with print-runs rising from 30,000 to 42,000 over the decade. There were also some 120 subject bibliographies for members pursuing studies.

Moreover while there was substantial growth, the total membership was still very small when seen in relation to the total number of managers, somewhere close to two million, in Britain even if it is borne in mind that other institutes had a claim over many specialized managers and that there was no pressure at all to be a member of the Institute. The table below shows the numbers during Bolton's period in office.

The new membership structures voted through in Bolton's period but taking effect after it were designed to provide a means of progressive advancement from point of entry to Associate Member to Member, while Fellow continued to be by invitation. Affiliate, Graduate, and Representative member

Table 5.1   Categories of membership, 1964–1966

Categories	1964	1965	1966
Honorary Fellows	6	7	8
Fellows	430	466	475
Founder members	59	36	39
Members	1,640	1,586	1,680
Associate members	4,854	5,326	5,946
Graduates	763	911	1,045
Affiliates	7,550	6,059	5,323
Sub-total	15,302	14,391	14,516
Company representative members	6,604	7,808	8,772
Total	21,906	22,199	23,288

Source: BIM Annual Reports

would disappear. It was also expected that the branches would form effective links with educational establishments to facilitate the progression. Over the next 20 years there was considerable growth in the new categories, so that by 1986 there were 14,151 Fellows, 52,021 Members, 6,758 Associates and Students, for a total of 74,416. This latter figure includes the later category of Companions, most of which were transferred from the ranks of Fellows; John was one of the first Companions and indeed an ex-officio member of the Board of Companions, which met to discuss issues of the economy as well as those of the Institute.

LATER INVOLVEMENT WITH THE INSTITUTE

Standing down from the Chairmanship was not by any means the end of JEB's activities for the BIM. Indeed only a couple of weeks after standing down, he was giving an address to the Wessex Branch on 19 October 1966 on 'BIM in the National Scene'. But he also served in several roles over a much longer period. He was a director of Management Publications Ltd from 1966–73, its chairman 1969–72; and on the Editorial Advisory Panel, Management Today from 1966 to 1974. We have seen that he became a Life Vice-President, and was a member and for a period chairman of the Board of Companions, and also the chairman of the BIM pension fund trustees. Taken together, these were a significant set of commitments. He also tried to attend the BIM Boardroom Discussion Sessions well into the 1980s. On the honours side, he was awarded the Bowie Medal for 1969, which is given in recognition of a significant contribution to management education.

The Mead Committee to review the 'aims and organization' of the BIM was set up soon after Bolton stood down as Chairman of Council and he may well have had an influence on its setting up. He gave oral evidence to it, and in many respects its report, published in November 1968, reflected the changes that had taken place in the Institute during the 1960s:

- An emphasis on attracting younger managers with training
- Regional and local activities should be strengthened
- Members in the regions should be able to participate creatively in BIM affairs
- Providing a bridge between the educational system and industry.

All these were a long way from the centralized, 'good and great', and corporate focus of the 1950s. Another move from the 1950s was its attention to small firms, which is taken up in more detail in Chapter 7. The BIM did have some interest in small firms issues before John's Chairmanship of Council—there was a joint conference for smaller firms in Manchester on the topic of developing managers, run together with the National Association of British Manufacturers in September 1964, but John almost certainly boosted that recognition. Indeed, small firms became a perhaps surprisingly substantial part of the BIM, although on reflection it is understandable that many small firms felt the need for some representative agency, and at that time there were no small business federations.

Bolton also soon became involved in a difficult issue of decision-making. David Ducat, his successor as Chairman, wrote in reply to John's letter at the end of Ducat's chairmanship in 1968: 'I really do not deserve the credit for the achievements of the last two years. I took over from you when things were going extremely well and on the up and up and I just got carried along by the flood'. But Ducat nevertheless also reflected on the internal management of the BIM: 'I feel that the internal management of BIM ought to be beyond reproach and I am afraid that it is far from that at the present time'. This comment had to do with John Marsh and internal relations within the management, given that Marsh was spending a lot of time on international activities but nevertheless had a significant number of departmental managers directly responsible to him, raising questions of efficient operation. The issue came to a head in 1972 with the removal of John Marsh from much of the Director-General's role in 1972. The comment about the BIM's internal management quoted above by David Ducat indicates that there was unease at least within senior members of the Council. Brech notes:

> Private consultations among the Vice-Presidents after the January session brought to a head their own misgivings and whatever doubts the proceedings may have added. In consultations with the Chairman of Council they came to the decision that the internal general management needed strengthening, but that could be best attained by removing John Marsh from the role entirely, though retaining his services for public relations and on the international scene. (Brech 2002: 530)

This situation shows that the importance and power of the Vice-Presidents as elder statesmen and previous chairmen of Council could be considerable. It is almost certain that Bolton was involved in these developments, as a recent Chairman of Council and as someone who could be relied upon to find the time to be available for such issues; in addition, there were only a very limited number of Vice-Presidents, and some of them would have been out of touch or elderly. Marsh actually kept the title of Director-General but was replaced in most of his previous duties by PJS Churchill, who took the title of 'Executive Director and General Manager' responsible to the Chairman and the Council for managerial and administrative activities. Nevertheless, Marsh seems to have wanted to maintain good relations with Bolton and wrote a very reflective letter in 1984 to him as the Senior Vice-President on the state of the BIM, the potential successor to Roy Close as Director-General and the management arena more generally, and even sent a book of his poetry. Indeed it sounded as though John was the person to whom he wanted to unburden himself.

Working as Chairman of Council in the BIM was a very substantial and high profile role, even if assisted by the vice-chairmen. It was also an unpaid one. The Institute was to go through some additional vicissitudes during the rest of the 20th century, but John Bolton's period of office was arguably a high-water mark in its fortunes. And for John Bolton himself, it seems likely that his strong performance in the role led to some of the very significant public service roles over the following years, as well as making him a candidate for various non-executive directorships. He continued his involvement with the Institute until the late 1980s: as an ex-officio member of the 28-member Council; as an active member of the Board of Companions; attending the occasional Boardroom Discussion; and doubtless as an informal consultant in his role as Senior Vice-President. However by that time he was dropping activities and Gay's death in January 1989 greatly accelerated this process.

Photo 2   John Bolton in naval uniform at the end of the War

Photo 3 Bolton after collecting his DSC in 1946, accompanied by his mother and sister

Photo 4   John and Gay Bolton at the 1st and 3rd Trinity Boat Club Cambridge
May Ball, 1948

Photo 5   Bolton welcoming the Prime Minister, Harold Wilson, to the British Institute of Management Conference in 1966

Photo 6   Bolton receiving the British Institute of Management Bowie Medal for contributions to management education from Lord Watkinson in 1970

Photo 7 Bolton making a speech at Cutlers Hall, Sheffield, in 1975. This is his typical posture when making a speech.

Photo 8 Bolton at the 10th anniversary dinner for London Business School, also featuring Harold Wilson and Margaret Thatcher

Photo 9   John and Gay Bolton together with Harry and Carolyn Hansen meeting the Duke of Edinburgh on the occasion of his talk to the Advanced Management Programme International Club in March 1978

Photo 10   An interlude on the Scottish moors. Bolton with friends and his daughter Athalie.

Photo 11A   Bolton showing a friend a cartoon depicting small business

Photo 11B   A Richard Wilson cartoon depicting Bolton as a monk preaching to the unconverted while two Chancellors of the Exchequer, Tony Barber (Conservative) and Denis Healey (Labour), are roasting an archetypal small businessman on the spit

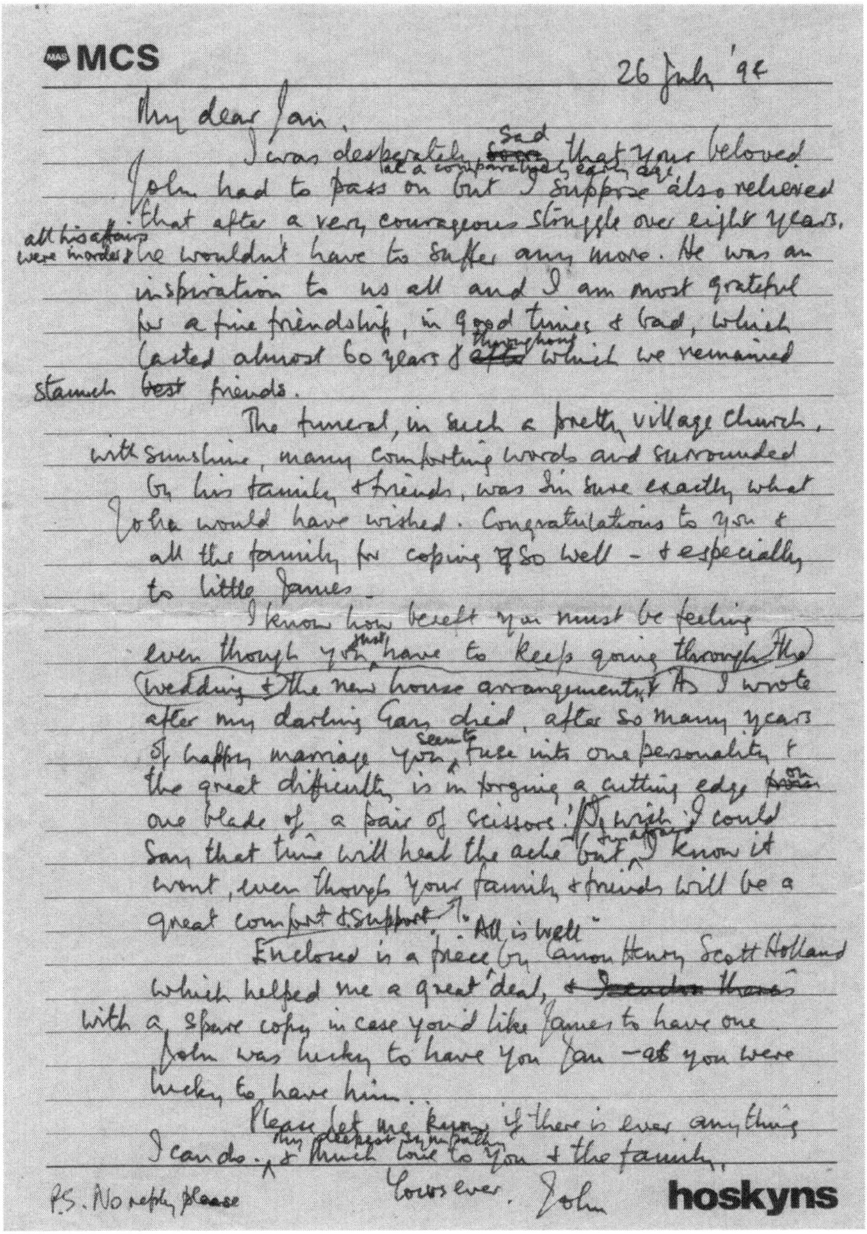

MCS 26 July '94

My dear Jan,

I was desperately sad that your beloved John had to pass on but I suppose also relieved at a comparatively early age that after a very, courageous struggle over eight years, all his affairs were in order, he wouldn't have to suffer any more. He was an inspiration to us all and I am most grateful for a fine friendship, in good times & bad, which lasted almost 60 years & throughout which we remained staunch best friends.

The funeral, in such a pretty village church, with sunshine, many comforting words and surrounded by his family, & friends, was I'm sure exactly what John would have wished. Congratulations to you & all the family for coping so well — & especially to little James.

I know how bereft you must be feeling even though you have to keep going through the wedding & the new house arrangements. As I wrote after my darling Gary died, after so many years of happy marriage you seem, fuse into one personality & the great difficulty is in forging a cutting edge from one blade of a pair of scissors. I wish I could say that time will heal the ache but I know it won't, even though your family & friends will be a great comfort & support. "All is well"

Enclosed is a piece by Canon Henry Scott Holland which helped me a great deal, with a spare copy in case you'd like James to have one. John was lucky to have you Jan — as you were lucky to have him.

Please let me know if there is ever anything I can do. My deepest sympathy & much love to you & the family,

Yours ever, John

P.S. No reply please

hoskyns

Photo 12   A draft letter of condolence to the widow of Bolton's friend John Crosse to illustrate the time and trouble Bolton took in creating such letters

Photo 13   Bolton on his 70th birthday, October 17, 1990

6 Public Service Roles

INTRODUCTION

John Bolton carried out a wide variety of public service roles; his strong sense of public duty, his breadth of experience, and far from least, his lack of a full-time executive job made him an ideal candidate for these activities. They became in effect a second career after Solartron. This chapter for the most part discusses the institutions and roles with which JEB was involved, rather than his specific contributions, largely because, with the exception of Surrey University, his personal role is difficult to evaluate.

There are of course others who make something of a second career out of public service roles; just to take some of those mentioned in this book, Sir Peter Parker, Sir Monty Finniston, and Lord Robens all had multiple public service activities, but John was certainly right up there with the leading group of his time. Some roles have already been mentioned in previous chapters, and the most important single role of this kind, that to do with small business, will be the subject of the following two chapters. But that still leaves a substantial number of important roles, together with some less important, which are listed below as he gave them in his entry in *Who's Who*:

General Commissioner of Income Tax 1964–2003
President, Engineering Industries Association 1981–84
Member, Executive Committee, Automobile Association
Chairman of Council and Hon. Treasurer, Surrey University

Member of Organizing Committee, World Research Hospital
Member of UK Automation Council 1964–65
Member of Advisory Committee for Management Efficiency in NHS 1964–65
Member of Committee for Exports to New Zealand 1965–68
Member of Advisory Committee, Queen's Award to Industry 1972–92(?)
Member of Council, Institute of Directors
Chairman, Economic Development Committee for the Rubber Industry, 1965–68
Vice-Chairman, Royal Commission on Local Government in England 1966–69
High Sheriff of Surrey, 1980–81
Deputy Lieutenant of Surrey from 1974
Member of United Kingdom Automation Council, 1964–65
County Sound—local radio station
Member of Grand Council, CBI, 1974–77
Vice-President, European Year of Small and Medium-Sized Enterprises 1983
Tate and Lyle, Customer Safeguards Committee, Ministry of Agriculture, Chairman, Fisheries and Food, 1977–80
Positions on the boards of schools, notably Cranbourne Chase School, Knighton House School, and Port Regis School

There is insufficient space to deal with all these roles in detail, so it is proposed to select a few of the more important ones for greater examination.

ECONOMIC DEVELOPMENT COMMITTEE (EDC) FOR THE RUBBER INDUSTRY

Set up in 1962 by the Conservative Government of the day, the National Economic Development Council (NEDC) was a consultative body, presided over by the Prime Minister or the Chancellor of the Exchequer, designed to discuss matters of national economic policy with representatives of interested organizations including the TUC, CBI, nationalized industries, the Bank of England, etc. The National Economic Development Office (NEDO) provided the full-time staff for research and assistance, and there were also regional and sectoral structures. Its status was much downgraded in the 1980s, with the Conservative government giving it a much lower priority than did their predecessors and they also significantly reduced its staffing levels. In 1992 the government announced the abolition of the NEDC, leaving the UK without any forum for discussion of economic issues between government, unions, and employers.

The role of NEDC (Caves 1968: 118) incorporated the creation of consultative bodies for specific industries, the Economic Development Committees, of which more than 20 were eventually created. Their function was to help shape the projections for their industries and to explore problems at the industry level and suggest ways to reduce or overcome them, producing reports for consideration. They were best known as 'the Little Neddies' and were composed of business, union, and government representatives with an independent chairman. Caves (1968: 322) in his team's enquiry into Britain's economic prospects noted:

> Our analysis of the deficiencies in the performance of British industry is certainly consistent with a need for something more than general increases in effective competition. Excessive product differentiation, inappropriate degrees of integration, sub-optimal use of research and development, and inefficient marketing and investment planning are deficiencies which might melt slowly and incompletely before the heat of increased market rivalry. Furthermore, they might well respond favourably, at least in some cases, to the treatments now dispensed by the little Neddies and the Industrial Reorganization Corporation.

It is now fashionable to decry the relevance of such corporatist bodies, but Caves' group of dispassionate heavyweight American academics clearly saw virtues in their approach (Caves 1968: 317): 'Individual Neddies have contributed valuable studies of comparative productivity and efficient scale in their industries and have pressed for increased standardisation, better coordination between makers and users of capital goods and the like'. Appointments to be chairman of the 'Little Neddies' were based on the rule that the chairman had to have no vested interest in the sector concerned and therefore tended to be, as Parker (1989: 160) put it, 'dangerously unencumbered with any experience of it'. Nevertheless they were people of distinction and would have needed the confidence of the members for the Committees to be effective.

The 'Little Neddy' for Rubber was the 14th to be announced, on June 18, 1965, with Bolton as Chairman, announced by George Brown, Minister for Economic Affairs. His position was designated as the Deputy Chairman of Solartron Electronic Group (it is as well to remember that he was already Chairman of Council of the BIM, so was taking on a good deal of external work, although he would have known that he was leaving Solartron). His colleagues, reflecting the tripartite approach, were:

Mr. C. H. Beckett, National Union of General and Municipal Workers
Mr. ACH Cairns, Department of Economic Affairs
Mr. W. Clark, Director, John Bull Rubber Company
Mr. J. G. Davies, Director, Pirelli
Mr. R. Davis, Transport and General Workers Union
Mr. S. G. Deaves, Director, BTR Industries
Mr. E. Holt, Director, Dunlop Rubber Company
Mr. D. D. Marshall, Chairman and Managing Director, Greengate and Irwell Rubber Company

Mr. A. H. Pendree, Deputy Chairman, Goodyear Tyre and Rubber Company (Great Britain)
Mr. P. G. Potts, National Economic Development Office
Mr. R. G. Room, Personnel Manager, Avon Rubber Company
Mr. C. B. Selby-Boothroyd, Board of Trade
Mr. Z. A. Silberston, Fellow, St John's College, Cambridge
Mr. I. Walsh, United Rubber Workers of Great Britain

Rubber was not a particularly large or important industry in Britain at the time, but nevertheless the status of the EDCs were all similar. The Rubber EDC had internal working parties and paid visits to various firms in the industry. It also had at least one substantial three-day conference for the industry in the Royal Garden Hotel, Kensington, in early 1967.

Bolton in his role as Chairman signed and probably in part wrote letters of report. One such was on December 23, 1965, to George Brown, the First Secretary, dealing with several issues raised by Brown some five months previously. One of these was about increasing capacity for exports through greater standardization, to which the response was negative in both the tyres and general rubber goods sectors, primarily because export markets themselves demanded a wide variety of products. A second was about increase in exports by cooperative action, for which the answer was also dubious; and a third negative view was about a pick-a-back scheme whereby larger companies could help smaller ones. Some other possibilities that were suggested for increasing exports were seen as having more potential, namely: collective efforts to increase exports; a movement of exports economic development committee; export trading corporations; and government services for exporters. And in a final section dealing with additional measures and general comments, one of which has a familiar ring: 'My personal experience is that export sales bear a direct relationship to export selling effort applied', repeating what Bolton had said in the Solartron context a decade or so earlier. In this final section, two other points are worth noting, one urging help for small businesses in matters of computing, and the other the need for more resources for NEDO, especially in three areas, exports, statistics, and work performance analysis.

In its issue of March 1967, the trade journal *Rubber and Plastics Age* had a very complimentary editorial about the EDC:

> Just over a month ago the National Economic Development Office's (NEDO) Little Neddy for the Rubber Industry held a most valuable conference in London. Great credit is due to the organisers and to the Chairman of the Rubber Neddy, John Bolton, for an interesting selection of topics and for persuading the Industry's leading executives to attend the conference. Its success obviously cannot be judged only by the excellent representation of all branches of the Industry; the only possible yardstick will be whether some of the ideas put forward will be acted upon by the delegates who have now returned to their firms. As

reported elsewhere in this issue, the conference highlighted the Rubber Industry's shortcomings with regard to productivity, profitability, marketing, machinery design, research, and education.

In other words the journal saw the EDC as performing a very valuable function, so much so, indeed, that it also went on to regret the lack of a Little Neddy for the Plastics Industry, and suggested the desirability of a combined Rubber and Plastics Neddy.

In his own contribution, John Bolton drew attention to the unsatisfactory profits earned, and said (as might be expected of him) that growth and profitability must come from improved management. He also noted that the imports of low priced footwear were being investigated by the Board of Trade.

He received a letter of congratulations in October 1968 from Fred Catherwood, the Director-General of NEDC, thanking him for his three years as chairman of the Rubber EDC:

> The task of an EDC Chairman in building a unified and constructive Committee from its several components is by no means easy, and your success in achieving this common purpose, with its productive results, has been outstanding. Indeed your Committee can be regarded as one of the more successful EDCs, particularly when one recalls that the industry was somewhat hesitant at the time of its formation.

He also had a very positive and similar letter from Peter Shore as Secretary of State for Economic Affairs and one from George Brown as First Secretary of State.

ROYAL COMMISSION ON LOCAL GOVERNMENT IN ENGLAND

Almost by definition, Royal Commissions deal with complex, difficult, and contentious issues, and the Royal Commission on Local Government in England 1966–69 was no exception. Much of local government had existed since medieval times with a plethora of some 1,300, mostly small, councils (not counting the 10,000 parish councils) and had instilled a strong sense of loyalty in many people, to say nothing of a set of vested interests in the existing office-holders and especially their representative associations such as the County Councils Association, the Association of Municipal Corporations, the Urban District Councils Association, and the Rural District Councils Association. On top of these there were perhaps 100 further national organizations with an interest in local government, mainly representing groups of professional workers in local government such as the Association of Chief Education Officers or the National Association of Local Government Officers. Central to the debate were trade-offs between difficult-to-define concepts, such as the balance between 'efficiency' and 'democracy'. The story of the Commission is well told in Wood (1976), from which this brief account is taken.

The Commission sat for more than three years when it was scheduled to take two, took on board 2,156 written submissions (given these, for obvious reasons, oral evidence could not be contemplated), contained within itself a wide range of vested interests, and produced a memorandum of dissent longer than the main report, the first Royal Commission to do so, as well as two notes of reservation by three members of the majority block. The critical issue of size alone resulted in the Commission being split into four separate camps, and although the most important issue, it was only one amongst many on which divisions arose. It was also the first Commission to have its own permanent self-appointed research team, a director supported by 10 planners, geographers, sociologists, and political scientists. It was indeed a formidable organization and operation. Later, when the matter reached the legislative stage, based on quite different principles from those recommended by the Royal Commission, the Government published 1,000 pages of explanatory notes with the Bill. Unsurprisingly the 1,000 pages of explanation did not produce a consensus; there were large numbers of amendments (indeed thought to be the largest number ever) not only in the Commons (1253) but also in the Lords (633), where villages such as Great Ayton and Poynton fought their corner and persuaded the Lords to overturn Government positions—in the case of Poynton by a single vote. Nine out of the 11 Commissioners (an unusually large total for a Royal Commission) had detailed knowledge of local government issues and indeed represented different perspectives on knotty issues. John Bolton did not; he was apparently there as a representative of industry, probably based on his Chairmanship of the BIM Council, while Vic Feather, the Deputy General Secretary of the TUC, represented the trade union movement. John was Vice-Chairman of the Commission, and must have found it a fascinating if often bewildering process. It is not entirely clear exactly what role he played, although it would have been in his instincts to back up the very able chairman, Sir John Maud (later Lord Redcliffe-Maud, hence the name frequently attached to the Commission's Report) and help to achieve a consensus, albeit a fragile one, of 10 of the 11 members. Nevertheless, he would have made a good fist of the vice-chairmanship, for otherwise it is unlikely that he would have been asked to chair the almost immediately following Committee of Inquiry on Small Firms. The experience of the Royal Commission almost certainly had an impact on Bolton in trying to seek consensus on the later Committee and may also have led to him insisting on a research staff. The Royal Commission was very hard work but its conclusions were not very popular.

The Redcliffe-Maud Report (1969) recommended the abolition of all the existing county, county borough, borough, urban district, and rural district councils, which had been created at the end of the 19th century, and replacing them with new unitary authorities. These new unitary authorities were largely based on major towns, which acted as regional employment, commercial, social, and recreational centres and took into account local transport infrastructure and travel patterns. There were to be 58 new unitary authorities and three metropolitan areas (Merseyside, South East Lancashire/North East Cheshire or 'Selnec', and West Midlands), which were to be subdivided into lower tier metropolitan districts. These new authorities, along with Greater London were to be grouped into eight provinces, each with its own provincial council.

In arriving at their recommendations, the commissioners were guided by a number of principles which they had themselves devised. These included:

- Town and country are interdependent, therefore the separate administration of urban areas and their rural hinterlands should cease.
- 'Physical environment services' should be in the hands of a single authority. Examples of these services included planning and transport. In order to provide these wide area services, the authority should have boundaries that reflected geographical patterns of population and movement and provided a coherent area of administration.
- 'Personal services' should likewise be administered by a single council. These included education, social services, health, and housing. The optimum population range over which to provide these services was 250,000 to 1 million.
- Wherever possible, both types of services should be in the hands of a single unitary authority.
- Areas for the new authorities should be capable of being effectively and democratically administered by a single council.

A principle which was not explicitly identified because it only came into general parlance in a European context some two decades later was that of 'subsidiarity', namely that a function should be performed at the lowest level of government at which it would be effective. The way that the Commission put it was that where functions *can* be provided by local authorities, they *should* be performed by them. Accordingly the different categories of council would have the following powers and responsibilities:

- Provincial councils: Drawing up of strategic development plans. They were to take over the functions of the existing Regional Economic Planning Councils.
- Unitary area councils: Both physical environment and personal services.
- Metropolitan area councils: Planning, transport, and general housing policy.
- Metropolitan district councils: Education and personal social services.

It had originally been envisaged that parish councils should also be abolished, but the Secretary of the National Association of Parish Councils

(NACP), Charles Arnold-Baker, convinced the Commission that they should be preserved. The Commission was nearly unanimous, with some reservations as to the exact geographic details. However, one member of the Commission, Derek Senior, dissented entirely from the proposals, and put forward his own in a Memorandum of Dissent (Cmnd. 4040-I), which was slightly larger than the Report itself. He would have preferred a two-tier system, with 35 city-regions of varying size, along with 148 districts. These were to be further grouped into five provinces.

Immediately after the report was published, Prime Minister Harold Wilson said that he accepted the recommendations 'in principle' and committed the government to 'press ahead quickly' on the legislation necessary to implement it, later clarifying that legislation would probably follow in the 1970–71 or 1971–72 Parliamentary session. The Labour government issued a White Paper entitled 'Reform of Local Government in England' (Cmnd, 4276) in February 1970, broadly accepting the recommendations of the report. The Government had however added two new metropolitan areas: West Yorkshire (with the five Bradford/Leeds/Halifax/Huddersfield/Mid-Yorkshire unitaries as districts), and South Hampshire based on the Southampton and Portsmouth unitaries, with the Isle of Wight being a separate district.

Observers felt that the Conservative Party, then in opposition, had no urgency in defining their position. The shadow spokesman Peter Walker did not commit himself but instead held a series of regional conferences to ascertain party grassroots opinion. Reports suggested these conferences were overwhelmingly hostile and the Conservative Party conference in 1969 passed a highly critical motion, while suggesting that some reform of local government was supported. Walker decided that a future Conservative government could not implement Redcliffe-Maud, but refused to disown the report completely. In the event the new Conservative government went ahead with an almost entirely different piece of legislation.

Bolton remembered the issues well almost 20 years later, writing in 1985 in response to a letter from Sir James Swaffield after they had met by chance at Claridges and Sir James had recognized John—John for his part had not 'placed' Sir James and had apologized for this:

> I remember that we were most impressed with the AMC's representations to the Royal Commission on Local Government and our preferred solution was medium sized single tier multi-purpose authorities, with exceptions for those services such as roads and traffic planning, refuse disposal and longer term structural planning etc. where a regional scale was needed. We were pressed by our friends in the Conservative Party to adopt a compromise solution which would involve larger districts which we were convinced, after looking at many possible models, would not be a starter, partly because no-one identified with the districts and their scale would not be adequate for the job—on the other hand,

people identified closely with their parishes which could have been given increased local responsibility. We agonised hard and long over whether to tell the truth as we saw it or whether to trim our recommendations to what we were told would be politically possible but, for better or for worse, decided that since local government reorganization was only looked at about every century, we just had to state our firm convictions and I am glad that you feel that sooner or later they will have to dust the old Report off and see what use can be made of our analysis.

Sir James Swaffield was the Secretary of the AMC at the time of the Royal Commission and later the Director-General of the Greater London Council from 1973–84. His own comments in his letter to John are worth recording here, in regretting that so much work had been put in and effectively ignored, when the report had provided many of the solutions which if applied would solve many problems:

> Let us not forget why the exercise of local government is so important. Local authorities are a vital ingredient even of a unitary state; they are the only bodies other than Parliament itself elected by universal franchise and they provide an essential check and balance within the distribution of power. . . . I happen to think that the themes of John Redcliffe-Maud still ring true and that, having had so many variations over the last few years, we should now return to him and enthusiastically endorse what he had to say.

The Royal Commission was a learning experience for John which he was to put to good use in his Chairmanship of the Committee of Inquiry on Small Firms soon afterwards, as we will see in the following chapter.

SURREY UNIVERSITY

The University of Surrey was established on 9 September 1966 with the grant of its Royal Charter but its roots go back to a late-19th-century concern to provide greater access to further and higher education for the 'poorer inhabitants' of London. Surrey University's history has been well described by Roy Douglas in his *Surrey, The Rise of a Modern University* (1991) and this section owes much to this source. The forerunner of the University, the Battersea Polytechnic Institute (founded 1891, first students admitted 1894) began concentrating on science and technology from about 1920 and taught day and evening students for degrees of the University of London. Its academic reputation steadily grew to the point in 1956 where it was one of the first colleges to be designated a 'college of advanced technology'. It was renamed Battersea College of Technology in 1957.

By the beginning of the sixties the College had virtually outgrown its main building in Battersea Park Road and in 1962 it had already decided to move to Guildford. Shortly afterwards (1963), the Robbins Report proposed that Battersea College, along with the other colleges of advanced technology, should expand and become a university awarding its own degrees. The greenfield site for the University-designate was acquired from Guildford Cathedral, Guildford Borough Council, and the Onslow Village Trust in 1965, and the move from Battersea was completed in 1970. Dr. Peter Leggatt, the Principal of Battersea College of Technology from 1960, became the first Vice-Chancellor of the new university until replaced by Professor Tony Kelly in 1975.

John Bolton became involved with Battersea before the move as a result of his connections with John Marsh of the BIM, who was on the Battersea Council and promoted the idea of John taking his place. Dr. Leggatt was also an alumnus of Trinity College, Cambridge and indeed was wearing its tie when John first met him, something which must have brought about an immediate bond. (By coincidence Kelly was also a Trinity man.) Even more to the point, however, John was very impressed with Leggatt's vision and as he put it in an interview in 1989 'I felt privileged to help him pursue it'. As John also said: 'I saw the need of several MITs in Britain and it was appropriate that they should grow out of the colleges of technology'. As we have already seen, he was also passionately interested in education, and was on the governing bodies of various schools as well as, of course, Harvard Business School. But of course it was by no means plain sailing. Battersea had been rooted in local authority systems with long tenures of interlocking groups of friends on the Council, and a technical college culture and many established staff to match. This transition was inevitably difficult for many long-serving people who tended to perpetuate their own kind and culture. This was not what John wanted, but even so, he was very surprised to become Chairman of Council within a year of joining, when Sidney Rich retired. John was present at the first meeting of the Council of the University, on September 30, 1966, held in the Council Room, Battersea Park Road. No doubt Leggatt (and others) had soon spotted him as someone to change the culture and transform Surrey into a university. Radical steps were needed. One was to introduce a three-year rotation on Council; another was to have members of the Royal Society on senior appointments boards; another was to ensure that degree ceremonies were worthy of a university. On this last point, when the second degree ceremony had to be held in the local Odeon, with its fleapit atmosphere, John said that mustn't happen again, so it was transferred to Guildford Cathedral, which many academics didn't like either. Inevitably, many academics didn't like quite a lot about the new situation. As John said rather ruefully: 'The same people who criticised Peter Leggatt for not taking enough decisions then criticised Tony Kelly for taking too many'. But he failed to persuade either of the VCs to have a house on campus, as at Trinity or HBS. He was to say later 'having seen it rise from the mud at Stag Hill [the location of its campus], it will always hold a special place in my heart'. As the first Chairman of Council, he was very involved with the physical move to Guildford.

Nevertheless, John felt that the structure of the University Council and its committees worked pretty well, with not too many ruffled feathers (although he did admit to losing his cool with one student petitioner). Everyone on Council had an interest in building a great university, so there was no factionalism. The key issue was raising enough funds. The Government provided initial funding for some aspects of the new university, but by no means all. It was still necessary to set up an appeal fund to purchase the site, to provide student residences and to provide a number of ancillary facilities. There were a number of functions at which financial help was sought from various organizations, and John was one of the key people in the appeal, along with Lord Nugent (ex-local MP), Col. Wells, Chairman of Surrey County Council, and the three High Officers of the University, Lord Robens, Sir George Edwards, and Sir William Mullens. All these people had interlocking circles of friends. Some £2 million was raised as a result of the appeal, a great deal of it from local industry, based on identifying a key person in each industry and persuading them to take the lead. John himself held dinners at Brook Place in the tithe barn at which he tried to get people to commit £5,000 a year for 10 years, very successfully, although one tycoon with a Rolls-Royce sent a cheque for £5. The initial very successful appeal used professional fundraisers, but a second one, which the university organized raised only half its target. Inevitably there was never enough money for all that might have been done. However he was proud of many of the things that were done, mentioning the Institute for Educational Technology, the leadership course, the Institute of Health, and the Science Park. The University's sandwich course was a great success, with almost everyone employed by the companies they worked with. The links with the town also became good. A unique development was the Managing Directors' Club, which John was instrumental in setting up. It had monthly meetings with a speaker and had three main roles: to discuss mutual problems; to introduce new techniques; and to provide interaction with the University. It was a great idea and a great success, with a membership of some 125 in 1983. But John would have wanted to raise more money through alumni organizations, as in the American way.

Many members of the public do not appreciate the important role that eminent outsiders can play in the operation of a university, especially at key periods such as its formative years. John carried out a range of important roles for Surrey University, from its inception as a new university, through its period of rapid growth, to its established maturity almost a generation later. He was Chairman (1968–1971) and Vice-Chairman (1971–1975) of Council in the early days, he was Honorary Treasurer for some seven years (1975–1982), he was a member of the Finance and General Purposes Committee, a member of the University Court, and he carried out some very important leadership roles outside the formal hierarchy, notably as Chairman of the Surrey Industry Appeal Committee and his own particular contribution, creating and being Chairman of the Surrey University Managing Directors Club. He was also a key figure in the selection for key posts, such as the Vice-Chancellorship when Tony Kelly was appointed, and the Chancellorship when The Duke of Kent was appointed. These were all huge contributions, requiring significant amounts of time not just for the inevitable meetings, but for other University events such as degree ceremonies, if they were to be carried out diligently. In 1981 he apologized that he had missed his first degree ceremony since the foundation of the University. However according to Surrey's Vice-Chancellor of the time, Professor Tony Kelly, he gave something even more, namely in creating partnerships with local business and industry and providing a credibility and a recognition for the University in the higher reaches of a Surrey society which was a little suspicious of this new institution and its origins.

In a university's operating system, the Council is responsible for all financial matters, the buildings, and the appointment of the Vice-Chancellor, while academic affairs are the responsibility of the Senate. The Council has a deliberative role and a representative role of various constituencies. The Treasurer is a two plus days a month role to maintain an overview of the University's finances and to chair the Finance Committee, which is responsible to Council for financial strategy, budget setting, investment activity, and capital expenditure. While not a specified constitutional function, fundraising can also be expected to be a part of the Treasurer's role, and sometimes quite a big one. It is, therefore, a substantial job, even if called 'honorary'.

The correspondence about John's resignation from the Treasurership is interesting in that it illustrates his role as a 'fixer' for the University as well his very strong sense of duty. At the end of 1981 he wrote to Tony Kelly expressing his wish to retire as a result of the pressures of the Presidency of the Engineering Industries Association, which he had just taken on. But he also felt that:

> it would be a good thing for a new Treasurer to be able to tackle the remaining phases of this appeal . . . and I sincerely hope that you will be able to persuade someone like Sir David Orr [an ex-Chairman of Unilever] who has the requisite industrial contacts at the highest level and experience of fund-raising to take over as Treasurer. I do not consider that there would be any conflict with Sir Ernest Woodroofe's [another ex-Chairman of Unilever] membership of Council, not only because he is near retiring age but because he turned down my approach to him to become Treasurer when Sir William Mullens died. Having promised Sir William personally that I would take over if I could not find

a suitable candidate, I found myself breaking Bolton's law. That is, briefly, that we must use our High Officer positions as trump cards to bring new talent of high calibre into the University's orbit—having been around since the beginning I was 'hooked' anyway as a faithful supporter of the University and always will be so. That is why I hope, in your wisdom, you and the other High Officers will not regard it as merely a post to 'promote' an existing staunch supporter into, however worthy he may be.

Those mentioned were all very distinguished men in public life, whom any university would have been happy to have associated with it. Surrey indeed was very well served by its High Officers. While there is an element of being situated in the right geographical context to attract eminent retirees, Surrey also owed a lot to Bolton (and one or two others) in their ability to identify and 'nobble' such people.

Unfortunately resigning was not to be so easy, since Surrey was one of the Universities most hard hit by the Government's 1981 cuts in University financing via the UGC; there was widespread concern about potential redundancies, and not only in Surrey. So Tony Kelly wrote back at the beginning of 1982 asking John to revoke his resignation because 'the resignation of the Treasurer is inevitably connected in our people's minds with the finances of the University, and can only give rise to adverse comment inside the University no matter how good your reasons for resigning at this juncture'.

So like the good trouper that he was, Bolton replied:

> Of course I would never dream of doing anything detrimental to the interests of the University and I sincerely believe that 'by handing on the torch' the University will be strengthened. However it is quite clear from your letter and from letters or phone calls from the other High Officers, that my resignation as Treasurer should neither seem to be precipitate, nor come at a time when the redundancy issue is being resolved. So I unreservedly withdraw my letter resigning as Treasurer on 21st January 1982—but on the understanding that immediate steps will be taken to find a suitable (and hopefully much better) replacement, so that the change can be announced at the special meeting of the Court, which I understand will now be necessary when all the present reorganization has been completed and probably before 31st March 1982.

It was in fact to be the end of July before he was able to step down from the Treasurership.

The University gave a dinner in his honour when he resigned from the Treasurership, and later in 1982 awarded him an honorary degree. In this latter, Sir Monty Finniston the ex-Chairman of British Steel, at that time the University's Pro-Chancellor, introduced him as 'the epitome of the busy businessman who finds time to do things where others find excuses not to do things', going on to add

> the financial difficulties created as a result of the cuts by the University Grants Committee . . . would have been substantially greater had we not had the sound financial groundwork, foresight and activity of John Bolton to fall back on. It was Keynes who said: 'Sound finance may be right psychologically but economically it is a depressing influence'. John Bolton proved that sound finance can also be economically rewarding at the right time.

This was the end of his formal roles, but he didn't lose contact with Surrey. On a personal level, he was instrumental in having the VC, Tony Kelly, appointed to the board of Johnson Wax in 1981, and the two of them were on the board together until Bolton's retirement in 1990.

There were other, more specific, ways in which he helped the University. John was instrumental in Black and Decker striking up a relationship with the Bio-Mechanical Department at Surrey; the Department designed new orthopaedic joints, while B&D were introducing battery-operated drills, saws, etc. He was willing to lobby on behalf of Surrey at the request of the Vice-Chancellor to Kenneth Baker, Minister of State for Industry and IT when Racal Electronics proposed to set up a chair in IT. The creation of the first British chair in Leadership Studies at Surrey also sounds like the sort of thing he would have suggested. John Adair was the incumbent.

ENGINEERING INDUSTRIES ASSOCIATION

The Engineering Industries Association (EIA) website states: 'We aim to be the Centre of Information, Trade and Support for the Engineering Industry', which involves a range of services, notably to do with overseas trade and parliamentary representation. It was founded in 1945 as a trade association for small and medium sized companies in the engineering industry and in this it differed from the Engineering Employers Federation, founded in 1896, and the British Engineering Manufacturers Association and the other 150 or so specialized trade associations, of which Parker (1989: 131) said:

> Most were arthritic with the pride and prejudice of their trade, many were run by senior citizens sitting on the edge of their pensions . . . The history of Britain's ramshackle array of trade associations is an industrial tragedy, a powerful cause of the downfall of our manufacturing.

Bolton took over the presidency of the EIA at a difficult time when the industry was in deep recession. As he put it in a letter to Tony Kelly of Surrey University:

> The additional work load of being President of the Engineering Industries Association is more horrific than I had envisaged when I agreed,

some two years ago, to take over that office from July 1981. Because the industry is in deep recession, over 10% of our members have gone bust in the last 12 months and employment in the engineering industry has reduced by some 20% in the past 18 months, so we have a fight for survival on our hands and I have the task of leading that survival. Since the engineering industry represents the 'main engines' of the economy, this task is of supreme importance to UK Limited and it is one which I cannot escape.

His daughter also remembers that the role took a lot of his time; although he was not paid for it, he thought it was important for the country. The current incumbent in 2013, Sir Ronald Halstead, finds that it takes some three days a week, so it is hardly surprising that John felt pressured by it. It is also worth noting that the current incumbent remembered that John had made quite a name for himself and had been highly regarded in the role. John also wrote to the Dean of Guildford Cathedral, in a letter which will be further quoted in Chapter 9:

As the new President of the Engineering Industries Association, which is also in the red, I am at present snowed under with the job of writing letters to companies, large and small, around the country asking for support, and with the disastrous conditions prevailing in the industry, one feels a bit like a mini-Gulliver towing four thousand or so 'small engineering ships' towards the safe shore of 1983.

These two comments also suggest a significant level of commitment and sense of duty.

After his presidency from 1981–84 he continued as a member of the EIA Council until 1993. He gave a talk at the F.I.F.E. General Meeting, York, in June 1981 'The Challenge for Trade Associations in Promoting Free Enterprise in the present European and World Environment'. It was given as incoming President of the Engineering Industries Association and the title indicates one of the main roles of the EIA, with others being to achieve standardization of products, to pursue market development, and to provide consumer information.

GENERAL COMMISSIONER OF INCOME TAX

John was a General Commissioner from 1964 until his death. General Commissioners of Income Tax are the oldest tribunal. They were established in 1799 by William Pitt the Younger's Income Tax Act, a temporary measure to finance the Napoleonic Wars. Many of the characteristics of income tax we recognize today, such as the tax schedules and taxation at source, were introduced in the early years of the 19th century. Traditionally, the value of the locally recruited Commissioners was that they have an understanding of the businesses and economy of their area. General Commissioners also had tax collecting and administrative powers, but these finally disappeared in 1946. The Special Commissioners, who were created in 1805, to assist the General Commissioners have now developed into a specialist, legally qualified tribunal, whereas the General Commissioners remain a lay, unpaid, and local tribunal. Each General Commissioner might expect to be involved perhaps six times a year.

General Commissioners are appointed to a division, based on the old tax divisions. Each division appoints a chairman for the division (as distinct from the hearing chairman), and there is no regional or presidential structure above that. Commissioners are appointed by the Lord Chancellor, on the recommendation of county advisory committees, which are usually chaired by the Lord Lieutenant.

Each division's administration is carried out by a clerk who gives the Commissioners legal advice. Administration that needs to be carried out centrally, such as policy, training, and finance is being carried out by the Tribunals Service.

Commissioners hear appeals from taxpayers on income tax, corporation tax, National Insurance, and some capital gains tax matters. Typical cases will be appeals against penalties and surcharges, tax status, applications to close tax inquiries, and amended assessments to tax. They also hear ex parte applications from Her Majesty's Revenue and Customs (HMRC) requiring taxpayers (and others) to provide information and tax returns. The appellant may appeal the General Commissioner's decision on a point of law to the High Court.

QUEEN'S AWARD TO INDUSTRY ADVISORY COMMITTEE

The Queen's Award to Industry was instituted by Royal Warrant in 1966. In the 1970s the scheme became The Queen's Awards for Export and Technology, with separate awards for outstanding achievement in export or technology. The Queen's Award for Environmental Achievement was added in 1992. A further change to the Queen's Award for Enterprise recognizes outstanding UK companies and encourages the development of British business. There are two types of award—for individuals and for businesses in three categories: international trade, innovation, and sustainable development. The Queen's Awards for Enterprise Promotion are intended to recognize individuals who make outstanding contributions to enterprise culture in the UK.

The Awards are made each year by The Queen, on the advice of the Prime Minister, who is assisted by an Advisory Committee that includes representatives of government, industry, and commerce, and the trade unions.

John was a member of the Advisory Committee from 1972. Winners are announced each year on 21 April, the Queen's birthday, and receive a range of benefits including worldwide recognition and extensive press coverage. The Queen also invites winners and members of the Advisory Committee to a reception at Buckingham Palace. John attended such a reception every year during his tenure on the Committee

HIGH SHERIFF AND DEPUTY LIEUTENANT OF SURREY

John was the High Sheriff of Surrey for 1980. A high sheriff is, or was, a law enforcement officer in England and Wales (and other countries). The high sheriff was originally allowed to kill suspects resisting arrest; this was still legal in the 17th century. The jurist Edward Coke noted that when the high sheriff employed constables to assist in his duties the law was also extended to them.

The post is unpaid and partly ceremonial, appointed by the Crown through a warrant from the Privy Council. Contemporary high sheriffs have few genuine responsibilities and their functions are largely representational:

* Attendance at Royal visits to the county;
* Proclamation of the accession of a new sovereign;
* They usually act as the returning officer for parliamentary elections in county constituencies and see to the annual appointment of an undersheriff;
* Attendance at the opening ceremony when a High Court judge goes on circuit;
* Execution of High Court writs;
* Appointment of under-sheriffs to act as deputies.

Most of the high sheriff's work is delegated; for example, the local police now protect judges and courts, so that in effect the post of high sheriff is essentially a ceremonial post. Theoretical responsibilities include the well-being and protection of High Court judges, and attending them in court; and the maintenance of the loyalty of subjects to the Crown. Nevertheless the role is still one which carries prestige and recognition.

The high sheriff was traditionally responsible for the maintenance of law and order within the county, although most of these duties are now delegated to the professional Chief Constable of Police. As a result of its close links with law and order the position is frequently awarded to people with an association with law enforcement (former police officers, lawyers, magistrates, judges). John as High Sheriff held two big garden parties at Brook Place, one at the beginning of his tenancy and another shortly afterwards, for some 150–200 people, mainly connected with law enforcement and the good and the great of Surrey, but also, for instance, the American Ambassador. It was for these that the garden at Brook Place was at its very best. In addition to these, John had to attend a lot of other social functions as well as the more formal responsibility of opening both the Kingston and Guildford High Courts. All told, he probably spent half a day a week on the role.

In England and Wales and in Ireland, the lord lieutenant was the principal officer of his county. The office's creation dates from the Tudors, being first appointed to a number of English historic counties by Henry VIII in the 1540s, when the military functions of the sheriff were handed over to him. He raised and was responsible for the efficiency of the local militia units of the county, and afterwards of the yeomanry and volunteers. The official title of the office at this time was His or Her Majesty's 'lieutenant for the county of x', but as almost all office-holders were peers they were referred to as 'lord lieutenant'.

The modern responsibilities of lord-lieutenants include:

- Arranging visits of members of the Royal family and escorting royal visitors;
- Presenting medals and awards on behalf of the Sovereign, and advising on Honours nominations;
- Participating in civic, voluntary, and social activities within the lieutenancy;
- Liaising with local units of the armed forces and their associated cadet forces;
- Leading the local magistracy as chairman of the Advisory Committee on Justices of the Peace; and
- Chairing the local Advisory Committee for the Appointment of the General Commissioners of Income Tax.

As the sovereign's representative in his or her county, the lord-lieutenant remains non-political and does not hold office in any political party. They are appointed for life, although the customary age of retirement is 75 and the sovereign may remove them.

The lord-lieutenant is supported by a vice lord-lieutenant and deputy lieutenants that he or she appoints. The lord-lieutenant appoints between 30 to 40 deputy lieutenants depending on the county's population size. They are unpaid, but receive minimal allowances for secretarial help, mileage allowance, and a driver. Deputy Lieutenants (DLs) tend to be people who either have served the local community, or have a history of service in other fields. They may represent the Lord-Lieutenant in his or her absence. This would include local ceremonies and official events, from opening exhibitions to inductions of vicars. DLs must live within the county. Their appointment does not terminate with the changing of the Lord-Lieutenant. They usually retire at age 75.

In practice, as is implied by these descriptions, both the High Sheriffs and the Lord Lieutenants and their deputies have very limited roles and indeed tend to be as much ceremonial and social as political, giving a focus to social and charitable activities within their county. John certainly had a substantial place in Surrey society and these posts reflected this as much as any professional qualifications for the roles.

7 The Committee of Inquiry on Small Firms

Introduction
The Origins of the Committee
Committee Processes
The Content of the Report
The Main Recommendations
The Research Reports
The Launch of the Report and Immediate Responses

INTRODUCTION

In spite of everything else he did, the Committee of Inquiry on Small Firms 1969–1971 is arguably John Bolton's greatest legacy. It is important to recognize that before the Committee, the small firm sector in Britain had little representation, few spokesmen, and virtually no voice. There has always been a vast preponderance of small businesses in all open economies, but with the coming of the Industrial Revolution there also came increasing concentration as large firms became increasingly dominant with the growing availability of economies of scale and the growth of international trade. There was also a tendency for the more advanced industries to be those which had higher levels of concentration. Indeed many saw this increased concentration as a natural process and disregarded the small firm as increasingly obsolete. This is not to say that the small firm was entirely ignored; the Macmillan Committee on Finance and Industry (1931) identified the 'Macmillan Gap', a chronic shortage of long-term investment capital for small and medium-sized companies. The Industrial and Commercial Finance Corporation (ICFC) was set up to meet that need, and in the post-war period it became a substantial source of funding for the sector. However, in post–World War II Britain, it became increasingly fashionable in both the major parties to say that Britain needed larger companies in order to compete on the world stage. Thus by the 1960s, industrial policy was heavily biased in this direction, with the Industrial Reorganization Corporation being specifically created to bring about large-scale mergers, while the Monopolies and Mergers Commission also supported this perspective. Overall, it was not so much a rejection of small business as a felt need to sponsor large firms. But it meant that there was virtually no support for small business from Government, unlike the situation in several other countries, while the small business community, again unlike several other countries, had no cohesion or sense of identity in political or economic terms.

THE ORIGINS OF THE COMMITTEE

How did the Committee come to be set up? The Labour government of the time had no great interest in the sector; this was the high watermark period of the corporate state. Britain had become dominated by mergers and acquisitions in the 60s, and as Parker said (1989: 174) 'We are the most concentrated of advanced economies, and I believe that, whatever the reasons for what has happened so intensely in the UK, it has not done British industry that much good'. Capitalism essentially meant big business, even if small business operated in a truer market economy. So what kick-started the interest in small firms? There are four contenders. One was Bernard (Jack) Weatherill's Private Member's Motion on February 10, 1967, which had had an input from John Bolton, and which spoke of the increasing difficulties of small firms and called on the Government of the day to relieve them. For a second possibility we noted in Chapter 5 the recommendation of para. 94 of the BIM's Mead Report (1968).

> In the course of our enquiries we have been left in no doubt that many small firms find it difficult in terms of time and cost to take full advantage of the existing reorganizations which are capable of assisting them with their management problems. We believe that this issue is of sufficient importance nationally to justify further study and we suggest that this Institute, together with other interested bodies and if necessary with Government support, should initiate an enquiry to consider what could be done to assist and improve management in the small firm.

A third contender is from the CBI, which claimed in its October 1971 Small Firms Bulletin that the Committee on Small Firms

> was the result of the representations made by the CBI both direct to Ministers and through the National Economic Development Council . . . and by the publication of the CBI booklet *Britain's Small Firms; their vital role in the economy*.

The article also intimated that the CBI might have been consulted about the make-up of the Committee and indeed this seems likely. A final possibility is from small business itself. Industry Week, in March 1970, while the Committee was still meeting, said

> The Bolton committee enquiry grew out of the discontent of 1967–68. That was no accident. The credit squeeze was beginning to bite and its teeth sank hardest into small businesses. Naturally they squealed. They felt unwanted by a Government whose ministers said that the practice of family businesses passing on from one generation to another was unjust (Mr Crosland) and that they were purveyors of trivia that the country neither needed nor could afford (Mr Harold Wilson).

Perhaps all four of these alternative explanations had an influence, but it seems unlikely that a Labour Government would set up an inquiry solely on the motion of a back-bench Conservative MP or on the basis of background discontent of a sector in which they had little interest or political capital. But the CBI claim seems strong, while the BIM had been to the trouble of contacting the CBI and then the Board of Trade and these two candidates seem most likely to have been the immediate cause of action. Both the CBI and the BIM had substantial small business memberships, perhaps in the absence of more specialized representation. Indeed in the BIM's case more than half initially and by 1968 three-quarters of the Collective Subscribers were small businesses within the BIM definition of under 500 employees (although many were also subsidiaries of larger companies), so that there was a definite BIM stake in this area.

And why Bolton as Chair? Obviously his work for Solartron, but also his other public activities. In particular it seems likely that he must have performed well in his chairmanship of the Rubber EDC and in his vice-chairmanship of the Royal Commission on Local Government, the most similar role. And of course his activities for the BIM, in which he would certainly have voiced his interest in the small firms sector, especially if the origins of the Committee did indeed lie in the Mead Committee's recommendations. His availability would also have been a factor; it would have been far too big a commitment had he still been at Solartron. There would have been discussion within government about the appointments, extending out to the CBI, the City, the NEDC, and probably the TUC.

The members of the Committee were: Bolton; Edward Robbins, a management consultant in Industrial Administration and Vice-Chairman of the Industrial Training Foundation; Professor Brian Tew, Midland Bank Professor of Money and Banking at Nottingham University; and Larry Tindale, a chartered accountant and Director and General Manager of the Industrial and Commercial Finance Corporation (ICFC). Of the four, John was the only one with any substantial managerial experience of working in small firms; of the others, Tew's intellectual interests were in monetary theory and the international monetary system and had no connections with small firms, although he had previously worked for ICFC and had some industrial experience as a part-time member of the Iron and Steel Board and the East Midlands Electricity Board. Tindale was an accountant by training and joined ICFC as an Assistant General Manager in 1959 before rising to become General Manager and a director in 1964. As General Manager he set about professionalizing ICFC and became the architect of the transition to 3i and its later success. He had a very strong free market ideology and his management style is described as follows in the history of 3i: 'Larry Tindale . . . with a less involved Chairman, brought to bear his own individualistic approach, running the whole organization and planning its direction with a minimum of delegation' (Coopey and Clarke 1995: 278). Tindale, not inappropriately, saw the ICFC as the dominant institution in the small business field and came to the Committee with views taken from this high vantage point. Robbins had a training background and no direct involvement in small firms; he was less influential in the discussions than the other members. Apart from John, the Committee was quite unlike the Royal Commission on Local Government, where almost everyone except John had a passionate commitment to local government from some perspective. The Secretary was David Hartridge from the Board of Trade, together with a further six in the secretariat; Hartridge proved to be an excellent Secretary, producing a colossal output at a tremendous speed. The Research Director was Graham Bannock, who also had six additional staff in the Research Unit, including importantly Professor S. J. Prais, on leave from the National Institute of Social and Economic Research, who made a notable intellectual input. Initially there was not intended to be a Research Unit, but at the Committee's first meeting Bolton requested one, probably based on his experience of the value of one on the Royal Commission on Local Government as well as the emerging immensity of the task before them. Perhaps a little surprisingly given the generally parsimonious way in which such committees were funded, the sponsoring Minister, Anthony Crosland, was not only willing to meet this request with a fund of £250,000, but told his civil servants that the Committee could have more if they needed it.

The Terms of Reference were:

> To consider the role of small firms in the national economy, the facilities available to them and the problems confronting them, and to make recommendations. For the purpose of this study a small firm might be defined broadly as one with not more than 200 employees, but this should not be regarded as a rigid definition.
>
> In the course of the study it will be necessary to examine in particular the profitability of small firms and the availability of finance. Regard should also be paid to the special functions of small firms, for example as innovators and specialist suppliers.

This was a broad remit. Indeed the most specific thing about it was the definition of 200 employees, at a time when such a definition was by no means universally accepted. The Committee has been criticized for its definition, but in fact the starting point was built into the terms of reference. Indeed others have taken a wider definition; thus the Centre for Policy Studies took 500 employees in mining construction and manufacturing and included sections not included by Bolton such as agriculture and the professions, thus reaching 40 per cent of GNP, 53 per cent of the output of the private sector and 33 per cent of employment. Other countries and indeed groupings such as the EU (250) and the American Small Business Administration (500) often used different criteria and this became a difficult issue in international comparisons or agreement.

COMMITTEE PROCESSES

When John first attended for the Committee, he was amazed to find himself in a huge room with 29 civil servants. And if that created a sense of scale, this was rapidly enhanced by the recognition of what was being taken on, as the Report noted in its opening paragraphs:

> It soon became obvious that we had undertaken a massive task, and one of great difficulty, for the small firm sector is extremely large and remarkably heterogeneous. On any reasonable definition, small firms account numerically for the vast majority of all business enterprises. Their diversity is even more striking than their number. Small firms are present in virtually every industry and the characteristics that they share as small firms are sometimes not apparent because of the differences arising from the contrasting conditions of different industries. A proper understanding of the whole small firm sector therefore requires study of many industries. There is also extreme variation within the sector as regards efficiency, methods of operation, the nature of the market served and the size of resources employed.
>
> (Para. 3)

There was however one characteristic shared by all small firms as the Committee used the term, and that was that they were managed by the people who owned them. Thus the first decision was that the Committee's 'proper concern was the owner-managed business'. The second decision was about the scope of the inquiry, since it was clearly impossible to consider the whole economy. Thus the Committee decided not to study the agriculture, horticulture or fishing industries, or the professions, and did not collect detailed information about them.

The next issue concerned what the Committee called 'the startling lack of information' on the general state of the sector, and thus rather than 'pronounce judgement on the strength of a body of generally accepted fact, we were ourselves obliged to assemble the basic information'. This was done in four ways:

- Issuing a general invitation to all interested parties to submit written evidence. Letters were sent to some 2000 reorganizations, of which some 400 submissions were received, mainly from trade associations and individual firms. Some submissions were specifically invited but not many.
- A postal survey sent to some 16,000 small firms, incorporating two questionnaires, one covering history, managerial characteristics, and other background information, and the other relating to financial accounts over a number of years. The first questionnaire was replied to by 3500 firms and the second by 2115.
- Because neither of these two methods could have provided the answers to some important questions, an internal Research Unit was set up to undertake a programme of research. This was partly carried out by the unit and partly by external consultant researchers working under the direction of the Committee's Director of Research. Eighteen Reports were published as a result of this programme, and are listed later in this chapter.
- As the issues came into clearer focus it became helpful to hold discussions with a range of interested parties, from MPs to academics to representative bodies. Oral evidence was taken in formal session for 21 full days, and there were numerous less formal meetings, with visits to many parts of the country and to the United States, Canada, Japan, France, and Germany.

While the decision to set up the Committee was doubtless based in part on short-term considerations, including the difficult economic circumstances for small firms at the time, it was made clear to the Committee that its major purpose was a longer-term one, 'the collection of information on the place of small firms in a modern economy' as the basis for future policy. In this it made a major contribution. Indeed the main driver of the whole Committee was the research effort from the internal research staff and the externally commissioned papers, rather than any ideological or even policy perspectives; without the research the 'policy' chapters would have been little more than the expressions of opinion.

In total there were 100 ordinary Committee meetings. These were not always based on consensus, and indeed there was something of a division within the Committee. Tindale and Tew generally argued against any intervention in the status quo, while John was more alive to and concerned about the difficulty of running small firms, with the support of his Research Director. John's preconception was that the Government was a great burden on small business and that this needed to be rectified. His favourite cartoon, indeed, was of a donkey bearing boxes of weights with Government sitting on it and whipping it along. He was later to regret that he had not been more insistent within the Committee. Tindale was arguably the most forceful personality, highly intelligent and with his own clear view as to where the Committee should be heading. He also used his position at ICFC to host discussion meetings with MPs and others to good effect. All of the members were surprised by the magnitude of the task. They had to give more time than they had expected at the beginning and this probably created some impatience. Everybody would have preferred a short, succinct report, but a list of recommendations without the backing research would have carried little weight. Moreover all the members were genuinely surprised at the importance of small firms within the economy that emerged, and this helped to drive them. In addition the Committee in its drafting tended to err on the side of comprehensiveness, making the Report perhaps longer than it might have been. In this situation John Bolton was a kind, patient, and diplomatic chairman of the Committee according to one of its key figures—very much a conciliator and moderator. He was not the main intellectual driver—Tindale and Tew were that, but he was the balancing force, with a good feel for the politics of the issue. And in spite of the pressures, he was never an impatient or unreasonable chairman vis-à-vis the staff, for whom it was an enjoyable experience outside the normal run of Departmental work.

THE CONTENT OF THE REPORT

The Report was a very substantial document of almost 450 pages (without the research reports) and was presented in two parts. The first, 'An Economic Analysis' predominantly written by Graham Bannock, the Director of Research, provided 'a description of the small firm sector, its place in the national economy and social fabric, and of the forces operating on it'. The second part, 'Problems and Policies' which was written predominantly by the Committee's Secretary, David Hartridge, dealt with the implications of the findings and discussed the effects on small firms of various external factors, including Government. The Committee's recommendations flowed from the discussions in Part II, and many of them called for changes in legislation or policy.

Central to the Report was recognizing the importance of the sector.

There are at least 1.25 million small firms in the United Kingdom; they give employment to some 6 million people or 25 per cent of the employed population, and are responsible for nearly 20 per cent of the gross national product. That part of the sector we have studied in detail . . . includes some 820,000 small firms, employing 4.25 million people and produces 14 per cent of the GNP. Still more important than its quantitative contribution is the fact the small firm plays a vital role in the preservation of a competitive private enterprise system. We believe that the small firm is in fact an essential medium through which dynamic change in the form of new entrants to business, new industries, and new challengers to established market leaders, can permeate the economy. . . . The real issue is what part have small firms to play in preserving a healthy industrial structure and in creating the kind of society we want for the future.

(Para. 13)

And also:

We are conscious that our Report may at times appear to reflect inadequately our regard for the contribution of the small business to the vitality, variety and humanity of our society, because these things can hardly be measured in statistical terms. But that contribution is enormous: without small firms this country would be an infinitely duller, poorer and less happy place.

(Para. 12)

The importance of small firms differed considerably between sectors, even though they were to be found in all industries. Thus they were extremely important in catering, retail, and miscellaneous services, much less so in manufacturing and wholesaling. They tended also to be in those industries concentrating on local markets, although it is worth noting that in those small firms that did export, the average proportion of exports was 32 per cent. This is not the place to recount the facts or the arguments or indeed the problems of defining a small firm in the first place in any detail, but some key factual outcomes are important.

One was the finding that the small firm sector was in decline, with substantial but uncertain implications. The decline was found in most industries with the possible exceptions of road transport and some of the miscellaneous service trades. Moreover the decline had been continuing since at least before World War II and there were indications that it had continued since the middle 1960s. The causes of this decline were examined in Chapter 7, which identified the following issues:

- The emergence of the very large company and a trend to oligopoly
- The increased role of the State and the side effects of this
- The loss of social standing of small business
- Marketing and the provision of economies of scale
- Transport and communications and the widening of markets
- Managerial skills enabling large firms to become more efficient
- Research and development costs and economies.

A second was that Britain had a smaller small firm sector than other countries, although comparisons were difficult. It was found that the process of declining share of small enterprises in economic activity was a general and continuing trend in all countries, but that this had gone further in Britain than elsewhere. The most significant comparison available, albeit out-of-date and somewhat misleading due to rather different definitions, was the proportion of manufacturing employment in small establishments, which showed Britain with 31 per cent, Germany 34 per cent, the USA with 39 per cent, all with a date of 1963, and most other Western countries with over 50 per cent (para. 6.2).

A third area of findings was to examine performance in the sector by examining various aspects of efficiency. One of these was in the use of resources, in which the finding was that when output was related to labour inputs, productivity rose with firm size, but that the reverse was true when profits were related to capital employed, and thus concluded that there were no grounds for thinking that small firms were less 'efficient' than large in their use of resources. Both findings, however, could be at least partially explained by the ratios of labour and capital in production. A second dimension of efficiency was in the contribution of small firms to competition, and here it was found that industries needed a substantial group of small firms, some of which might be expected to grow into rivals to the existing large firms. A third lay in the contribution to innovation and invention, and here again it was found that small firms made an important contribution, although probably more in invention than innovation.

A fourth main finding was to identify eight separate economic functions performed by small firms:

- They provide a productive outlet for enterprising and independent people who are not suited to employment in a large organization but have much to contribute to the vitality of the economy.
- They are the most efficient form of reorganization in industries where the optimum size of the production or sales unit is small.
- They can flourish in a limited or specialized market where it would not be worthwhile for a large firm to enter.
- They can act as specialist suppliers to large firms with lower costs than large firms could achieve.
- They provide competition and therefore some check on monopoly profits.
- They are an important source of innovation in products, techniques, and services.
- They are the traditional breeding ground for new industries, i.e. innovation writ large.
- Perhaps most important, they provide the means of entry into business for new entrepreneurial talent and the seedbed from which new large companies will grow.

A final finding was the widespread weakness of management in small firms, although with some brilliant exceptions. This was a constant theme in the research reports, in the view of specialists in the field and in the evidence of 21 large companies who were asked to comment on small firms as suppliers or sub-contractors. A consistent pattern emerged of weaknesses in the following areas:

- Finance, both a lack of knowledge of sources of finance and lack of skill in presenting a financial case
- Costing and control information, as in unawareness of impending difficulties, or in evaluating different levels of activity
- Reorganization, with poor delegation, job specification, or lack of adequate procedures
- Marketing, with a tendency to be product or service oriented with neglect of the marketing function
- Information use and retrieval, with ignorance of potentially useful developments and failure to make use of available information
- Technological change, with an inability to keep abreast of change, partly through lack of qualified staff, partly through ignorance of developments
- Production scheduling and purchase control, making it difficult to meet delivery dates and optimize stock levels.

In addition, there was a general hostility to outside interference and even advice.

THE MAIN RECOMMENDATIONS

The debate leading to recommendations started from whether the small firm sector needed discrimination in its favour. Although there was probably some disagreement about this, with John opposed by Tindale and Tew, the judgement was that the decline of the sector had not reached the point where deliberate discrimination would be justified. Thus the principle adopted was one of neutrality as between firms of different sizes. That decided, 'with considerable misgivings' (para. 8.13) the next issue, which took up the majority of the Report, was to identify and rectify 'a number of inequitable and unnecessary disabilities, mostly imposed by Government, which amount to discrimination against them' (para. 8.18). Individual chapters then took up various topics and provided recommendations as to what ought to be done.

Chapter 9, dealing with 'Reorganization in Government' provided the single most important recommendation. It noted that small businessmen had been 'extremely ineffective as a pressure group (para. 9.4) and that this was one of the main reasons for the ignorance of Government and its apparent indifference. The Committee felt it necessary that such a large sector should have a more powerful voice in public affairs, in spite of the other fact that small businessmen themselves were fiercely independent and appeared to feel that any Government attention would be a threat to this. Other countries, such as the United States, Japan, and France, had much more structured representation within government and the Committee therefore recommended that there should be a Small Firms Division within the Department of Trade and Industry and that there should be a designated Minister to be responsible for small firms and to oversee the Division.

Other major topics that the Committee considered were: management skills and advisory services; sources of finance; the impact of taxation (these last two were the largest chapters with the most complex issues in Part II); industrial training; statistical and administrative returns; monopolies and restrictive trade practices; disclosure; and development and planning controls. Overall, there were some 58 recommendations, discounting some implicit suggestions in areas such as sources of finance. As the Report said in its conclusions: 'This is a fairly formidable list of recommendations', and while the Committee felt that 'adoption of them all would alleviate in considerable measure the current difficulties of the small firm sector', they added 'as we know from our experience of the last two years, new problems and difficulties arise almost as fast as the old ones are solved' (para. 19.20).

Another significant recommendation was that there should be a network of Small Business Advisory Bureau in large industrial centres to act as a 'signposting' or referral service to appropriate sources of professional, commercial, or official advice. This would work in areas like finance, where in spite of the recognized importance of the topic the Committee decided not to make any recommendations given their view that there was no institutional deficiency in the finance market (para. 19.13).

On taxation, the other topic of much discussion, there were by contrast a considerable number of recommendations. The Committee (para. 13.13) found that

> the current regime of high taxation operates differentially against the small firm sector in two respects. First, high taxes on capital (especially death duties) undermine incentives in small firms, which are frequently family businesses, more seriously than in large; and second, high taxation of profits and rapid inflation have combined to make the financing of expansion more difficult unless recourse is had to external finance on a scale which the small businessman is unwilling to accept and often unable to achieve.

While the Committee, in accordance with its general approach, did not propose to give small firms specially favourable tax treatment, it did make 13 recommendations in this area, most of them designed to ameliorate particular difficulties and many of them quite detailed.

Another significant recommendation was to exempt small firms from the levy/grant system of the Industrial Training Act, while another area of numerous (15) recommendations was the burden of form-filling, and here the intention was to ensure that the full cost, and particularly the cost to industry, of statistical or administrative requirements should be considered before imposing them. In this connection, and doubtless mindful of the poor information base they had had to work with, they also recommended that planning should begin for an integrated system of official records about business. A final significant suggestion in this area was that statisticians should be more closely associated with policy makers to make policies more firmly based on a quantitative analysis of the issues.

Two other areas where the Committee made several recommendations were competition policy, where they were not satisfied that existing policies gave sufficient weight to the power of the competing units, and planning controls, which created a number of problems for small firms.

Alongside what they called 'this fairly formidable list of recommendations', there was also a constant reiteration of the difficulty of analysing and monitoring the sector due to the absence of systematic information.

There were also eight appendices, half concerned with the giving of evidence to the Inquiry, another two about foreign treatment of small firms, one on closed trading companies, and one on estate duty and family businesses.

THE RESEARCH REPORTS

Given the paucity of information available on the sector, the Committee found it necessary to commission 18 research reports running to over 1250 pages. They are listed as follows:

1. The Small firm in the Road Haulage Industry. B. Bayliss
2. Scientific and Engineering Manpower and Research in Small Firms. J. G. Cox
3. Small Firms in the Manufacturing Sector. J. R. Davies and M. Kelly
4. Financial Facilities for Small Firms. Economists Advisory Group
5. Problems of the Small Firm in Raising External Finance. The results of a Sample Survey. Economists Advisory Group
6. The Role of Small Firms in Innovation in the UK since 1945. C. Freeman
7. Attitude and Motivation. C. W. Golby and G. Johns
8. The Small Unit in the Distributive Trades. M. Hall
9. The Small Firm in the Motor Vehicle Distribution and Repair Industry. J. Hebden and RFR Robinson
10. Small Firms in the Construction Industry. P. Hillebrandt
11. Three Studies on Small Firms. P. Lund and D. Miner

    i Previous surveys of small firms
    ii Comparisons between firms of different size using the CBI Industrial Trends surveys
    iii The investment behaviour of small firms

12. Dynamics of Small Firms. Merrett-Cyriax Associates
13. Aspects of Monopoly and Restrictive Practices Legislation in Relation to Small Firms. S. Moos
14. The Small Firm in the Hotel and Catering Industry. J. F. Pickering
15. Small Retailers: Prospects and Policies. A. D. Smith
16. A Postal Questionnaire Survey of Small Firms: An Analysis of Financial Data. M. Tamari

17. A Postal Questionnaire Survey of Small firms: Non-Financial Data, Tables, Definitions and Notes. Research Unit
18. The Relative Efficiency of Small and Large Firms. D. Todd

There are far too many reports to review them in any detail, but one example helps to illustrate the complexities involved. Report No. 6, on the role of small firms in innovation, was written by Professor Christopher Freeman of the Science Policy Research Unit at Sussex University with the aid of his staff. The research involved 120 named reorganizations, mainly industrial but including a dozen universities, which assisted with the compilation of the lists of innovations, 'while a large number of firms, too numerous to mention' verified information. In total 1100 innovations were surveyed, and the report included an experiment in 'weighing' for the quality of innovations in four industries, while the team carrying out the research under Freeman's leadership consisted of 10 people. Even then their survey did not cover by any means the whole of the economy. Nevertheless this was quite a large-scale research project in its own right, requiring a considerable amount of organization, communication, and analysis, including a substantial discussion of methodology. Indeed the methodology issue was a significant one; as the research report noted:

> In attempting the measurement of the innovative contributions of various classes of firm, the Unit was faced with the basic problem that no systematic primary data was in existence. There is no list of innovations available for any branch of industry, or for the economy as a whole, still less any systematic data classifying innovations by size of firm.

This was the kind of problem shared with many of the research reports, and indeed the Committee as a whole.

The research reports added a great deal to the stock of existing knowledge about small firms, and were certainly taken into account by the Committee. Their main role was to assist the Research Director, Graham Bannock, in the writing of Part 1 of the Report. They also appear to have been used as a research source elsewhere, in both Britain and in other countries. Indeed the reports taken together can be argued to have been excellent value for money in terms of the information they created. It is not clear how many sets were printed, but all the 18 reports were out of stock and out of print by 1983, when John tried to order a full set for Harry Hansen, so there was obviously interest in them.

THE LAUNCH OF THE REPORT AND IMMEDIATE RESPONSES

On November 3, 1971, John Bolton hosted a press conference to launch the Report. After introducing his colleagues Robbins and Tindale (Tew was absent in Australia), JEB said that they had found the small firms area exciting, interesting and complex, requiring two and a quarter years' work rather than the expected one and producing a rather large egg in the form of a quarter of a million words and more than that in the research reports. He then went on to cover what he saw as the three main issues: what is so important about small firms anyway; why are their problems any different from large firms; and the major recommendations and the follow-up required. On the first, he said that he had been astonished at the size and vital contribution of the sector in economic terms, for quality of life and for the public at large. On the second, he instanced various factors which made for a hostile environment in which nobody was looking after small firms' concerns, while large firms were more able to control their environment and lobby for their interests. On the third, their recommendations were aimed at giving small firms a fair crack of the whip by closing the 'policy gap' in Government, by closing the information gap, and by relieving the sector of unfair burdens. The Report, he finished, was at the same time a charter and a book of reference which only scratched the surface of this vital sector of the economy, and that much more needed to be done. And in all this, he hoped the Press would help.

Enterprise (1971, Vol. 1, Issue 12) said in its editorial:

> getting reliable and representative opinion did not prove easy. Indeed despite press advertising which called for as much personal evidence as possible, the bulk of evidence came from representative bodies rather than individual firms. This was undoubtedly the Committee's biggest failing. Their surveys had low response rates, supplemented with limited interviews with small businessmen.

Bolton himself said in his introduction at the press conference:

> Our task proved to be far more complex and difficult than we had expected, mainly because of the paucity of economic and statistical data about the sector as a whole. . . . The main finding of the Committee is that the UK small firm sector, although still a large and vital component of the industrial structure, is declining steadily in size and in its share of economic activity.

When the report was published, there were various letters of congratulations, some from old friends such as Sir John Rodgers and Bernard Weatherill, but others such as John Davies at Ministerial level as well. A special letter was from the Secretary, David Hartridge, who started by thanking John for giving the team such an enjoyable dinner. He noted that some of the staff had worked in the Civil Service for 20 years but never been taken out before. Hartridge added:

> Thank you also for your kindness and forbearance throughout the two years and more of the Inquiry. Over such a long haul it means a great

deal to have a Chairman who can be absolutely relied on to never blow his top or to indulge in recriminations when problems arise and I, more than anybody, have benefited from your tolerance and understanding. If I may say so, it says a great deal for you that so big and difficult a job has been done without friction of any kind. I can't expect to get many jobs as enjoyable and rewarding as this one . . . I know the Report is well regarded in the Government and that your immense labour in the public service is greatly appreciated.

(It was something of an exaggeration to say that there was no friction, but this was after all a thank you letter.)

Hartridge's note about John's generosity and thoughtfulness was echoed by several who had received his letter thanking them for their evidence. As the Chairman of Lansing Bagnall said, 'Far from your thanking me for help, I feel I must thank you and the other members of your Committee'. On a different tack there was a letter from Brian Tew immediately after the report, noting that para. 10.49 about the ILO (Industrial Liaison Officers) services should not have been included in the form it was, and that it should be disowned.

John Davies, the Secretary of State for Trade and Industry, introducing the Report in Parliament at the same time as the press conference, said: 'They have provided the first authoritative study of the place of the small firm in our economy. It will stand as a landmark for many years to come'. As indeed it has. He also committed the Government to accepting most of the recommendations, to relieve 'the disabilities which small firms now suffer, usually as a result of unintended neglect by Government . . .'.

The issue of how many of the recommendations were accepted is not without its ambiguities due to somewhat different policies actually being implemented. But certainly the Report was largely accepted, and much changed as a result of it; moreover governments for many years thereafter felt obliged to issue statements about how much they were doing for small firms, using the Report as a point of reference. Conversely, there were various 'score-sheets' about what had and had not been done, and as one put it several years later: 'the cynic might say that successive Governments have cleverly managed to implement the quantity but have missed the important quality issues'. In particular it complained that what had been done often lacked 'teeth'. But sometimes the score-sheets misinterpreted the Report, as did this one in saying that the Report had recommended a Minister at Cabinet level; what the Report actually said was that the proposed Minister should have the backing of a Cabinet Minister, a rather different thing. A reasonable accusation of what did not happen was the lack of any move to provide hard factual data about the sector, an issue about which the Report commented on numerous occasions. However what happened over time is the subject matter of the following chapter.

There was substantial recognition of the Report in the newspapers; *The Times* and the *Financial Times* had editorials, while *The Guardian* had a whole page of coverage. But there was no real sense in these comments of the momentum that was to emerge as the decade unfolded. In the parliamentary debates on the Report, as was not unusually the case, the debate in the House of Lords was more measured and reflective than that in the Commons, even if one noble lord did refer to 'Professor Bolton', and although more than one reference was made to the limited number of speakers and numbers present for the debate. The general thrust, as Lord Mottistone summed up, was that 'Bolton has charted a splendid course', and that it would now be up to Government.

Some eight months after the launch there was a further debate in the House of Commons as part of a Private Member's Motion by Robert Redmond on 12 June 1972 in which he argued, following on the Government's reaction to the Bolton Report: 'Like Oliver Twist, I am coming back for more, but unlike Oliver Twist, I expect to get it'. The motion was essentially bipartisan. The lead Labour speaker, Robert Maclennan, said:

> The Bolton Committee is to be congratulated on having produced such a comprehensive, in some respects controversial and in some respects novel, report, which contains a vast amount of information about the problems of small industries and a number of very useful suggestions, some of which have already been acted upon.

There was little academic analysis at the time because the subject was not studied in universities. The most considered review of the Report was by Professor B. S. Yamey of the London School of Economics in the *Three Banks Review* (1972). Yamey, a well-known industrial economist, was surprised that an inquiry had been set up, given the indifference or even hostility toward small business for the preceding 25 years. But he was gratified that the Report, unlike others dealing with industry, did not recommend major Governmental expenditure or favouritism. He noted that the Report 'charts terra incognita with skill and verve', which would serve as an agenda for some time to come from 'this disinterested and authoritative source'. His criticisms were mainly two:

> for failure adequately to specify the distinctive sources of the discrepancy between public and private benefits in the small firms sector upon which its interesting analysis is made to turn; and it does not spell out fully the nature of the links in the chain connecting the fate of the relatively few potential fliers in the small firm sector with the fate of the entire small firm population.

But these were big asks, he admitted, and overall he commended it.

In the amount of letter-writing to the papers which followed, there is a fascinating glimpse of small business anxieties which finished up in the Bolton archives. Mrs. Worster from an engineering company in Cirencester wrote two letters to the *Financial Times* pointing out that it should not be too difficult to maintain financial controls, whereupon two small business-men, one an agricultural contractor from Newtown, Montgomery and the other a central heating engineer from Keighley in Yorkshire, wrote to Mrs. Worster asking for her system. It seems quite probable that neither knew where else to go for such information.

The Institute of Directors quickly produced an eight-page pamphlet, *After Bolton What?* arguing that 'the importance of the Bolton report can hardly be overstated' and coming up with a 10-point plan of general and specific proposals:

General

1. Taxation policy: exempt part of profits
2. Enquire into the effects of EEC entry on small firms
3. Co-ordinate advisory services
4. Make better use of retired directors' skills
5. Ensure that small premises are available

Specific

1. Abolish short-term assessments
2. Allow small firms, by choice, to be taxed as partnerships
3. Abolish gains tax on companies
4. Extend 45 per cent estate duty relief to net trading assets
5. Allow for tax interest on loans generally but in particular on loans used to buy into small firms

Not all reviews of the Report were sympathetic, *The Economist* (November 6, 1971) had a half-page piece headed 'Bolton Report—No Case for Aid' which drove Bolton to do his own editing of the review. When the article started off 'Because there was so little of substance to tilt against, the Report was a disappointment', this had a big Bolton question mark against it. Then: 'if numbers fall too low, they might become too small to be effective, but it produces not a shred of evidence that this is happening'; this has a Bolton mark beside it with 'not true'. As for 'So no actual money is asked for (for which the government should be grateful) beyond that needed to set up an export service and an advisory centre in all major towns. Neither can really be justified'; this received a stronger mark, with 'Balls' against it. Plus another couple of indignant question marks later. *The Times* (4 November 1971) was also mainly concerned that small firms did not need special support, and while it underlined the Report's emphasis on the significance of the small firm sector in the economy, it argued

Economies of scale and technology itself have created an inexora-ble trend towards gigantism in industry. This trend is a natural and desirable development and it is something that small firms must learn to live with . . . In recent years there has been a detectable neurosis among small businesses in Britain which has built up into a sort of persecution complex. The complaints of small firms are well known and have been repeated ad nauseam.

Its editorial finished:

> The new Minister at the Department of Trade . . . should be able to ensure that discrimination is within reason eliminated. It is doubtful whether these and the other Bolton Committee proposals stand up as a 'charter' for small firms or whether indeed it is appropriate for small firms to have a charter.

Moreover, for all the positive immediate response from the Government, Alan Peacock, who had been Chief Economic Advisor to the Department of Trade and Industry between 1973 and 1976, noted in 1989:

> I remember very well when the Bolton Committee on Small Firms first appeared and how sceptically it was regarded by powerful politicians and civil servants who had all too readily accepted the Galbraithean thesis that the small person in business was a tedious anachronism (Bannock and Peacock 1989: 3)

Nevertheless a final and more personal short-term outcome of the Report was that John was appointed CBE in 1972, for which he received more than 150 letters of congratulation.

Table 7.1 Proportion of manufacturing in small establishments

Country	Year for data	Percentage
UK	1963	31
Germany	1963	34
USA	1963	39
Canada	1968	47
Belgium	1962	51
France	1963	51
Sweden	1965	53
Netherlands	1962	58
Australia	1963	60
Switzerland	1965	61
Norway	1967	64
Italy	1961	66

Source: Report of the Committee of Inquiry on Small Firms, p. 68

8 Small Firms after the Committee of Inquiry

Introduction

Part One: Bolton's Contribution to the Debate on Small Firms after the
      Report

  The 1970s
  Major Speeches—the RSA, Marlow, and Manchester Bankers Lectures
  Venture Capital Activities
  The 1980s and Beyond

Part Two: Changes in the Small Firm Sector in the Aftermath of the
      Report

  Sectoral Growth
  Government Policy
  Financing Small Firms
  Representation and Recognition
  Improved Information
  Attitudes
  The Report in International Debate and Comparisons

Conclusions

INTRODUCTION

From a low level of recognition and knowledge, the small business sector
became fully accepted as a critical part of the British economy in the 15
or 20 years following the Committee. In no small part this was due to the
impact of the Report of the Committee of Inquiry and of John Bolton's own
passionate pursuit of a role which was effectively foisted onto him after his
chairmanship of the Committee. This chapter is therefore the story both of
John Bolton's own contribution to the debate after the Committee and the
way the sector developed after the Report, when there was an unprecedented

flourishing which could be measured in many different dimensions, and is therefore split into these two separate parts.

PART ONE: BOLTON'S CONTRIBUTION TO THE DEBATE ON SMALL FIRMS AFTER THE REPORT

It is very doubtful if John Bolton anticipated what followed the Committee's Report. He probably imagined that the Government would respond in a positive way and hoped that the Report would be remembered as a landmark, but that people would soon move on to other things. He almost certainly never imagined that well over a decade later he would still be seen as the spokesman for the sector, indeed 'Mr. Small Business', and be expected to lead an ongoing debate and reaction, involving dozens if not hundreds of commitments, mainly through lectures, to a wide variety of organizations and audiences, constantly trying to get over simple messages. This is the period when he did most of his writing and lecturing, and became a substantial public figure. His talks were not off-the-cuff but carefully prepared, usually with more than one draft, although presented in a relaxed manner, while articles would have several drafts. There are pictures of him in a characteristic pose, left hand in his pocket, half-moon glasses perched on the end of his nose, right hand holding his small key-point cards. He probably did not expect, either, that he would become more radical in his perspectives and demanding in his prognoses, to the point where the Thatcher Government, as it became in the 1980s, probably saw him as an irritant which it wished would go away. This transition can be noted in his own words. In 1985, he wrote a letter to Sir James Swaffield comparing the small firm committee decision-making with that on local government which we have already quoted in part in Chapter 6, but which continued:

> For interest, when I chaired the Committee of Inquiry on Small Firms from 1969–71 I had no difficulty in deciding that to make any impact at all we must follow the evidence of the Whitehall mandarins and their political masters on what would be practical politics, rather than suggest a more radical solution. The good news is that virtually the whole of our recommendations were accepted by the Government of the day. The bad news is that time has shown that a more radical solution involving positive discrimination in favour of small firms was necessary to redress the imbalance and succeeding 'great leaps' forward announced by successive Ministers for Small Business have still left the small firm sector in the same unsatisfactory situation that it was in when we reported in 1971. . . . Sadly, we now have four million people unemployed with all the misery and loss of GNP which that entails, whereas a thriving and expanding small firm sector would have greatly ameliorated the situation—as it has so successfully in the United States.

The 1970s

Bolton's commitments started almost immediately after the Report was published, with a talk to the Bristol Polytechnic Small Business Centre on December 16, 1971. On such initial occasions, his main objective was to repeat the message of the Report and its implications for various parties, not least the need for self-help by the small firms themselves. Chairing the Committee also made him very desirable (and effective) at balancing the range of issues concerning small business and being able to pull together the various threads, and therefore being good at summing up, as at the Financial Times conference in January 1972. Similarly, his role as Chairman of Judges in the TDC/Guardian Innovator of the Year Award, 1972 almost certainly derived from his chairmanship of the Committee on Small Firms. But it was not to be long before he moved away from these sorts of neutral roles and became more critical and demanding.

In February 1972 John wrote a short piece for the magazine *Engineering* to make the point about the importance of small firms, starting with: 'Napoleon referred to us contemptuously as a nation of small shopkeepers. If he was right it didn't prove such a bad thing as a basis for overthrowing his particular brand of imperialism' and finishing rather apocalyptically: 'Time is running out fast and what is at stake is one-fifth of Gross National Product, 30 per cent of the employed population and perhaps the very future of our free enterprise economy'.

Even by 1973, in addressing the 'Management Tomorrow' Conference, he was saying 'our analysis remains true today, in spite of many positive measures taken by Government in the past two or three years to remedy this situation of neglect'. He was arguing that it the entrepreneur who is governing success or failure, and it is his needs and problems that ought to be considered, covered by the five 'M's: the Man, the Market, Margins, Management Information, and Money'.

The *Financial Times* on July 4, 1973, had a substantial article picking up on the Bolton issues of small firm financing, and especially the dominance of bank loans, accepting the point that 'official controls over bank lending have had a disastrous effect on the small firm', largely because they are the first to suffer when money becomes either short or expensive, and concluding that 'English risk investors are far more risk averse than their North American counterparts'.

An important feature of the situation was the increasing problems of the small firm sector after the oil crisis of 1973, in which declining business profitability hit the small firm sector particularly hard. In such times of low demand and liquidity problems, large firms usually transmit their pressures down the line with tighter trade credit terms, whilst themselves stretching their payments as long as possible. The rapid rise in inflation was also hurting; in addition to the increase in costs and the difficulty of increasing prices commensurately, loan limits in banks were far behind inflation, while interest rates on loans had gone up sharply. As Bolton pointed out in *Industrial Management* in 1976, 'A typical bank manager after the War used to have a ceiling for small firms of £3000. The same bank manager now operates with an increase to only £5000. Really it should be £15,000 just to level peg, and £20,000 would be more realistic'. At this time, due to such features, there were record numbers of bankruptcies and receiverships, adding to the general sense of decline in the sector. Moreover this was also a period of new legislation having a disproportionate effect on the administrative burden of the small firm sector. It was in considerable part these adverse developments which led Bolton to revise his views about what was needed for the sector.

His talk to the ICFC-NUMAS Press Conference in March 1976 set up something of a template: first the report, then the still-existing problems; then the development in the situation since 1971, and finally what the small firm can do to stay afloat. The heart of the talk was to say that in spite of Government acceptance of most of the Committee's recommendations, 'by 1976 we are back to square one. The patient's condition continues to decline—witness the record number of bankruptcies and receiverships. Not enough is being done and not quickly enough'. The main problem was still the availability of working capital, with the onus with the clearing banks. In many cases lending limits had stayed static or were even reduced in spite of the double squeeze of higher inflation requiring more working capital and the depreciation in the value of the assets available as security for an overdraft. He pointed to a case of a profitable high technology company with world beating products and know-how, with Government blessing and £200,000 of private capital, where in spite of a need for high working capital the overdraft limit was £5000 because the company had low fixed assets. He felt that more authority needed to be given to the local bank manager, and indeed this was to become a refrain over several years.

He then moved on to the tax front, where in spite of some useful, if marginal concessions, largely resulting from the Report, there had been a major adverse change with death duties replaced by a combination of capital gains tax and capital transfer tax, putting a premium on 'playing it safe'. He wanted inheritance taxes to be no worse than in Britain's competitors, where consanguinity rules permitted assets to be passed down within the family, and to reduce capital gains tax by say one per cent per year so that transferring a business at the end of a career would be subject to little capital gains tax. He also pointed to anomalies in the taxation of new unincorporated businesses, in effect penalizing risk-taking. Other areas he criticized were excessive paper work; again in spite of some reduction as a result of the Report, there had been a tide of new requirements, with VAT being a major culprit with the complexity of its definitions. A final area for criticism was the sheer amount of legislation in areas like health and safety and employment for business in general, perhaps desirable in their own right but causing huge problems for small businesses. As to what small businesses needed to do to stay afloat, he had some useful comments encapsulated in the following paragraph.

In March 1976 the Ship and Boat Builders Federation News reproduced 'A Small Businessman's Survival Kit', Bolton's 10 'do's and don'ts', which were:

1. Better debtor control to keep cash flow healthy
2. Stock monitoring with an age analysis to dispose of old lines
3. Cash flow projections and a friendly bank manager
4. Margins must be maintained
5. Concentrate effort on the most profitable lines
6. Look for new markets
7. Know your nearest Small Firm Information Centre
8. Call in expert help before it's too late
9. Have an outside 'confidant' with whom you can discuss problems
10. If in real trouble, see your main customers, who will often help

He wrote the first part (the second part was by Graham Bannock who had become MD of Economists Advisory Group Ltd) of an article for a management symposium in 1977 entitled 'Government and small business: a case of benign neglect' in which he started by noting that there had been 'a sublime state of indifference' about the small firms sector in Britain at the time of the Committee, contrasting the situation with other countries in a highly evocative way:

> The Japanese couldn't believe that we didn't have a specialist department in Whitehall to monitor the health of the small firm sector; the French couldn't understand why a British M. Poujade had not arisen to give small firms some political clout; the Germans were astonished that we didn't have a network of training facilities geared to small enterprise, and the Americans knew we were just crazy not only to fail to place small firms, as they do, on the same emotional plane as 'motherhood and the flag' but also to arrange our tax affairs so as positively to discriminate against innovation and wealth-creating enterprise.

He admitted that the indifference had diminished with recognition by the Government and the political parties, but 'it would be folly to imagine that the wealth-creating small firm sector rates in the same league as issues such as environmental pollution, trade with South Africa, or Abortion law reform'. Actually, small business was becoming by this time 'a cause' along with these issues, in no small part due to the continuing efforts of Bolton himself. Indeed it had become a crusade, with JEB as its leader. But discrimination, he argued, still continued, especially in taxation and finance. Outside Government, there had been more encouraging developments, especially with the growth of venture capital, while the banks, the media, and the academic world had taken more interest in the sector. Nevertheless,

In retrospect, the recommendations of the Committee of Inquiry's Report should have been stronger—leaning more towards positive discrimination in favour of small firms. . . . The fact of the continuing and perhaps accelerating decline of the small firm sector is now plain for all to see. To permit this to continue would constitute a national disaster of the first magnitude.

Actually, unbeknownst to Bolton, the decline had stopped, as is noted in the second half of this chapter, even if the statistical recognition of this had not yet penetrated.

In the second half of the article, Graham Bannock started by asking what had in fact happened. One of the recommendations of the Committee had been that Government should monitor the position of small firms, but nothing had been forthcoming and was indeed 'extraordinarily difficult', both due to unsatisfactory returns and also identifying the existence of small firms. Nevertheless he suggested that 'the weight of evidence is that the decline of small business has continued slowly', and that 'small firms continue to be much less important in Britain than in other advanced countries, mentioning the USA, West Germany, Japan, France, and Belgium and noting that 'these countries are also all far more prosperous than Britain', with, of course, the implication of a causal connection.

By 1977 there was a considerable debate about small business, and certainly there was a massive amount in the newspapers on the subject. In addition there was a lot of evidence on small business submitted to the Wilson Committee to Review the Functioning of Financial Institutions in 1977, which published an interim report 'The Financing of Small Firms' in March 1979 (Cmnd, 7503). It produced an analysis which differed little from the Bolton Report and 15 recommendations which again closely resembled those in Bolton. This was also the period of the Harold Lever Report, which found that small firms were as efficient in the use of resources as large, less efficient in labour, more in use of capital—18 per cent on capital employed as opposed to 14 per cent for large, essentially repeating what the Bolton Committee had said. Both these reports were indications that the role of small business was being taken seriously.

Bolton was not, of course, the only one to take up the small business agenda. Another key figure to become involved at this time was the Governor of the Bank of England, Gordon Richardson. It must be doubted if many previous Governors had devoted a talk to small firms, as Richardson did in contributing to an ICFC Conference in October 1977. Moreover, he was very much singing from the same song sheet as Bolton at this time, if not so argumentatively. He recognized the Bolton Report as the starting point for any analysis of the small-business sector, including its functions in the economy, both in terms of innovation and its contribution to the lowering of unemployment. He also recognized the worsening conditions that had led Bolton himself to reflect that his Committee's recommendations should have been stronger. And he followed Bolton in suggesting two keys areas of potential improvement, one in the field of taxation, and the other in lowering the cost of finance for small firms. He saw venture capital as a difficult area in which to make money, instancing ICFC, but also noted:

> I also sometimes wonder whether the experience of those who have entered the venture capital field might not have been happier had they developed a greater capacity to monitor and judge markets and products, rather than just balance sheets and cash flows.

The *Business Graduate* devoted a special edition to small firms in Summer 1978, which at first sight seems rather surprising, given the small number of business graduates in small business, but may perhaps be better understood by recognizing that John Bolton was on its advisory council and indeed had been its first chairman.

In a *Guardian* article of October 14, 1977, curiously titled 'What a way to run a bassoon factory!' JEB noted that 'the message is forcibly getting home' and 'there is a real sense of national emergency that we must do something positive'. But more was required, and he explored the paradoxes and contradictions of existing policy: In particular he attacked tax policies and especially VAT. Taxation was the key area because the amount of outside finance depended primarily on the level of profits retained in a small business. However too often the vast majority of small businesses were clobbered by taxation provisions designed to catch the relatively few abusers of the system. The availability of outside finance was the next important priority and here he noted that the big institutions such as the pensions and insurance companies were only putting 0.3 per cent of their funds into the small firm sector. Why was this so small? Well, Bolton pointed out, the provisions of the Insurance Companies (Valuation of Assets) Regulations 1976, issued under the Insurance Companies Act 1974, which provided that an unquoted firm must be making regular profits before an investment in its equity capital can be counted as an admissible asset for Department of Trade valuation purposes. In the case of a new company, or one in its early build-up phase, any investment by an insurance company thus had to be valued at nil on the insurance company's books, adding substantially to the more commonly mentioned disincentive of administrative difficulties in dealing with small firms. Meanwhile, private investors who had been the traditional source of risk capital were now powerfully discouraged by capital gains tax (based in part on inflationary paper gains) if their hunch is right and a total loss if their hunch is wrong. And finally, he had a go at Value Added Tax, criticizing especially the lack of a single rate, which added greatly to the administrative burden. But he also suggested going further and raising the exemption limit to £50,000, because below this, as he finished by saying, 'I'd further wager that an investigation would show that this 20% of tax collected from smaller firms costs more in administrative expenses than its gross yield in revenue. What a way to run a bassoon factory!' Almost certainly some of the points in this article had been drawn to his attention because of his almost unique role in the field. Such points as these needed to be brought out into the open, and Bolton was a valuable means of doing this, because after the Committee he was certainly listened to. These issues continued to bubble away. And an emerging theme pursued by Bolton was the ability of the small firm sector to solve the unemployment problem if only they could employ one extra person. Even within large businesses, Bolton advocated decentralization to smaller units, instancing Dawson International, of which he was a non-executive director, where centralization had not worked.

Financing small firms became the biggest single issue in the 1970s and beyond, hence the Wilson and Lever Reports. A lot of the debate was based on the banks not doing enough and the need for entrepreneurial bank managers. One of JEB's most provocative (if tongue in cheek) titles of an article was 'The bank manager: entrepreneur of the 1980s', in *The Bankers' Magazine*. In it he challenged bank managers to make their contribution to the task of regenerating Britain by recognizing the needs of small businesses. He started by noting that 'the sector was overwhelmingly dependent on their friendly local bank manager for 'outside' finance—more than 90 per cent of small firms had never, in fact, approached any other source'. Looking at the national economic situation, with declining mass-production industries and high unemployment, there was an urgent need for the small-business sector to play its part in economic regeneration through job growth and this in turn required adequate financing, which depended on the clearing banks in general and each individual branch manager in particular. He didn't want to knock the clearing banks because in spite of small business horror stories 'there is counterbalancing evidence of banks going to great lengths to back a man in whom they believe'. But more still needed to be done. Perhaps it was time for higher limits, better control figures, a measure of government guarantee or a change in the loan to asset ratio in excess of the 1:1 so often quoted as normal. And finally, even more tongue in cheek, he wrote

> I've made a New Year's resolution—to sing in front of my shaving mirror every Monday morning and to the British Grenadiers' tune—
>
> > 'Some talk of ICFC and some of NEBs,
> > Of Wilson and of Lever, and such great names as these;
> > But of all the world's brave heroes, there's none that can compare
> > With a tow, row, row, row, row, row
> > Of the British branch bank pioneer.'

He wrote an article for *The Times* (October 31, 1977) with a title taken from Shakespeare 'For this relief much thanks . . .'. This was also the article when he seems to have begun his transition to ask for more than the original report. To complete the quotation, spoken by Francisco in Hamlet, 'For this relief much thanks; tis bitter cold, and I am sick at heart' summed up the response of the average small businessman to the measures announced by the Chancellor in his recent mini-budget to boost the morale of the small firm sector. Bolton felt that the measures needed to bring about the necessary transformation must match the enormity of the problem and so

> even allowing for the fact that creating new jobs is relatively cheaper in the labour-intensive small firm sector, my judgement must at present be that Government does not appear to have *begun* to contemplate measures which are far-reaching enough to solve our problems.

He continued in a quite aggressive tone:

> much thanks for the improved CTT relief, but before the mini-budget, the tax burden of a father transferring a business to his sons in Britain was estimated to be some *six times* that prevailing in Germany—perhaps it is now only two or three times higher than the German level. . . . much thanks for the changes raising the level of profit that can be retained in a close company without compulsory dividends from £5000 to £25,000 and for substantially raising the top limit for abatement— but how about the dead weight of deferred tax on stock appreciation still showing on . . . balance sheets . . . Much thanks for the hope of measures in future to help people starting businesses by allowing initial losses to be set against later income, but if this only applies to *un*incorporated businesses it will prove to be an illusory incentive for the men we hope will create the new businesses capable of growing into the next generation of large businesses. The need is for a complete tax holiday for say five years of life of a genuine start-up company provided profits are ploughed back.

And so on for quite a lot of other issues; the Minister might have been forgiven for thinking that nothing would be enough to satisfy the champion of the small firm. But at least he finished 'Tis *still* bitter cold and I am *still* sick of heart. But at last there is a warm glow on the horizon'.

As well as the lectures above where John had something important to say, there were others where he was not saying anything different, but was asked because of his presence in the field. Some of these latter must have been fairly boring for him, such as a day conference in 1978 run by the Charnwood Section of Leicestershire Chamber of Commerce in which John had only a small role to play; moreover the letter of thanks by the Chief Executive was extremely bland. Nevertheless he was showing the flag, and this was important to him. And before moving on to his major speeches we should note that he wrote articles for influential publications such as 'The Banker's Magazine' and 'Professional Administration', as well as for the broadsheet newspapers and introductions for pamphlets or other publications.

Major Speeches—the RSA, Marlow, and Manchester Bankers Lectures

In addition to his many talks to a range of bodies, Bolton made three major speeches, designed to set out the small business case to maximum effect, namely to the Royal Society of Arts, to the Engineers and Shipbuilders Institute in Scotland, and the Manchester and District Bankers' Association. Perhaps not coincidentally these were given to different audiences in different parts of the country.

His address to the RSA in January 1982 was probably his most important speech, which was also published in the RSA Journal. For it he asked for 86 people, many of them with their wives, to be invited. The evening was a particularly nasty one weather-wise, and there was a rail strike, so to have an audience of over 250 was quite a feat. In his talk he argued that capital intensive investment in large companies would not solve the unemployment problem. He therefore wanted to persuade his audience that no solution to the economic and social problems of the country was likely without a very substantial expansion in the number of small businesses and the growth of the existing ones. To do this, however, would require 'relatively massive measures' by Government to shift the balance further in favour of small firms, and that while there had been moves in the right direction, these were likely to be one or two orders of magnitude too small in their effect. After reviewing the Report, its recommendations, subsequent Government action and what he called 'the sublime state of indifference' to small business that had alarmed the Committee, he went into the heart of his message with a number of points:

- The Report had failed to emphasize sufficiently the importance of the small firm in creating a more balanced industrial structure, both regionally and within industries and especially in the new high technology sectors.
- The spectre of rising unemployment and the expectations of further job losses due to the impact of technology on job structures, especially in large companies.
- Small firms have a much higher leverage than larger ones, quoting American research showing that per dollar spent on research and development, small firms provided four times as many innovations as medium-sized firms and 24 times as many as large firms. He also quoted the Birch research on job creation (to be reviewed later in this chapter).
- The British education system had shown itself excellent at spawning new inventions, and he quoted the success of Solartron to this effect.

However the potential levels of investment were at least 10 times lower than the £3–6 billion needed to create the hundreds of thousands of start-ups required.

- The 1979 Interim Report of the Wilson Committee to Review the Functioning of Financial Institutions had confirmed and reinforced the analysis of the Bolton Committee, and had made a number of valuable recommendations.
- While the financial world had changed its attitude, there was no information to show whether the level of bank lending was rising or falling, or how profitable it was. There had been a considerable growth in venture capital institutions and the large institutions such as pension and insurance funds had channelled increasing amounts of their resources via these intermediaries. The Loan Guarantee Scheme seemed to be working well. Nevertheless 'the 14,000 clearing bank branches remain the only practical vehicle for a massive increase in start-ups.'
- The media had shown greater interest in small businesses, with the *Guardian* and the *Financial Times* having introduced regular weekly features on small business.
- Management education and training and research on small firms had all advanced considerably; prior to 1971 there had been virtually nothing.
- Many large companies (Shell, ICI, Pilkington, BP, and IBM) had recognized their self-interest and social responsibility.
- Professional advisors had tailored their services to the needs of small business.
- Trade associations had taken account of the needs of small business, while new and vocal organizations had emerged to represent the sector.
- Public recognition and esteem for small business had grown.
- Government, which he had left to last, had taken an increasing interest in small firms, as had Members of Parliament generally. An interesting figure was the number of entries in *Hansard* dealing with small business, whether questions or debates: in the five years 1964/5 to 1968/9 there was an average of four entries a year; in the six years 1969/70 to 1974/75 it rose to 20 a year, while in the five years 1975/76 to 1979/80 it had advanced to 80 entries a year. And there were more government initiatives to be noted, seeking to improve the climate for small business.

Many of these points were clearly steps forward. Yet his final message was pessimistic, that they would go only a very small way to providing a solution. He had a few additional points which he thought could make an impact: a fulltime Minister at Cabinet rank; the expansion of the Loan Guarantee Scheme; trading profits retained for expansion should be free of tax; capital grants for re-equipment; and something like the Japanese system of a compulsory moratorium before liquidation. Then, 'In conclusion I believe there is a future for UK Ltd and its creative and skilled population in tomorrow's world, so I am certain that there is a particularly promising future for small business'.

There was a very good response to the speech. Robert Beldam, ex-chairman of the Smaller Firms Council of the CBI asked for six copies of the RSA speech to send to his successors and finished: 'It was good that on such an unfavourable evening so many should have the interests of smaller firms at heart to come to seek yet further enlightenment from "Mr Small Firms". He also added 'I think it should have been made clear that gigantic strides have been made on behalf of Smaller Firms as a result of all the work you did so thoroughly and in such detail'. There was also a letter from Neil Falkner of Development Capital Services Ltd (which John chaired):

> This is just to say how much I enjoyed your splendid talk last night. I cannot imagine a more sincere compliment to you that over 250 people should turn up in the midst of the snow and the rail strike. If I may say so I always feel it to be a privilege to be associated in business with someone of your perspective and wisdom.

It was not just in Britain that the RSA speech was noticed. His old friend from Harvard Business School days, Bob Malott, chairman of FMC, recommended John's RSA speech to the head of the American Small Business Administration and asked John by letter to send the latter a copy, adding 'it was one of the best analyses of the problems and opportunities for small business that I've ever read'.

The Marlow Lecture some nine months later was in many respects the Scottish equivalent of the RSA lecture, given in Glasgow to an Institute of Engineers and Shipbuilders in Scotland audience, to whom he was able to pay tribute for the performance of his World War II destroyers, HMS *Wilton* and HMS *Childers*, both Clyde-built and where he had spent some time in their final building stages. Inevitably there was some overlap with the RSA speech; as he had said in opening that earlier speech: 'It is exceedingly difficult to say anything fundamentally new about small businesses and their future', and anyway, he had the same message that he wanted to put over. However he started by casting his net even wider, beginning 200 years previously with British domination of steel, ships, and engineering but then its subsequent decline. Nevertheless he wanted to reassure his audience

> that we are witnessing the beginning of a new industrial revolution, every bit as far-ranging in its potential effect as that of two hundred years ago, based on the new catalysts of new technologies, new products, even new sciences, but for its flowering dependent upon the same basic ingredients, which thank God we still possess in abundance— inherent creative skills, craftsmanship and perceptions of a world market.

And while he went on to make essentially the same points as in the RSA lecture about the progress that had been made, instead of returning to the scale of what needed to be done, he finished by emphasizing the range of recent inventions in Britain, noting some of the 'firsts' celebrated in the Queen's Awards for Technological Innovation, and quoting from *The Director Magazine's* recent 'Survey on Scotland', concluding 'Where Scotland leads, perhaps the rest of Britain will soon follow'. Overall, it was less demanding and more optimistic than the RSA Lecture.

The other major lecture was to the Manchester and District Bankers' Association, which actually preceded the other two, in November 1979. In this he started with the Interim Report of the Wilson Committee, emphasizing the similarities of analysis and recommendations to his own Report. He then said that with hindsight his Report had given insufficient importance to the importance of small firms in creating a more balanced industrial structure, instancing Dundee as a city that had attracted large American companies, notably NCR and Timex, to replace the jute industry, but had then found that technological change in these new companies had greatly reduced the numbers of jobs. He went on:

> If Dundee had been able to build up a more balanced structure of small, medium and large companies, with some expanding as others were declining, and providing a stable matrix across several industries, its acute problems of unemployment would have been averted.

He then extended this argument to a spectre of rising unemployment across the whole country before positing a solution based around small firms; to create three million jobs in the 1980s, up to 250,000 new start-ups would be needed. With this as a target, he looked at some of the issues raised by Wilson. On sources of start-up capital, he argued for changing the risk-reward ratio by special tax concessions, such as the US ability to allow losses on small firm investments against individuals' income tax, or a start-up tax holiday of three years. On the role of the clearing banks, he praised the Wilson recommendation for a Government-backed loan guarantee scheme for additional lending. But the most interesting possibility raised by Wilson, he felt, was the idea of 'Small Firm Investment Companies' with tax exempt status avoiding capital gains tax within the companies together with relief of personal tax for the purchase of their shares, offering prospects of long term growth in income and capital. Taken together, however, he felt that Wilson had not offered remedies sufficient for the needs of the situation and that an opportunity had been missed. He saluted the pioneering stance of the Cooperative Insurance Company in financing highly risky small ventures through Small Business Capital Fund, which he chaired. But, he added, 'in ten years we've only been able to start some 25 new firms—and they have suffered the normal mortality rate'. Even ICFC, overwhelmingly the largest provider of venture and development capital, had only invested in around 3300 firms during their 33 years, or about 100 a year. He welcomed the Post Office Superannuation Fund's pilot scheme to help two new firms start up every month. But he noted that Bolton Committee research had found that the large financial institutions were investing only some 0.3 per cent of their total funds into a sector representing 20 per cent of GNP and 30 per cent of the employed population. So now addressing his audience more directly:

> Gentlemen, this is *your* challenge . . . if only *every* branch manager could be given a requirement—edict if you like—to start up two new firms a year in the 1980s, salvation seems possible . . . And because the combined force of local bank managers is the only means capable of assessing projects and watching them effectively, in sufficient numbers to make a difference, you are our only hope of salvation.

And in closing, he offered a Bolton Entrepreneurial Banking Award—'it will go each year to the Branch Manager who has been responsible for financing the most start-up situations—always provided your head offices and regional offices accept the global target'. As far as is known, though, they did not take him up on this.

Venture Capital Activities

Bolton did not only give speeches and write articles about small firms. As Professor Ray Thomas said of John at his honorary degree ceremony at Bath, 'he practised what he preached', and nowhere more so than in his activities in providing the capital which he had argued so forcibly for, becoming personally involved in funding. By February 1972 he was Chairman of Small Business Capital Fund Ltd., which was backed by the Cooperative Insurance Society. After three years in operation (written on 25.2.73) the group was backing 16 private ventures. SBCF's policy was to take an equity stake usually between 30–40 per cent in return for the funding, while the organization also stressed the importance of offering management support. He saw it as a 'mini-ICFC' for small firms, which also set up the Sunday Times Small Business Award with a minimum of £75,000 in equity and loan capital for the winner.

In addition Bolton became Chairman of Development Capital, a company founded in 1973 which pioneered investment by large institutions and pension funds in the small business sector, with an office at 88 Baker Street and six other directors. It also owned eight secondary companies, all of which JEB became a director of as they were created between 1974 and 1982. John became President of the company and its subsidiaries from 1984 to the end of 1988. Finally, he had a small family company, Growth Capital Ltd, whose directors consisted of John, Gay, Nick, and Athalie.

The 1980s and Beyond

Bolton's feeling that not enough was being done continued well into the 1980s, as manifested in the letter to Sir James Swaffield at the start of this chapter, and as the seminal RSA lecture exemplified. He continued to respond actively to invitations for small business functions and organizations, he was used by the Department of Industry as a discussant on finance for new technology-based firms—Keith Joseph was the relevant Minister by this time, and he was a great supporter of research into small business and became a Trustee of the Small Business Research Trust, attending its launch in December 1982. Sir Charles Villiers was the initial chairman of the Trustees, but John remained a Trustee until his death. In January 1987 he was invited to join the RSA Award Scheme for the Management of New Ideas, which his old contact from the BIM John Marsh was behind. In June 1980 he received a long and interesting letter from Ted Choppen, head of the Petroleum Industry Training Board, ex-Chairman of Esso and FME Council member, talking about how to use the Training Boards to train for small business and inviting the help of FME.

He wrote an important article in the London Regional Management Centre News for June 1981 on 'The need for more management education and training for small business and entrepreneurship'. In it John noted that an American study by the National Science Foundation showed that $1000 invested in R&D in a small firm produced four times as much 'innovation' as in medium size firms and 24 times as much as in a large firm.

He was often asked to chair meetings, especially in the small business / innovation area. Thus when being asked to chair an 'Aspects of the Future' lecture at the Polytechnic of Central London, the organizer noted in her letter of invitation: 'Your being there will give the event a great sense of occasion, and we are deeply honoured'. He would also be asked to attend discussions on small business such as the Financial Institutions Group of the Department of the Environment in 1982 or more grandiose affairs such as the International Small Business Congress Gala Banquet in 1986.

In an interview in the *Financial Times* on October 14, 1986, when Bolton was almost 66 and semi-retired, the journalist, William Dawkins, noted that the Bolton Report 'was instrumental in galvanising successive governments into supporting the sector and is largely responsible for the public importance . . . accorded to small business development today', while

> events like the birth of the Unlisted Securities market six years ago, the explosion in the availability of venture capital and the existence of a voice for small business in the Cabinet in the form of Lord Young, the Employment Secretary, are all fundamental steps in establishing a wider dispersal of economic power and a more entrepreneurial industrial culture.

Nevertheless John suggested he was far from happy with the situation and indeed that there was a new set of problems not envisaged when the Report was written. By this time, the conventional wisdom was that small business had a pivotal role in job creation, but Bolton noted that because large businesses were reducing their labour forces faster than ever, small businesses could be the only source of reduction in unemployment. His key point was that by concentrating on fine tuning the small business measures already in place, the Government ignored the fact that its efforts fell several orders of magnitude short of the mark. He instanced the Business Expansion Scheme (BES), arguing that the Treasury had fundamentally misunderstood the real value of the BES in its stringent attempts to stop investors exploiting the scheme as a tax haven and indeed the BES was quite quickly ruined by the trend to dependence on property. He pointed out that the Netherlands, with only a quarter of Britain's population, had four times as many small businesses, while the comparison with other countries was also poor. In order to create 3 million new jobs in Britain over five years, 150,000 new companies would be needed every year. (This was about what was being achieved in the mid-80s; however very few of the new company registrations were in manufacturing (3 per cent) and a lot were for non-trading purposes.)

After his wife Gay died in 1989 John largely withdrew from active involvement in small business, as with his other activities; he was in any case almost 70. However he still maintained an interest in some organizations such as the Small Business Research Trust. Obviously small business issues did not stop, but by that time the major momentum of the 1970s and 1980s had diminished and small business had achieved a stable position in the economy and political attitudes toward it were generally positive. It is only now, following the financial crisis of 2008, that interest in small business as a solution to the problems of the economy is becoming active again. Notwithstanding this, it is time to move to Part Two of the chapter, which takes us away from Bolton's own role in the debate to what was actually happening in the sector in the 1970s and 1980s.

PART TWO: CHANGES IN THE SMALL FIRM SECTOR IN THE AFTERMATH OF THE REPORT

The Bolton Report and its follow-up led by Bolton himself generated a great deal of momentum in the 1970s, and this continued into the 1980s, providing an opportunity to take stock of what happened to the sector after the Report by examining a number of different dimensions. While it would be unwise to argue purely on a 'post hoc ergo propter hoc' basis, the connection between the Report and the transformation of the sector cannot be denied. Thus in spite of John keeping up his demands for the support of the sector there was also much to be positive about by the mid-1980s, when John wound down his personal campaign. Much of what follows is taken from the next authoritative research-based analysis of small business, a sub-stantial programme funded by the Economic and Social Research Council, with David Storey (1994) publishing a very comprehensive review of its outcomes and other research, exactly a quarter of a century after the Bolton Committee began its work. On the very first page of Storey's book, there is the following comment, written without irony: 'Even the casual newspaper reader knows about the key role which small firms play in employment creation, their overall importance in the economy, their role in innovation, the importance which government attaches to "enterprise", etc.' That this could be written shows what a complete transformation there had been since the Bolton Committee had begun to fill the vacuum in information and awareness.

Sectoral Growth

Bannock and Peacock (completed as a report in 1987, published in 1989) wrote a study entitled 'Britain in the 1980s, Enterprise Reborn?' in which they argued the case for profound changes, statistically, organizationally, and attitudinally, toward enterprise in Britain. Most importantly was the recognition of a turnaround in the decline of the small firm sector which had been such a feature of the Bolton Report. Indeed there is something of a paradox in the Committee's discussions as to whether positive discrimination could be justified, concluding not unless the role of a seed-bed for new enterprises was threatened, and the fact that unknown to it the decline in small business was already beginning to be reversed. Bannock and Peacock (1989: 87) tell the story of an overall trend strongly upwards from 30,262 new registrations in 1970 to 114, 831 in 1986, although with a glitch in the mid-1970s at the time of the oil crisis. Liquidations also rose but at a much slower rate, so that there was a net gain of some 85,000 new enterprises by the mid-1980s. This was a huge change from earlier periods.

While the Bolton Committee (1971) had calculated that there were some 1.25 million small firms in Britain, Storey (1994; 21) reported some 2.7 million for 1991; even allowing for the difficulties of definition and counting, that represents a huge increase. Not surprisingly, Britain had caught up to the average number of enterprises per thousand inhabitants in the European Community (Storey 1994: 22) and also had the highest birth rate as a pro-portion of the active labour force (except for Denmark where the statistics are anomalous) (Storey 1994: 54). Unsurprisingly again, a large percentage of this growth was accounted for by self-employment. In employment terms, out of a total employed labour force of 14.633 million in 1987, 4.741 mil-lion were in firms with less than 20 workers and a further 2.468 million in firms of 20–99 workers, with 1.966 million in firms between 100–499 employees (Storey 1994: 166). Although the categories are not the same, this compares with some 6 million in small firms as defined by the Bolton Report. Associated with this resurgence of new business formation were other economic changes, including a decline in the share of the largest firms in output and employment, an increasing rate of organizational change, and a proportional move to the service sector, which tends to have more small firms. What came to be a key political issue, the contribution of small firms to job creation, will be examined later in this section.

Government Policy

A second area of progress was in government policy from both Conservative and Labour governments, where there was a very substantial shift, a rebalancing in fact, away from the almost totally large business focus of all governments up to the Report. It may not have satisfied an increasingly demanding John Bolton, but its momentum was not in doubt. In 1981 the Government produced a list of 63 ways in which it had helped small businesses, excluding macroeconomic issues such as the attack on inflation and the consequent high cost of borrowings, while in 1982 a Small Firms Division listing had raised this to 96 ways. But the most explicit statement by Government came when the Small Firms Division of the Department of Industry wrote a response in November 1981 for the 'Bolton Ten Years On' Conference. Its intention was 'to remind the conference of more recent Government measures [i.e. after the initial response to the Bolton Report] to aid the small business sector, most of which derive directly or indirectly from Bolton recommendations'. It noted that the drive by central government to support and inform small firms and to examine their legislative and administrative burdens had been intensified in recent years and especially in the last two years (i.e. since the Conservative Government took over). Its main points were:

- The introduction of the Business Start-Up Scheme to increase the reward/risk ratio in investing in new firms.
- The introduction of the Venture Capital Scheme to allow losses from investment to be set against income rather than capital gains.
- A pilot for facilitation of business formation by unemployed or redundant people by the Manpower Services Commission.
- The Loan Guarantee Scheme to help banks finance projects, with the guarantee covering 80 per cent of the loan, with the lender covering the remaining 20 per cent. The lender assesses the viability of the project and applies to the Department of Industry for the guarantee.
- A Business Opportunities programme to make people aware of the new measures.
- The rules governing employment legislation had been changed to relate to the administrative resources of small companies.
- Planning procedures had been speeded up and controls relaxed for small-scale activities.
- Changes in rating laws enabled the payment of rates by instalment and eased the eligibility of premises for domestic rate relief.

- Encouragement of the construction of small industrial buildings, together with generous benefits in Enterprise Zones.
- Relief from statistical forms and the reduction of financial information requirements.
- The Small Firms Service lead in identifying advisory resources to draw on, together with the strengthening of the teams of counsellors.

Following on from this list there were other developments, most notably: tax advantaged Venture Capital Trusts; the simplification of the administration of VAT for small firms; and a major effort to reduce compliance burdens. A system of Regulatory Compliance Cost Assessments was introduced, policed by the Cabinet Office and under which all new legislation imposing costs on business must have such an assessment before it was passed. The Business Link centres which took over from the Small Firms Advisory Service grew to give advice and support, not merely act as signposting services. The Government also took soundings, some of which John was involved with, such as the Department of Industry meetings on finance for new technology based firms chaired by Sir Keith Joseph. Joining the European Union also made a difference, given the generally higher level of interest in small business affairs in other countries before Britain joined; there was a special department, DG23, to take account of the interests of small business. To be fair to those in the higher reaches of Government, it must also be noted that both Harold Wilson and Harold Lever took a personal interest in small business to the extent of chairing their own committees of inquiry into small business finance, Wilson of course after he had stepped down from being Prime Minister.

Having said this, a remaining problem was still a lack of coordinated thinking, whereby policy changes for reasons not related to small business often had unintended consequences for the sector, especially where departments operated independently and on the taxation front.

Financing Small Firms

Bolton's continual hectoring of the banks was one of his main themes, but in fact the high street banks did a good deal to change their ways in the 1970s; at least at the senior level; making change effective at the branch level might have been more elusive. Bank loans to small firms also increased substantially. Storey (1994; 219) notes that lending in 1992 was twice what is had been in the mid-1980s, and moreover that since the Bolton Report there had been a growth in the relative importance to term loans as opposed to overdrafts; term loans, which were generally much more favourable to small business, had been almost unknown at the time of the Report. Moreover, as least for manufacturing and business services companies, there was a marked increase in those seeking external finance, and a decline in those not being able to access any finance. In addition, the banks set up separate small-business divisions, were willing to second people to small business institutions, and helped to fund research.

A further dimension of change was the substantial rise of venture capital at this time, with the numbers of venture capital organizations providing financing facilities growing considerably after the Bolton Report. Bannock and Peacock (1989; 80–83) charted the growth of the venture capital market in Britain from two companies just after World War II, including ICFC, to 20 by 1979. Thereafter growth was almost exponential, rising to 126 only seven years later in 1986, of which 55 were independents and 71 were subsidiaries of other financial institutions; an industry association, the British Venture Capital Association, was founded in 1983. The amount invested by these organizations also grew by leaps and bounds, from £195 million in 1981 to £671 million in 1986 to a peak of £1.6 billion invested in over 1500 companies in 1989, 86 per cent of them in the UK. *Investors Chronicle* produced a guide to 85 of these bodies in 1983, together with a listing of their characteristics such as amount of capital earmarked, type of client, equity stake, etc. Some of these were set up by the clearing banks, some by the insurance and pension sector, some from merchant banks, some were independents, and some were public bodies, such as the Highlands and Islands Development Board or the Greater London Enterprise Board. And reflecting the interest in venture capital, in 1987 the Stock Exchange launched 'The Third Market' for the 'minnows in the corporate pond' following on the success of the Unlisted Securities Market set up in 1981. We have already noted Bolton's own not insignificant contribution to venture capital.

Similarly, the amount invested by venture capital grew very rapidly, although it should be noted that most of this was in management buy-outs or buy-ins rather than start-ups or other early stage investment; nevertheless, investment in these latter did also grow to be over £100 million per annum by the late 1980s. In addition to the formal industry, there was also a growth of informal venture capital, sometimes known as by 'business angels' or more colloquially 'Aunt Agatha', and this may well have been even more than from the formal industry, especially in the 1970s, when it was estimated that some £400 million annually was raised in this way. This capital was also particularly helpful in the difficult early stage of development.

Financial help also came from the Government, mainly in the shape of three different schemes. The Loan Guarantee Scheme, initiated in 1981 after lobbying by Bolton. Basically, it provided a guarantee to banks on defined loans to small businesses which would not have received finance on commercial terms, primarily due to lack of appropriate security, with the firms paying an interest premium on the loans. It was immediately successful, with 177 advances in the first year of operation, but was used less when the guarantee was reduced and the premium raised. The Business Expansion Scheme was introduced in 1983 to provide tax relief to individuals investing in qualifying companies. However after a useful start it degenerated by becoming dominated by property and by being used as a tax avoidance vehicle. A third way was through the Enterprise Allowance Scheme in which £40 a week was paid over a year to individuals wishing to start their own businesses, amounting to 106,000 in the peak year of 1987–8. This may seem a small amount, but to many entrepreneurs it made a substantial difference.

Representation and Recognition

On a different side of the organizational front there were new bodies to represent and support small businesses, such as the National Federation of Self-Employed and Small Businesses, the Forum of Private Business, the Association of Independent Businesses, the Small Business Bureau, and the Union of Independent Companies, as well as the CBI's Smaller Firms Council, together with increased interest in the Institute of Directors and local Chambers of Commerce. Indeed there may well have been too many such developments, since they were competitive and did not always sing from the same hymn book. Large companies also realized fairly quickly and then increasingly into the 1980s that Small- and Medium-sized Enterprises (SMEs) were important markets for them as well as important for the economy with companies such as Shell, ICI, BP, and IBM leading the way. Some large companies set up SME departments and/or divisions to promote SMEs directly, especially in places where they had closed down facilities and created unemployment; British Steel and Pilkington were examples. The Chairman of Shell Oil led the way with an important speech titled 'Small Firms a Big Problem' and funded quite a lot of research into SMEs. There was a growing realization that large firms shared some concerns with SMEs including regulation and they lobbied government accordingly. This new interest by large firms may also have extended to paying their bills on time, a perennial complaint of small firms.

Science parks became very popular in the universities (including very notably John's alma mater Trinity College, Cambridge), while many local authorities set up enterprise zones with subsidized premises for small firms. There was a growth, with considerable impact, of local Enterprise Agencies, and the emergence more formally through government policy of Training and Enterprise Agencies with a particular remit for training. There were also specialist programmes for entrepreneurs, especially the New Enterprise Programme and its counterparts. Representation at Cabinet level, something that John had long argued for, was also achieved under Lord Young, Secretary of Employment in the mid-1980s. It is possible that the small business lobby actually became too strong. Storey (1994: 229) raises the possibility that some unwise policies were introduced solely due to small business lobbying, instancing the introduction of the Enterprise Investment Scheme, a virtual re-creation of the BES, in 1993.

Improved Information

Another category of developments from the Bolton Report was in improved information, both of the statistical variety and in research and writing about the small business sector. There were massive improvements in small firm statistics, an area of which the Bolton Report had been highly critical. The introduction of VAT in 1973 provided a new source of data with the government funding a study into ways of using VAT statistical records in conjunction with other data to create comprehensive figures on numbers of SMEs. These methods are still in use today and are the basis of the official statistics on SMEs. The result was that enterprises in the SME sector were found to be considerably more numerous than previously thought. Outside the official statistics the invaluable quarterly small business surveys, initiated by Graham Bannock in 1984, and carried out by the Small Business Research Trust with funding by the banks continue to this day at the Open University.

The aftermath of the Report saw a huge increase in writing and research about small business, with the Bolton Report being very influential in setting the research agenda as well as providing a legacy of legitimacy to a previously under-researched area. Perhaps most significant were three rather different publications at five year intervals called by similar names, namely 'Bolton 10, 15 and 20 Years On'. The similarity of name indicates the importance of Bolton as a catalyst for writing about the sector. The first was the papers of the Small Business Research Conference in 1981 (Stanworth et al. 1982), in which, however, there was no editorial control, little coherence in terms of the themes covered, and the relationship to the Bolton Report was limited, to say the least, in many of the papers. Nevertheless, as already quoted, there was a significant response to the conference by the Department of Industry, and John Bolton was not only the principal guest speaker, but took an enthusiastic part in running the conference, extending to a letter of thanks to the other guest speakers. He saw it in part as a 10th birthday party for his Report as befitted the Conference title 'Bolton: Ten Years On' and a chance to fly the flag. The second publication was a review of research written by James Curran of Kingston Polytechnic for the Small Business Research Trust (1986). Bolton wrote the Preface, commending the amount of research which had been done and Curran for presenting it in a comprehensive and easily readable form. It pointed out the weaknesses of research, at the top end the lack of a national data base to permit the macro-analysis of the contribution of small firms to the economy, while at the other end of the scale it noted the lack of ability of much research to get close to the day to day activities of small firms. Nevertheless, it was a very valuable contribution. The third publication (1991), edited by John Stanworth and Colin Gray, was a substantial book generously financed by the National Westminster Bank and coherently planned by the Small Business Research Trust. Again, John Bolton wrote the Preface. The chapters provide a comprehensive state of play in small business 20 years on from the report, showing the resurgence of small enterprises, much of which we have already noted.

There was in addition an expansion in how-to-do-it books and magazines for small companies, while the BIM had a substantial working party on the fiscal environment for new and small firms. Small business clubs and enterprise agencies sprang up. The *European* (later *International*) *Small Business Research Journal* was started in September 1982 by Clive Woodcock of the *Guardian*, who had been running a column on small business for some time, with an emblem of an acorn. And of course there was much more coverage in the media, perhaps especially the small business page in the *Guardian*, but including useful listings such as that in the *Investor's Chronicle* of February 11, 1983 providing a guide to capital facilities, something which was also provided by other agencies such as the big accountants. There was also a lot of debate in the letter columns. Even the BBC produced a list of small business clubs.

Attitudes

From the above there was also a substantial change in attitudes toward small business, as identified by Bannock and Peacock (1989: 84). They argued that there was a transformation of public attitudes in the 1970s toward a more entrepreneurial society and industry and away from the traditional careers based on the professions and the civil service. Management was becoming an increasingly attractive subject to study, and much of the growth of the business schools was driven by demand from managers themselves rather than by universities themselves initiating courses in advance of demand. The move toward self-employment, the increased desire to become rich, the spread of share ownership, and above all a recognition of the need for wealth creation for a successful economy were all dimensions of changing values which encouraged small business.

Indeed there were signs of change everywhere, even if with some geographical disparities. But because enterprise is a social phenomenon as much as an economic one, social attitudes are key, and while most indicators are anecdotal, Bannock and Peacock pointed to the growth of an enterprise culture through such indicators as the content and genre of publications, better research and teaching about them, new small business organizations, increased sponsorship of business promotion, new interest by local authorities, as well as an increased interest in self-employment and more positive attitudes toward wealth creation. Also important was the more progressive attitudinal response from the small business community; thus demand for the Small Firms Service doubled from 108,000 in 1980/1 to 212,000 in 1981/2. On a rather different level, a cult book of the period, attracting much attention, was E. F. Schumacher's *Small Is Beautiful: A Study of Economics as if People Mattered* (1973) which challenged the prevailing economic doctrine of size, scale, and increased specialization, proposing instead a system of what he called 'Intermediate Technology' based on smaller working units and technology with a human face. While not necessary compatible with traditional small-business attitudes—it became something of a manifesto for the nascent 'green' movement—it nevertheless provided a philosophical backing for small scale.

The Report in International Debate and Comparisons

What was happening in Britain also needs to be put into an international context, both in international comparisons and influences from abroad. The Bolton Report had a significant impact abroad as well as in Britain, as the President of the Executive Committee of the International Congress on Small Firms, in inviting John to the 1982 Congress in Madrid, noted: 'We are familiar with the "Bolton Report" and are aware of the influence it has had on Small Business throughout the world'. Indeed the Congress had begun in 1973 and its origins may have had some connection with the Bolton Report. The 1986 Congress was held in London and John was a member of the Advisory Committee, while the chairman of the Organizing Committee was Sir Charles Villiers. John attended the gala banquet chaired by Lord Caldecotte and was addressed by US Secretary of Commerce Malcolm Baldridge by satellite link-up.

We have seen in the previous chapter the Report's account of the low proportion of small businesses in Britain as compared to other countries. What comparisons there were made were not to Britain's advantage. Graham Bannock (1991), comparing Britain with Germany, had a chance to look back at the Committee on which he had served as Research Director, and reflect on its strengths and weaknesses after the passage of a decade. He gave a number of reasons why the small business sector had declined further in the UK than elsewhere. An underlying one was taxation, where the relatively high level of direct taxation and especially the high marginal rates on profits made the environment more difficult for small business in Britain, while tax relief was available for some activities but not investment in small firms. He estimated that there might be 40 per cent more businesses in Germany after allowing for the difference in population. The Japanese professor Kikutaro Takizawa (1974) compared the United Kingdom, the United States and Japan in a pamphlet, a copy of whose results he sent to JEB, which concluded: 'In Great Britain, in comparison to the United States or Japan, there has been scant recognition of small business problems as being problems of the national economy', especially since, as he went to point out, small business in Britain was a relatively small part of the national economy.

A major impact on the way in which small firms were viewed across the world came from the United States through David Birch's 1979 study *The Job Generation Process*. As a result of his path-breaking research, small business became widely regarded as the principal generator of net new employment in the United States. When first introduced the idea was revolutionary. Few economists or policy analysts gave smaller firms a passing thought. Large entities were presumed to be the primary, if not the sole, source of economic vitality and the only units worth examining. Yet, the newfound utility of small business took hold quickly not only because it fitted America's self-image, but because the empirical data based upon Birch's work supported it:

- Small businesses create a vastly disproportionate share of the net new jobs in the United States.
- The smallest size class (1–19 employees) produces the most net new jobs relative to its share of total employment.
- The share of net jobs is related to the business cycle. Larger firms expand their share of net new employment toward the end of expansions, while small businesses provide a relatively stable supply throughout.
- Jobs created from small business births are about two to three times as plentiful as the number created from small business expansions.
- Small business jobs tend to be created by two types of firms. Birch refers to them as the 'mice' and the 'gazelles'. The mice are the new, small entries. The gazelles are a comparatively few rapidly growing firms that are responsible for the bulk of small business jobs created through expansions.
- The distribution of employment by firm size is changing rapidly across industries, with small businesses becoming increasingly important in manufacturing but declining in retail.
- The business population is characterized by extraordinary churning. Businesses open, close, expand and contract continuously. The success of the United States and the failure of Europe to create jobs appeared to be related to the high incidence of business births in the US.
- The nature of job generation, at least as it involves large and small, seems to have changed about 25 years ago. The focus shifted from large to small, although no empirical literature exists directly on this point.
- All areas of the United States lose jobs at approximately similar rates. Regions of economic prosperity, however, differed from non-growth or low-growth regions in their ability to create new jobs, which are in turn functions of achieving higher rates of technology innovation.

While this work is American, it is probably not far removed from how Bolton and his colleagues saw the role of small business in Britain. Moreover later British research using the same methodology as Birch reported broadly similar results, although not quite as striking as the American ones: during the 1987–89 period, 54 per cent of the increase in employment was in firms with less than 20 workers, whereas this size group provided only 32 per cent of the base year employment total in 1987 (Storey 1994: 165). This vindicated Bolton's claims about the sector providing a key part of the answer to the unemployment problem.

CONCLUSIONS

Bolton added a great deal in personal terms to the momentum created for small firms for a dozen or more years in the aftermath of the Committee. Not only following up on the Report itself, he helped to identify and publicize many other issues to do with small firms, and as the principal spokesman on behalf of small firms, he was listened to. The question must be asked, as we did over management education, whether the same outcome would have been achieved without Bolton's personal input, and again the answer must be no. People are important in history. He was also given credit for making things happen. Thus writing in 1981, Bill Adam from Brussels congratulated John on getting the bank guarantee scheme introduced—'You were right all along'. However a comment by John's good friend and later to be eulogist at his funeral, Lord 'Jack' Weatherill, writing to him after making his maiden speech in the House of Lords in 1992 after stepping down as Speaker in the lower house was more downbeat: 'You were responsible for creating a better environment but alas the weeds have covered much of the ground you cleared in 1971', raising the question of how short term the impact was.

The main question is whether the growth of small firms after the Committee was directly connected with the Committee or whether it was a 'natural' trend which would have happened anyway as large firms began to decline quite rapidly in their total employment. One point to note is that what was happening in Britain was also happening in many other countries, denying a unique cause. Nevertheless, the changes in Britain were more marked in relation to what had gone before, giving room for some potential for an impact such as that of the Report. Either way, a lot was being expected of small firms and a lot was delivered. The timing of the Report was significant because it provided a context for other forces to build on. Although Bannock and Peacock (1989) do not include the Bolton Report or the missionary role which Bolton played in the dozen or so years after it as factors in social attitude change, it is not unreasonable to allocate them some influence in the changes. What the report did was to bring the attention of the establishment to the significance of small firms, while Bolton's involvement thereafter helped to keep them there. There would have been some revival in the sector without Bolton and the Report, and indeed in retrospect it is apparent that this was happening by the time of the Report, but there can surely be little doubt that the scale of the revival owed something to the policy, attitudinal and infrastructural improvements that were sparked off by the Bolton Report.

However some things never change, even up to the present in 2014. Unemployment, compliance issues, and 'red tape' amongst others, have been ongoing issues which successive governments recognize but never solve and are at their worst when the economy itself is in trouble, as was

Table 8.1 New company registrations and liquidations, 1970–1986

Year	New registrations	Liquidations
1970	30,262	8,782
1971	39,445	8,412
1972	54,456	8,215
1973	67,349	7,240
1974	42,496	7,885
1975	45,678	9,795
1976	56,085	10,640
1977	52,214	9,974
1978	63,566	9,205
1979	66,472	9,019
1980	69,374	11,481
1981	72,416	12,920
1983	96,188	17,978
1984	97,908	18,250
1985	104,581	18,250
1986	114,831	–

Source: Bannock and Peacock (1989: 87) from Department of Trade and Industry

the case following the financial crisis of 2008. As to the perennial issue of finance, access to lending may have gone in cycles, but there has been little if any overall progress, as the centralization of decision-making has led to domination by computer-based formulae rather than the branch bankers who were optimistically seen by Bolton as the hope of the future. At the time of writing, the British banks are being separately investigated by the Treasury Select Committee and the Office of Fair Trade for their attitudes to small firms. Perhaps it is time for a new Bolton, both the man himself and the Report.

9 Mentor, Facilitator, and Non-Executive

INTRODUCTION

The background and range of contacts which John Bolton had developed by the mid- to late-1960s, together with his personality, made him eminently suitable both for formal roles as a non-executive director and for less formal contexts as a mentor/intermediary/facilitator. This clumsy description can itself be broken into three main groupings: helping organizations, usually with fundraising or appointments; advising individuals, usually with career issues; and events and invitations, covering speeches, meetings, activities, and bodies which requested his participation. His personal experience, network knowledge, his empathy, and not least his willingness to provide his time for people made him extremely popular to discuss their issues with, whatever they might be. He did so much for so many people and organizations, well above the normal call of duty and politeness, that this aspect of his life deserves appropriate attention. Indeed these services, kindnesses really, are an important measure of the man.

This chapter is about these dimensions of his career. The two parts of the chapter inevitably overlap. Thus many of his activities as a non-executive went considerably beyond his official duties and had a social dimension of being mentor and adviser to managers in the companies, while his role as a non-executive gave him the opportunity and knowledge to carry out services originating outside the companies.

BOLTON'S PERSONAL INVOLVEMENTS—ORGANIZATIONS

It is fortunate that Bolton left a folder of his personal correspondence from the early–middle 1980s, and from this we can both see what he did for people and infer that this was also very likely to be true across the rest of his career. Perhaps there was more in this elder statesman period of his career, but we have already noted that even in his Solartron days people from the shop-floor were very willing to ask his advice about their personal problems. The amazing thing is the range of correspondence he got involved in with a wide cross-section of people seeking his help in one way or another, some of them asking for referrals to jobs as high as chairman of a nationalized industry, others wanting holiday jobs while at university. But he was always courteous and tried his best to answer positively and at reasonable length, which must have taken a substantial amount of time within his already very busy schedule. And what is available is probably only the tip of the iceberg, because it would not take account of advice when phoned, or at casual meetings, or covered highly confidential matters which were unlikely to be left in open correspondence, and it is anyway very likely that the file does not contain even all the written correspondence.

We will start with some substantial vignettes which illustrate his helpfulness and generosity of spirit. A classic example concerned an out-of-the-blue letter from the Dean of Guildford Cathedral, Tony Bridge, in 1981 asking for help with their finances, to which he replied with the following charming and constructive response:

> I am sorry to have been so long in replying to your letter but I have been away in America.
>
> I would be delighted to help you and the cathedral in any way possible but unfortunately that excludes time. I am under a condition of serious 'overload' and am busy reducing my existing commitments and this would preclude me from joining your small group of people to approach companies, but I would be happy, of course, to give any general advice I can.

As the new President of the Engineering Industries Association, which is also in the red, I am at present snowed under with the job of writing letters to companies, large and small, around the country asking for support, and with the disastrous conditions prevailing in the industry, one feels a bit like a mini-Gulliver towing four thousand or so 'small engineering ships' towards the safe shore of 1983. I have no doubt that you have felt the same in towing a host of sinking souls with you from time to time and I hope I won't therefore be included in your sinking souls category.

What I can do, which is of more direct help, is to suggest that you contact Mr Stuart Sill Johnston (at Firn Cottage, The Street, Wonersh, Surrey—telephone Bramley (048 647) 2541) who is a friend of the Cathedral and who, I feel certain, you will have met at various University functions since he has for the past ten years been a most dedicated and successful secretary of the Foundation Fund, and in that capacity he reported directly to me as Treasurer. Stuart had a heart attack some six months ago and is retiring early (like in the next few weeks) and I would have thought that to help you in your mission would be the best therapy he could have. Though he cannot cope with the pace and politics of the University scene any longer, it would be equally harmful to him to do nothing, and I strongly advise you to jump in while he is still available. I have taken the liberty of having a word with him and he would not be averse to being approached. He certainly has expert knowledge of all the firms, national and local, who have been interested in the University, and hence in Surrey, and I believe would be a marvellous help to your fund-raising campaign. He would also know of people with time to spare who might therefore be of more practical help to you than chaps like me. In particular, I would like to suggest Sir John Pile, former Chairman of the Imperial Group, Munstead, Munstead Heath, Godalming—telephone Godalming 4716. Stuart knows him and would also be able to help you with that approach.

I am off to America again on Wednesday, returning on Sunday 20 December, and thence to Venice for a week's away from it all Christmas (we seem to escape about once every ten years) so that really takes us into the New Year. Might I suggest that when you have contacted Stuart, if he thinks I can be of any further help he might activate his skilful liaison link with my secretary so that we can fix a mutually convenient date for a drink at the cathedral.

With kindest regards and best wishes for Christmas and the New Year.

This letter tells us quite a lot about John. First his overload, which was significant. But in spite of the overload he went to considerable pains to write a very comprehensive and helpful letter, explaining his situation in detail but then going on to suggest not just people but a whole process, with addresses, telephone numbers and all. Note also that John had prepared the way by approaching Stuart Sill Johnston in advance, and also that he wrote the letter in a way which would make the Dean feel that he was doing Johnston a favour. Unsurprisingly the Dean was delighted ('I can't tell you how grateful I am for all the information you gave me and the suggestions you make, let alone saying you will help us in an advisory capacity'). Of course writing letters like this only made more people write to him for advice and help as he became known as someone who would respond in this way.

John was very supportive of Slimbridge, the West Country Wildfowl Trust run by Sir Peter Scott, the son of Scott of the Antarctic. He introduced prospective benefactors such as Sam Johnson, the Chairman of Johnson Wax, and his wife and Sir Colin Corness of Redland to Peter Scott at a lunch at Brook Place in 1985, following which he and Gay took the Johnsons to Slimbridge, where they had a very good day with Sir Peter. After it Scott wrote back: 'We are so very grateful for the way in which you are helping the Wildfowl Trust' and asked John 'what sort of letter we should write to Sam? The question is how to engage his long-term interest in our organization'. John himself paid for the concrete for the banks of the Slimbridge lake, while Redland also gave assistance. Later he suggested Richard Hill, a Bristol businessman as a Trustee and Scott responded: 'We cannot thank you enough for the advice and help you are giving us in finding benefactors'.

On a similar basis he was considerable help to The Society for Wildlife Art for the Nation (SWAN) in finding members of their council. John wrote:

> Naturally I would be delighted to help in any way I can with advice, though I ought to warn you that I am actively engaged in three appeals at present and my friends now cross the street when they see me coming.

He was indeed a natural to approach on appeals. He held a large gathering at Brook Place for the Woking Nuffield Hospital Appeal as well as several for Surrey University. But inevitably he couldn't support them all. He turned down a financial request for the centenary appeal from Port Regis School but the headmaster wrote: 'I fully understand the circumstances and would like you to know how grateful we are for all your support in the past, not only financial, but the wisdom you have shared with us which has enabled us to prosper'.

Then there was a letter from one of the Directors of Central and City Investments:

> Cistern Cay
>
> Thank you very much for being of such magnificent assistance at short notice over the matter of our application to the Foreign Investment Board of the Bahamas. Your letter was a real gem and if I believe even half a word of it, to say that I would be flattered would be a considerable understatement.

This was John Mactaggart, a friend of Nicholas, who was later to write a moving tribute on John's death.

He was good at suggesting others when not able/willing to do something himself. Thus when approached by Richmond College—The American International College of London—he recommended Larry Tindale from 3i and the Small Firms Committee for the Board of Trustees and Bowman Scott from Solartron for the Board of Governors. The Intermediate Technology Development Group wrote saying thanks for meeting them and leaving a list of possible Council members, i.e. various of his friends. They were also looking for £6000 to complete the funding of a handbook of small scale employment opportunities and asked if he could suggest any sources. From the managing director of Flomark in 1983: 'Thank you for your letter and for all the trouble you have taken on Flomark's behalf. I will certainly follow your advice'. A further letter asked for help with introductions for Flomark to the ship repairing industry in Britain. John was able to offer two names. A letter thanking him for his troubles came from N. L. Falkner's wife Maria, who was associated with Flomark. Occasionally the request was highly specific, as in helping Black and Decker find an appropriate orthopaedic surgeon.

He sent material to Control Data Business Advisers, an HR consultancy in Minneapolis which held the software licence of his son Nicholas' UK company; it sounds as though they saw John as an entry point to Britain. And, of course, the headhunters inevitably got into the act for suggestions. Eric Bull of Noble Lowndes was invited out to Brook Place in 1982.

A measure of his willingness to please several different organizations at the same time and to try to fit everything in came with a Marlar Venture Capital drinks invite, to which John replied:

> I'll try to end my FME Education meeting at Management House at 6.30pm. I hope to be with you from 6.45 until I have to leave for the Redland dinner at 7.15. Sorry that I shall be dressed in a dinner jacket.

But inevitably he was not always successful. He tried to solicit a donation for Midhurst Hospital, but was told via Freshfields the leading firm of solicitors, that the prospective donor was not well enough to consider this. He also tried to fix up a meeting with Sir Freddie Laker for Professor Richard Dooley of Harvard Business School, who wanted to write a case study on Laker Airways. John wrote what was for him an unusually ingratiating letter to Sir Freddie, saying that he would have right of veto over anything said, that a substitute company name could be used, that Solartron had gained a great deal by being an HBS case study, and that the world needed to know more about British business at its best. His intercession made no difference; he was put off twice, the second time definitively, by Laker's secretary. Dooley wrote plaintively: 'tell me that there really *is* a Sir Freddie Laker, Uncle John, that he wasn't just dreamed up by the fertile imagination of some PR-type'. On a similar tack, in 1982 Roger Collis, a case writer for

Harvard Business School, wrote to John to explore possible Johnson Wax and Dawson case studies. These don't seem to have proceeded either.

BOLTON'S PERSONAL INVOLVEMENTS—INDIVIDUALS

The vast majority of the Bolton correspondence was with individuals about their own affairs, looking for support, help, or advice, often in the context of wanting to leave their existing employer. Individually, these instances might not be remarkable but collectively they make an impact, especially when it is appreciated that they are contained within a few years and that as already noted they represent something of the tip of the iceberg of his personal interactions. He found it very difficult to say no.

Sometimes these were ongoing. He had a long relationship with Robert Appleby, who lived alone after his wife died in 1975, in which he kept Appleby informed about what was happening at Black and Decker. They seem to have met at the BIM in the mid-1960s; when John became chairman of Council in 1964, Appleby was a vice-chairman. In the 1980s Appleby was retired after having been Chairman and Managing Director of Black and Decker Ltd for almost 20 years and was frustrated both at his own personal immobility and also at Black and Decker policies in Britain and Europe, where he felt strongly that his own contributions as one of the principal architects of the Company's great growth between the mid-1950s and the late 1970s were being undermined. Moreover because he did not receive information, not even the annual report because he was not a shareholder, he depended on John to keep him informed of what was happening. He was a man of strong opinions on topics from astronomy to the laws of physics to the place of unions and indeed must have appeared distinctly cantankerous to many people. Since he was given to sending John voluminous documentation to support his arguments, it is not unlikely that John may have occasionally shared such views—one gets the feeling that Appleby would have tried the patience of a saint! Nevertheless John was always very forbearing toward him, even if not going to see him as frequently as Appleby would have wished. Appleby did however appear to realize that he might sometimes be imposing on John and wrote to him in March 1984: 'Thank you indeed for your interest and help in these matters. You are very kind. Sometimes I think you are too kind'.

Even the very top could ask for help. Larry Farley, Chairman and CEO of Black and Decker, wrote to John to seek external directorships on his retirement and asking for John's discreet referral to CEOs who might have need of a director. John replied

> I . . . can assure you that this type of involvement will prove to be most rewarding and personally satisfying. I often say it is like being a grandparent in that you give your advice freely (whether asked for or

not), have a feeling that nobody takes any notice then your heart takes a double beat sometime later when you find that some of your advice really has stuck.

The Farleys had eight daughters and Larry was only 50 on his retirement, so perhaps he felt he needed the money.

Ronald Fidler, President and Chief Operating Officer, also of Black and Decker, wanted to return to Britain and asked for John's help, thanking him for 'your interest and support of my development at B&D'. John suggested a possible chairmanship of a nationalized industry (but not British Steel) and wrote to Sir Peter Parker, then Chairman of British Rail, asking him to meet Fidler, which Parker duly did. This shows the extent to which John was willing to go to help others. In the event Fidler went into Oakland Management Holdings and launched a Business Expansion Scheme Fund, for which he asked for Development Capital syndication.

Judge John Ellison, a good friend from his High Sheriff years, wrote to John asking him to put his name forward as a Deputy Lieutenant for Surrey. John duly did this, writing to Lord Hamilton, but at the same time wrote back to Ellison saying that although he had put two very suitable names forward some time earlier, and was thanked by the Lord Lieutenant for doing so, nothing more was ever heard. So John advised him to contact other people as well, including the Vice-Lieutenant: 'If you know him I would be very happy to have a word with him as a preliminary and then bring in Michael Calvert and Judge Sir Carl Aarvold'. In other words he went to the trouble of not only suggesting a wider approach by Ellison but also offered to widen his own support by bringing in other people. He could well have just left it at a direct letter to Lord Hamilton, although perhaps he knew that a multi-pronged approach was necessary. No wonder people approached him for such favours.

Geoff Hudson, the Johnson Wax UK Managing Director wrote to John in December 1983:

> Just a note to thank you for the support you gave the British management team at the Board meeting yesterday . . . I was listening very carefully to what you were saying. If there is a bold stroke by any means that we can push this business ahead, that might be a good subject for an unscheduled board, as we have had in the past.

Clearly all was not well, and he was hoping that John would come up with something. But apparently things didn't work out, and by March 1984 Hudson was looking for a new job, on which John gave advice. Hudson wrote thanking him for his 'extremely nice' letter and offer of support. A year or so later, Brian Chandler of Johnson Wax Europe was made redundant and although he didn't know John wrote to him on the recommendation of Hudson. Chandler wrote a very grateful note on the discussion and information provided by John.

Sometimes his contacts would turn to him decades later. He helped Peter Hamilton, who had been with Solartron as product sales manager from 1957–59 and indeed had come to that role directly from a Harvard MBA before joining Firth Cleveland as Assistant to the Chairman between 1959–61, rising to become Chairman and Chief Executive from 1977–1979. Clearly he was something of a protégé of John's. Eventually he became Group Chief Executive of APV, the process equipment company, but resigned after a disagreement with the non-executive chairman and sought John's views. John suggested he apply for the Director-Generalship of the BIM when Roy Close retired in the mid-1980s. Sadly Hamilton died shortly before work began on this book, because he would have had some interesting insights on the Firth Cleveland and Schlumberger takeovers of Solartron.

On a somewhat different basis was this letter from David Murchison, a lawyer in Washington and Al Decker's shooting partner:

> I can't thank you enough for taking care of Stacy on her arrival in London. Trevor [John's chauffeur] was at the gate waiting, handled all her bags, took her in great style to Queen Mary's College and then got her perfectly settled in her room. He was superb in every way. What an incredible treat for a young lady in a strange country!

Another somewhat different one was that John had a request from an old friend the Speaker of the House of Commons, Bernard ('Jack') Weatherill, to have a look at his brother-in-law's company, which had taken on a new chief executive. The company had a cash flow problem and could John talk to the CEO about it? John put the CEO in touch with Plasmec and Neil Falkner of Development Capital and went out his way to help. As well as meeting the CEO, he wrote to Falkner laying out his own views on the situation to make sure that Falkner was prepared. All of this took place within a month.

But more frequently the requests were one-off. Those below are a sample which happened to have correspondence attached to them, and by no means all of such requests would. Indeed most would almost certainly have been oral, with John being asked at a meeting of some sort to have a word in someone's ear about something, or offering advice over a glass of sherry. A frequent comment in letters was something like: 'I thoroughly enjoyed meeting with you last week. It was good of you to give me so much of your time. I hope I did not outstay my welcome'. Some of the requests were not exactly humble, but came close to pressuring John. Probably they didn't appreciate how busy he was. People kept in touch with him, just in case they needed him in the future. He clearly took a lot of trouble for a lot of people. He was very courteous and generous with his time, always trying to suggest a positive outcome even when he could personally not do whatever was asked. Quite a lot of the letter-writers were rewarded by being asked to Brook Place for a meal or at least a chat. Denis Burton, an old friend from Wolverhampton and Solartron, helped to set up High Technology Consultants Ltd and had a meal at Brook Place telling John about the new company. However to avoid telling too many similar stories, the following is a list of others who wrote to him:

- He was approached by Bob Thomson, a retired director of NCR to give advice on how to be a non-executive.
- He was asked by a colleague on the Black and Decker Board to find a gap year place for an 18-year-old Etonian who wanted some experience in electronics before going to university. The colleague passed the request to John 'as the only person that I know with influence in the electronics field' and John duly obliged by contacting Oxford Instruments.
- An unusual request from an old acquaintance, Peter Falstrup, was to obtain two chromium GB signs, as John was also a Rolls Royce owner. John's response (and was there a touch of weariness and even asperity?) was to have the existing ones replated, for which he could 'check with any local engineering works, or use the Yellow Pages!'
- Michael Young at the Institute of Community Studies asked him to talk about the ways in which senior executives deal with time pressures, with Sir Bruce Williams having suggested him. It is not clear whether John actually did this, but his views would have been interesting given his capacity to pack such a range of activities into his life.
- Malcolm Black, general manager of SC Johnson's International Business Development Executive, wanted to stay in London after many years of travelling and living abroad, something with which Johnsons were being co-operative. But he asked to visit John to discuss ideas with him.
- Arthur Brooking of British Rail Investments Ltd wrote to thank John for a very enjoyable lunch and attaching his CV, at the age of 65! He wanted to become a non-executive director of John's Small Company Fund or in some other role.
- Wilfrid Fry, an ex-Solartron employee, set up his own company, Transducer laboratories, and invited John to visit, which John agreed to do. Fry was also looking for advice on how to fund the project.
- Patricia Good, ex-FME, wrote to John asking for his support in writing about her past activities at FME, and John was happy to agree her reference to FME.
- Peter Gorb of LBS asked John to be his referee for applications to senior academic positions.
- William Bree of BIM left to take up a position as Chairman of Charles Martin and wrote soliciting business in the executive search area. John replied, 'We shall miss you badly at BIM but I can well understand you wishing to move on to other things after all those years of "toil and tribulation" with the old firm'.
- At another level there were the completely cold approaches such as that by S. R. Cain, who had been advised by the BGA administrator, Meriel

Harris, to get in touch. Cain was a Stanford Business School MBA graduate (top 25 per cent of class) who wanted to move into a senior position in a small business, but wasn't aware of the venture capital market and therefore asked for help.

- Occasionally there was a brush-off, as when Ralph Haxby wrote about his idea for ASTUTE, on M&A seminars, and John replied: 'Alas I seem to be short of inspiration on suggestions for an appropriate audience for future test sessions'. But he still replied, as quite a lot would not have done.
- Frank Pyne of Problem Resolution—Consultants for International Venture, Project and Financial Problems, wanted a meeting to discuss the needs of small firms, having met John at the Surrey University Industrial Liaison Managing Directors Group.
- A letter from John Pulford let John know of a change in appointment to a car company, including Ferrari. John replied: 'When I can afford a Ferrari, I will certainly be in touch . . .'.
- Andrew Napier asked John to sponsor him as a member of the IOD, John being a Council member.
- Hugh Murphy wrote in 1987: 'Because you were so instrumental in my joining Johnson Wax some fifteen years ago'. John seems to have known his parents.
- Tony McCann wrote to explain why he decided to leave Black and Decker; he didn't want to go to the US and was concerned about how Europe should be run: 'lastly, I wish to thank you most sincerely for the great help and support you gave me and hope that you didn't feel too let down by the eventual decision'.
- Richard Munn wrote: 'As I wrote to consult you about banking jobs, I thought I would let you know . . . Thank you again for your advice'.
- Don Morley wrote in 1983: 'I would therefore like to express my sincere appreciation for the time and consideration you have given to my job search in recent months!' And in an earlier letter: 'I regretted not being able to speak with members of the Board prior to my departure [from Johnson wax] but can at least take this opportunity to thank you for your support during my eighteen months as Financial Director'.
- Robert Kellie wrote: 'I am really very grateful to you indeed for giving up so much of your time for a most useful discussion about the sort of job I should look for as well as the way to approach companies'.
- Lady Lisburne, whom he had met at an AA dinner, had asked for an HBS small business brochure, but he hadn't managed to get one, so he also suggested LBS and MBS as alternatives.

In addition there was correspondence for a miscellany of purposes. Thus following a casual meeting on the Edinburgh-London shuttle, John Diebold head of the Diebold Group, sent a follow-up letter 'I would like to reiterate my invitation to you to stay with us in the States when you are next in the country. Please do let me know when you are planning a trip. It would be a very great pleasure indeed to have the opportunity of having a longer visit'. This was quite a powerful invitation for a casual meeting and indicates the standing that John had.

He responded very positively to James Beattie of Wolverhampton who had written a booklet on management, agreeing that 'small business proprietors must work consciously to turn their employees into an efficient and happy team and I shall be delighted, spurred on by your example, to stress this aspect in future talks which I may give about the small firm sector'. Given the Wolverhampton link, it is not impossible that they knew each other.

Some of the letters seem pushy, but there may have been a personal dimension which justified them, such as sending CVs to see if they might be of interest. And he had several approaches of the kind: 'knowing of your interest in the smaller firm prompts me to set out a proposition which may be of interest to you'. One of them concluded:

> We appreciate that the propositions outlined above may not be directly in line with your normal investments but the early losses may be attractive to offset substantial profits elsewhere. Alternatively you may see this proposition as an arm's length income tax reduction arrangement.

Another one which may well have been replicated invited him to cast his eye over a pilot scheme to be supported by the DTI Encouragement to Entrepreneurs Scheme.

BOLTON'S PERSONAL INVOLVEMENTS—EVENTS AND INVITATIONS

He was also approached to chair meetings, give references, and to be involved with a range of issues, organizations, and activities. Here follows a sample from an early 1980s correspondence file:

- When John was being asked to chair an Aspects of the Future Lecture at PCL, the organizer noted in her letter of invitation: 'Your being there will give the event a great sense of occasion, and we are deeply honoured'.
- He was asked to advise on a questionnaire for SITPRO (Simplification of International Trade Procedures Board).
- Asked to become a member of the International Advisory Board of BDF Associates, which dealt with management buyouts finance for new technology-based firms.
- Keith Joseph when at the Department of Industry had two meetings to discuss the financing of new technology at which John was present, and he was invited to comment on the notes of the meetings.

- He was invited by the US Ambassador to a reception followed by the Chicago Symphony in September 1981, followed by dinner at the Savoy Hotel until 1 am, hosted by John H. Perkins, President of the Continental Illinois Corporation.
- After this he sent a copy of the Marlow lecture to the US Ambassador.
- He was also invited to opening of Institute of Business Ethics, led by Neville Cooper of the Christian Association of Business Executives and Top Management. There is a substantial correspondence with Neville Cooper through his Top Management Partnership.
- John was invited to 'give a hand' with an RSA award scheme for the management of new ideas. John Marsh was behind it.
- He was asked to join the Advisory Board Service set by Top Management Partnership and Neville Cooper. Two or three from the Panel would meet with a Board to review strategies and problem areas— February 1986. Cooper also set up a Government-Industry Partnership meeting with Lord Young, and later with other key Government and City figures.
- Other requests could involve writing or speaking. Keith Middlemass of the University of Sussex asked him to write a chapter about small business in government-industry relations. John suggested Graham Bannock.
- Lord Young of Dartington, from his base at the Institute of Community Studies, wanted to talk to him about the use of management time and the time management strategies used by executives.
- John gave PRONED (Promotion of Non-Executive Directors) a very full reference for John Reeves of F. J. Reeves of Totnes, who obtained a role with Crossleys the Builders Merchants. PRONED was sponsored by a very wide range of leading institutions from the Bank of England, BIM, and CBI to the Stock Exchange.
- Mixing in academic circles, he sent a letter to Peter Moore as Jim Ball's successor at London Business School, noting: 'I had a word in Sir Terence Beckett's ear at the time of Philip Nind's farewell party and advised him strongly against choosing a businessman, quoting my 30 years of experience of Harvard in support'.
- Leo Kramer hosted a lunch for the good and the great at the Berkeley in 1983. How did American companies get such high level attendance? With the help of people like John. British companies didn't do this sort of thing.

It was not all one way, of course; there were some things on which John took the lead. Thus he asked the Singleton to 'look after' Ron Fidler and his wife on their visit to New England. He wrote to the widow of Jack Laybourne, England and Pegasus amateur footballer and a Trinity man, the son of a Durham miner. Writing condolences was something which he clearly felt impelled to do and they were much appreciated. Sometimes it helped to be able to wear two hats, as when he wrote to Morgan Guarantee asking for a meeting for his Development Capital colleagues, using the contact who had sent him a paperweight on his role as Chairman of Black and Decker Investment Company in connection with a £35 million syndicated loan. He would also write notes to friends about events which affected them. Thus a letter from Sir Peter Parker, Chairman of British Rail, noted how 'reinforcing' it was to have had had John's note at the time of the train drivers' strike.

BOLTON AS A NON-EXECUTIVE

In his many non-executive directorships, John was not bringing a specific skill to his board memberships, such as an expertise in tax or technology, even if he was very good at reading balance sheets and finding issues to question, and even though he himself said 'All my directorships tend to have a technical bias and be of importance to the country'. Rather he was bringing his wisdom and accumulated experience as a general manager capable of thinking from a chairman's or managing director's perspective, together with an ability to be an emollient smoother of board interactions and to act as a mentor to younger members. He had a great knowledge of networks and how various boards operated, so that practices could be transferred without breaching confidences. Indeed he became something close to a professional non-executive; certainly his income must have been very substantial from the various companies which he was associated with, in fact representing a majority of his income by the 1980s. Often non-executives are picked because they have been seen to perform well in a particular role or are known in a particular network, and in John's case it would seem that his performance as Chairman of Council of the British Institute of Management might have been such a role, combined with his perceived availability at the time, while his Harvard network must have been invaluable for American companies looking for someone suitable in Britain. Others probably arose through headhunters; John wrote to Jim Parker Jervis of Spencer Stuart and associates thanking him for arranging 'my appointment to the board of your favourite company' which in this case was Redland. He picked up quite a range of non-executive roles, amounting to some 15–20 at any one time during the 1970s and 1980s, half of them being well-known public companies, until he retired from almost all around 1990 as he turned 70. His time commitments would have been substantial in total, amounting to at least a third of his total time. What is notable about almost all these companies is the length of time Bolton served them. Indeed he was seen as one of the main non-executives in the country (Spencer 1983: 64). On a related aspect he was also asked by PRONED to comment on the suitability of potential non-executives.

It is by definition difficult to analyse the influence of any particular member at a board meeting unless this is recorded somewhere, and this is a very rare event. Bolton's obituary in *The Times* says of his directorship roles:

> In this capacity he was well known not only for his straight talking and refusal to pander to what he thought boards wanted to hear but also for his little black book. This contained a wealth of jokes and stories, from which he used to draw a moral from his own experience.

This latter must have been a welcome relief to otherwise grave and serious board meetings. Thus while we can say that John was a long-term member of several important boards and was clearly a popular member, it is difficult to define precisely what he contributed or what particular line he may have taken. A partial exception in terms of information can be made for Redland, where a board member wrote a book about the company, albeit someone who joined the board after John's retirement from it (Young and Scott 2004). We will therefore use the Redland situation as a case study, and in addition introduce some other organizations with which he was associated, noting any interesting feature that is available from his records.

But before this we need to appreciate the context within which non-executives like John were working (McNulty and Pettigrew 1996). In the 1970s and 1980s there was a debate about the role of the non-executive, and their numbers were growing, both in total and as a proportion on company boards. British non-executives had tended to be friends of the chairman or other local worthies of celebrities, indeed often MPs, whose knowledge of management or the industry involved was often weak or negligible. Arguments in their favour start from the assumption that full-time managers cannot provide all the qualities required on a board, especially not the detachment and wider experience that outsiders can bring to bear. They can also provide special skills of a functional kind not represented on the board, give an independent view where there are conflicts of interest, and provide useful contacts in the outside world. Other potential contributions include advising the chairman on top management positions or structure, or on aspects of remuneration, where insiders might be biased. Personal qualities are important in the non-executive, being able to make an impact without antagonizing insiders and being willing to stand by his views to the point of resignation if he thinks a course of action is inappropriate. Whether he (or she and there are some she's) has specific skills or not, he should also have an understanding of business generally and an appreciation of the state of finance and the economy. And of course he should have common sense and the ability to devote a reasonable amount of time to the company, usually about two days a month. Young and Scott (2005: 52) noted that a survey of independent directors carried out in conjunction with 3i had shown that non-executives in companies with a turnover of more than £1 billion spent on average 26 days a year on their duties—16 formal meeting days,

7 preparing and travelling, and 3 on plant visits or other non-formal occasions. Multiplying up JEB's commitments on this rough basis, it can be seen that he spent a lot of time on his non-executive roles.

However as the Institute of Directors pointed out, non-executives 'who are independent, possess character and judgement and who have the skills of "knowing how" as distinguished from "knowing what" are quite rare'. JEB met all these criteria and more, so no wonder he became a very popular non-executive. Indeed, in effect he became a professional non-executive, one of a fairly small band in Britain. He wanted the British system to move in the direction of the American one, where independent directors had a more detailed role and helped in policy formulation as well as sitting on board committees.

However the American system was moving toward another dimension, which was taken up by the Institute of Directors in its own little pamphlet about its services as an intermediary in providing a non-executive search process: 'Increasingly, such [non-executive] directors are drawn from the ranks of chief or senior executives in successful, non-competing companies whose boards find such arrangements to be of mutual benefit'. Indeed the American system was moving even a stage further than that, using non-executives to be on audit committees of the board which regulators expected to oversee internal control practices; this was a step which expected a great deal of non-executives, arguably more than was feasible.

The issue was not confined to large companies. There is also a case for having independent directors on a small company's board. As W. F. Nesbitt wrote in *The Director*, running a small business can be a lonely and isolated position, and an independent director can give a sole or majority shareholder/ boss someone to confide in, who knows the company and can act as a sounding board. John had Nesbitt down to Chobham and had a long chat with him whilst also giving him advice as to his own career.

We now briefly examine some of the companies with which John was associated, initially taking up the idea of Redland as a case study.

Redland plc

Redland plc was a leading British building materials business. It was listed on the London Stock Exchange and was for some time a constituent of the FTSE 100 Index. The Company was established in 1919 as a manufacturer of concrete tiles trading as the *Redhill Tile Company*. In 1946 the Company changed its name to *Redland Tiles*. In 1954 it expanded into Germany taking a minority interest in *Braas*, a building materials business based in Heusenstamm. The Company was first listed on the London Stock Exchange in 1955. There is a very substantial history of Redland in a book by Don Young (a Redland director but after John had retired) and Pat Scott (2005), and this is used as the basis for much of the information provided here.

By the 1980s it had become a very substantial company with sales over £1 billion but was also a complex organization due to its mode of growth through takeovers and partnerships around the world. Over three decades this expanded its areas of operation into aggregates, roofing, bricks, road marking and maintenance, reinforced plastic pipes, building claddings, fuel, distribution, and shipping. In other words it had become something of a conglomerate, taking short cuts to growth rather than growing organically, and having some difficult relationships with its partner companies, notably Braas. Moreover its takeovers were not entirely assimilated, leaving fragmented sets of activities around the world and a centre emotionally remote from its subsidiaries, dominated by short-term financial considerations, and with less concern for production, marketing, or human relations skills. Its modes of operation were very good for the City of London service providers who helped with the financial aspects of the high level of merger and acquisition activity, but less good in terms of realizing longer-term value from this activity. Indeed it is arguable that considerable value was lost from this strategy, a result which is by no means uncommon in British industrial history. At the same time Redland was a very ethical company with very high standards of personal probity.

The problems in Redland that led to its ultimate demise were rather like a slow-growing cancer that took maybe 30 years to reach life-threatening proportions.

The company had chosen the route of 'partnerships' and acquisitions as its method of supporting growth. One effect of this was that Redland's core management did not have the opportunity to develop from the ground up the necessary management skills and perspectives across the substantial empire and were therefore unable and even unwilling to integrate acquisitions.

Acquisitions need strong investor support and Redland had to keep the financial markets on side—this was done through a dominant corporate office that valued financial skills above all else—and, arguably, it was here that the high status of the non-executives was most useful to the company, rather than in developing strategy as such. For the corporate office 'strategy' was how to raise money for the next acquisition and developing narratives to support this. The pressures from the financial markets meant inevitably that the mind sets of the senior managers became rather short term. This was a serious weakness in relation to Braas, which became by far the biggest profit earner. The Braas family had a completely different mindset and used the myopia of the Redland management to enhance their independence through a compendious shareholder agreement that accrued power to the minority by small increments over maybe 20 years. The idea of 'partnership' and leaving operations to the partners gulled the Redland management into believing that all was well with Braas. However, the Braas family quietly believed that Redland was a disaster, beholden to the City, that would take their Braas profit and spend it on another acquisition. However, Braas had its own problems to do with market fixing and over-investment in more and more elaborate plant—which was fine in good times, but a liability when downturns and increasing competition from outside Germany threatened.

In 1990 Redland diversified into the manufacture of plasterboard forming a joint venture with Lafarge for that purpose. By 1991 Braas was contributing almost half the profits of the Group. The Company acquired Steetley plc, a major competitor, in 1992, which it found difficult to assimilate, putting its share price under pressure and pressuring it to reduce its dividend. It sold its UK brick manufacturing business to Ibstock in 1996, but under pressure from the City, the Company was acquired by Lafarge in 1997, much against the wishes of several key directors. Until close to the end, Redland plc had no industrial strategy. Instead it managed to please the financial markets and grow by acquisition, without developing any synergies from common skills, culture from its fragmented operations. By the time this problem was recognized it was too late.

Last, on the surface the company had a commitment to recruiting bright graduates into corporate planning and then projecting them into operational leadership. This practice was lauded by many as a way of inducing 'bright' people into a rather boring set of industries. This practice caused resentment at the operating level and a way of managing that was characterized by formality at board meetings of subsidiaries, compounded by a culture of presentations. These were very like presentations to investors, and indeed the behaviour was very akin to managers accounting four times a year to shareholders. (Some corporate staff actually described Redland as 'the shareholder'.) Eventually, however, it became evident that creative accounting could no longer hide the fact that the company's cash flows could not meet the cost of capital and that the company was in trouble.

The point of this long background is to raise questions about what non-executive directors can possibly do about a slow burning underlying cancer that has many roots.

There is no doubt about the quality and independence of the distinguished array of non-executives, including John Bolton from 1975–1990, who served on the main board of Redland. Others who served on the board included Robin Leigh-Pemberton, later to become the Governor of the Bank of England, and Lord Ezra, the ex-Chairman of the National Coal Board. Should non-executive directors like John Bolton and his colleagues have been able to exercise a benign influence on the company and its strategies? When John was a non-executive, Redland appeared to be very successful. Non-executives are not supposed to go digging in the entrails of companies looking for problems.

But the key issue is really how non-executives can strongly challenge management without fomenting a crisis when on the surface the company is doing well. In British companies this is likely to create a situation where the non-executive is seen off.

There are far more blatant examples of non-executives sitting on their hands unable or unwilling to challenge a strong executive. Marconi and Rentokil come to mind.

So, maybe there is a systemic problem here to do with the domineering influence of the financial markets and the malign effects of the media, compounded by the current vogue for governance rather than stewardship; one that cannot be addressed by part-time, distant, and often short-serving non-executives.

When John retired after 15 years on the Redland Board, he was given a retirement dinner at Cliveden on May 31, 1990. Two of his colleagues followed up the speeches at the dinner with letters of their own. One was from Trevor Osborne of Speyhawk, a new external director:

> It has been evident from my year's service on the Redland Board that Colin and indeed all the Directors hold you in the greatest esteem. As the year has gone by I have understood more and more why that should be so. I have greatly enjoyed serving with you and I know from other Board members that for over 15 years you have played a very important and influential role in the development of the Company's policies and in the guidance of its executive. The purpose of my letter is merely to thank you for the enjoyment of your company, the example which you have provided and at the end of it all a very amusing speech delivered to a group who have and showed the greatest affection for you.

The second was from Peter, an internal director, who said:

> May I add my own best wishes for your retirement from the Board of Redland PLC to those you have already received.
>
> As a young analyst in the then Financial Planning Department I recall well the impact your arrival on the Board made. More recently, since joining the board, I have learned much from observing the contributions you have made and the manner in which you have made them. You have so often shown how a few carefully chosen words can sway an argument more effectively than a long and less well structured speech. I hope, one day, I will learn how to apply this lesson!
>
> I have also learned from you how a sense of fun can contribute to resolving many of the more difficult and contentious matters we have to address.

This sense of fun was manifested in endless anecdotes in his speeches. In the Redland one he thanked the chairman:

> Colin could not have been more constructive and helpful to a non-exec, though he can be a trifle more direct with his executives. There's the story of a cable from an overseas company to Robert—regret quarter's results very disappointing, please prepare Colin. Robert replied 'Colin prepared, please prepare yourself'. And he finished with 'which reminds me of my final final story, which must have a message somewhere for you husbands. There was a sweet young thing on a safari who had been ravished by a handsome young gorilla. On being asked how she felt, she

replied: How do you think I feel? He hasn't written, he hasn't sent me any flowers, he hasn't even bloody well telephoned!'

David Soskin recalls how Sir Colin Corness, chief executive of Redland, used to 'probe and probe again' when he worked for him. 'He was a highly intelligent man, who asked very difficult questions', recalls Soskin. 'He didn't take anything on trust. He really grilled you in the nicest possible way. You had to be very well prepared for conversations with him and that was very valuable'. Soskin again 'Colin had tremendous strategic ability combined with ruthless analytical talents and was always able to cut to the chase of any business issue. He also had a healthy scepticism of consultants, investment bankers and other advisers'. Corness was to become Chairman of GlaxoSmithKline and Taylor Woodrow after his Redland period, so must be considered one of the leading company chairmen of his era.

Black and Decker

Black and Decker was probably John's most substantial director role. He was on the British Board from 1965—this was how he knew Robert Appleby so well—and then the American board from 1972 until 1991 on reaching 70. He and Gay also became great friends with Al and Virginia Decker. Black & Decker Corporation was founded in 1910 by S. Duncan Black and Alonzo G. Decker as a small machine shop in Baltimore, Maryland, and rose to become the world's largest producer of power tools and accessories.

John was not just a director of the main American board, but four other subsidiary Black and Decker boards, Black and Decker Group Inc, Black and Decker Holdings Inc, Black and Decker Investment Co., and Black and Decker (Leasing) Ltd. To be invited to join the US Board was a real feather in his cap, and he used to go across the Atlantic on Concorde for six board meetings a year in Maryland.

The following interchange on Black and Decker's behalf says much about John's sense of duty and commitment. He had a letter from David Bowers of Manchester on 29 September 1985:

Dear Sir,

I am writing to you in your capacity as a director of the Black and Decker Group. Recently I took a Black and Decker hedge trimmer to your service centre in Manchester to be told that the model was obsolete and that your engineers would not attempt any repairs. Through my own efforts I discovered that the model required a new switch. This cost £2.00 and was fitted in a few minutes. I consider this to be too extreme an example of enforcing a sense of inbuilt obsolescence. In order to compete with German and Japanese imports British manufacturers must develop customer loyalty through better after sales service. However, my experience of your service centre has left me angry and more likely to buy from your competitors.

To which John replied:

Dear Mr Bowers,

I am sorry to hear of your dissatisfaction with the Black and Decker Service centre at Manchester and have taken the liberty of passing your letter on to the Chairman and Managing Director of Black and Decker UK, Mr Roger Thomas, Black and Decker, Westpoint, The Grove, Slough, Berks SL1 1QQ.

I am not a Director of the UK Company although, as a non-executive director of the parent Company, Black and Decker Corporation in the USA, I am obviously keenly interested that we always have satisfied customers and I am sure that Mr Thomas will send you a satisfactory explanation. However my unofficial response is that you don't mention the age of your Black and Decker hedge trimmer and, if it like mine, it will be 15 or 20 years old and therein lies one of our problems. We need to update our products to keep up with the latest technology—and with competition—but as you will realise, it becomes an extremely difficult task maintaining spare parts for all models around the world for an indefinite period, even though the Black and Decker Company has been built up on value for money, good service, good customer loyalty and holds to these principles firmly today.

Congratulations on your successful initiative in finding a suitable switch and having your hedge trimmer repaired in a few minutes. It gives me the thought that, if it has not already taken place, there could be a small business opportunity to carry a stock of obsolete product spares, much as they do in the case of obsolete models of special motor cars, and I will check through on that idea to see what the position is around the world.

Thank you for writing because it is only by hearing of any customer's dissatisfaction that the company can keep on its toes.

Yours sincerely

How many non-executive directors would have replied in this way? Even though John deftly changed the subject away from the source of the complaint, it is difficult to believe that Mr. Bowers did not receive the letter with a sense of having been properly responded to. And, of course, note the identification of a small business opportunity.

One initiative he did take as a non-executive director member of the pensions committee was to suggest by letter that the position of wives of those non-executive directors who had opted for 10 years' pension at half the fixed annual retainer fee should provide for a surviving spouse option.

Dawson International plc

Dawson was based in Kinross in Scotland until it went into liquidation in 2012 due to problems in financing its pension fund. It operated in three segments: UK Knitwear, US Knitwear, and Home Furnishings Private Label. UK Knitwear comprised the Barrie business, which manufactured cashmere and woollen garments, which were sold in the European market. It sold both to private label customers as well as under its own labels, which included Barrie, John Laing, and Glenmac. US Knitwear comprised the Forte business, which sourced cashmere garments from China, which were sold in the American market, primarily to large private-label customers. It also sold to smaller boutique customers under its own Kinross label. Home Furnishings Private Label segment designs and sources bed linen, primarily from Asia, which is sold to Private Label customers.

JEB was a director from 1971 until 1990 and had a good social interaction with the Chairman, Alan Smith, and his wife Alice. One of the key issues the company was concerned with in his time was its structure, moving toward decentralizing decision-making, something with which JEB strongly agreed.

NCR Ltd (National Cash Register)

NCR was attracted to set up a manufacturing plant in Dundee at the end of World War II in order to replace the declining jute industry, along with other American companies such as Timex. NCR produced electro-mechanical accounting machines in a highly labour-intensive, mainly male, production system with very little bought-out content. Thus Dundee for some time had an enviably low unemployment rate. By 1969 NCR Dundee had 6500 employees, but in the early 1970s a new economic environment brought drastic change to both NCR and Dundee, and under the leadership of Bill Anderson at its Dayton Ohio base, the firm responded by introducing a new computer based product line and shutting down electro-mechanical factories, which created a labour activity more suited to women and a high bought-in content. The impact on Dundee was severe; within 18 months the 6500 employees had dropped by more than 50 per cent and by the early 1980s by 90 per cent, even though exports and output continued to rise. Bolton used the example of NCR and Dundee in his arguments for small businesses as a source of jobs.

However this was not the end of the story. Dundee was given the role of designing a second generation ATM, the 1780, for the UK banking system. But after an initial success, the 1780 began to break down and the banks refused to accept delivery of new ones, indeed switching their orders to industry leader IBM instead. The future looked bleak, with closure on the cards, when Jim Adamson arrived in April 1980. What he achieved became a worldwide example of leadership in action as described by the Harvard leadership guru, John Kotter, in his '*A Force for Change: How Leadership Differs from Management*' (1990). Under Bill Anderson as chairman, NCR looked to give its plants both design and profit responsibility for the products they manufactured, and Adamson made 'quality' his key to all aspects of the operation. He had to sell this concept to his customers, to his product development group, and with the aid of his personnel director, Alan Murdoch, to the disillusioned and cynical workforce. To manage his ambitious programme, he began calling 7 am meetings of his directly reporting managers, two hours before the normal start time for managers. And in a PR master stroke to reassure the customers, at an ATM industry trade show in Chicago attended by nearly 2500 bankers and featuring products from almost every ATM vendor in the world, an elegantly dressed Dundee employee stood on a platform with the new 5070:

> by herself and without the aid of tools or an assistant, she proceeded to take the machine apart, placing the pieces on a nearby table, and then to put the machine back together again, all in less than fifteen minutes. At the end of each demonstration she pressed the start button, and in all thirty-nine demonstrations, the machine worked perfectly. Most customers were clearly impressed . . . And NCR management in Dayton, some of whom were not at all convinced that such a demo was worth the inherent risk, heaved a collective sigh of relief. (Kotter 1990: 27–8)

To cut a long story short, Adamson turned his ATM business into a world leader 'by offering a wide range of superior quality products that fitted customers' key needs, and by offering those products ahead of the competition' (Kotter 1990: 25). Kotter's example is about how Adamson turned what was initially a management role into a transformational leadership one.

JEB was a director of NCR from 1971 to 1991 and there through the transformation that Adamson achieved. How much of a role he played in the transformation is unclear and in any case would not detract from what Adamson did. But Bolton was very friendly on a personal level with Bill Anderson, the NCR Chairman, and his wife Jan, and it is not too much to surmise that in the period around 1980 when Dundee was teetering on the edge of closure, Bolton may have been quietly influential in persuading Anderson to give Dundee another chance. If so, it would show what a non-executive can contribute in a difficult situation. At all events, it was one of the great success stories of Bolton's time as a non-exec.

Johnson Wax

S. C. Johnson & Son, Inc. previously known as Johnson Wax, is a privately-held, global manufacturer of household cleaning supplies and other consumer chemicals based in Racine, Wisconsin, with some 12,000 employees in 72 countries around the world. JEB was appointed to the Johnson Board on 20 September 1971 and resigned in 1990. Sam Johnson and his wife Gene had lived at Frimley Green, quite close to the Boltons, for a couple of years while Sam was moving up the family business. The Johnsons were special people, very generous and gracious, huge benefactors, and strong environmentalists. As with some other cases John seemed to have a predilection for being involved with family businesses; he was very fond of Johnsons as a company and particularly the personal relationships with the other non-executives, engendered by the corporate motto which started 'together we . . .'. Sam for his part apparently saw John as something of a confidante for advice; the two had membership of the Harvard Business School Visiting Committee in common. The Johnsons were an extremely nice couple and became good if not great friends of the Boltons, although John apparently said that he would only go on the Johnson Board if he could say what he thought, not what he thought was expected. The European board meeting would be held at Frimley Green, where the UK business was situated, with a traditional agenda: dinner at the hotel on the Sunday night, a pheasant shoot on the Monday, and the board meeting on the Tuesday. Needless to say, this would be very convivial for John. He was instrumental in the appointment of Professor Tony Kelly, Vice-Chancellor of Surrey University, to the board of Johnson Wax in Britain from 1981–1996, something for which Kelly was very grateful.

The Automobile Association

On 29 June 1905 a group of motoring enthusiasts met at the Trocadero restaurant in London to form the Automobile Association, and by World War II it had 725,000 members and provided a wide range of services. John was brought into the AA by Alec Durie, probably as a result of their joint membership of the BIM Council, and his commitment was not just to the main AA, but also to several of its subsidiaries. He was a Committee member of the AA from the late sixties to 1990 and of AA Insurance Services Ltd over the same period, of Automobile Association Developments Ltd from 1985 to 1989 and of AA Pension Investments Ltd also from 1985 to 1989. It was a good source for networking, contacts, and friends, although unpaid whilst John was on the Committee.

Hoskyns Group

Hoskyns Group plc was a market leader in the supply of computer services in the United Kingdom and operated from Shaftesbury Avenue London; it was acquired by Cap Gemini in 1990 and eventually liquidated in 2001. Project services accounted for 47 per cent of its 1992 revenues; information systems management, 43 per cent; and consulting/education/training, 10 per cent. It had a remarkably successful period of growth between 1984 and 1991 during which the value of its shares rose 10-fold to more than £300 million.

John didn't join Hoskyns until 1987 and also became a management adviser, for which he was paid £12,000 a year, waiving his fee as a non-executive director. He seems to have been used as a go-between in Hoskyns' relations with the American company Martin Marietta. He also won the Hoskyns' starting price sweepstake.

A clearly heartfelt tribute was a handwritten letter from Tony Robinson, Joint Managing Director of Hoskyns, dated 30 April 1993, which refers to a takeover bid by GEC during which the young son of Arnold Weinstock moved the goalposts at a late stage of negotiations.

> Dear John,
>
> I am really sad that you are leaving Hoskyns. I have read your nice letter to Geoff dated 20.4.93 where you talk about. . . . the trauma of GEC. . . . It is in that area that I find myself most indebted to you.
>
> I expect you have forgotten it but there was a Board meeting where we were discussing how to handle GEC. I, since I carried prime responsibility for handling them, was paging a problem to the Board about how we should behave, given that they were behaving in a way that I found unacceptable.
>
> After half an hour's discussion you terminated the debate by advising me . . . 'tell them to fuck off . . .' you said, raising your fingers in a Churchillian V-sign.
>
> I took your advice, really heartened by your support, and it worked!
>
> Thank you
> Tony

He was appointed on 9 December 1986 and resigned in 1993.

FMC Corporation (Food Machinery Corporation)

John was not a non-executive director but rather a paid adviser for FMC Corporation of Europe. Bob Malott Jr., its chairman, was a good friend dating back to John's time at Harvard. From its inception in 1883, FMC Corporation has been one of the world's foremost, diversified chemical companies with leading positions in agricultural, industrial, and consumer markets. Under Malott's guidance, FMC's managers became more involved in policy debates and politics, and hence sought to meet key people in a country. One of JEB's roles was to organize occasional visits to Britain by FMC's senior officers, and the amount of preparation required was not unlike a royal visit. There are records of two such visits, one in 1984 and one in 1987. For the 1987 visit, a central feature was a dinner at Claridges in order to meet some key opinion-formers in Britain. Those attending (with their partners) were:

Justin Dukes, Managing Director, Channel 4 TV
Michael Grylls, MP
Robert Heller, Editorial Director, Management Today
Anthony Kelly, Vice-Chancellor, Surrey University
Sir Christopher Laidlaw, Chairman, Bridon plc
Sir Austin Pearce, Chairman, British Aerospace
Bob Reid, Chairman, Shell (UK)
Fred Smith, CEO, APV Holdings

Biographies of all the attendees were obtained and sent in advance to Chicago. For the dinner itself, there were two tables of 12 people each, one chaired by Ray Tower and the other by Jim McClung, both key players in FMC. John's duties included ordering the wines, port, and cigars. But it is the list of those who were invited but could not attend which makes even more impressive reading and gives a sense of what had to be done to obtain a reasonable cross-section of the good and the great of British industrial and political life:

Lord Ezra, ex-Chairman of the National Coal Board, Director of Redland
Sir John Hoskyns, Director-General, Institute of Directors
David Nickson, President, CBI
Sir Terence Beckett, Director-General, Ford of Europe
Sir John Harvey-Jones, Chairman, ICI
Sir Patrick Meaney, Chairman, Rank Organization
Paul Channon, Secretary of State for Industry
Sir Brian Hayes, Permanent Secretary, Department of Industry
Sir Peter Parker, Chairman, Rockware Group and Mitsubishi UK
James Ball, Chairman, Legal and General Insurance
Sir William Barlow, Chairman, BICC
Sir Michael Edwardes, Chairman, Chloride Group
Sir Ronald McIntosh, Chairman, APV Holdings and former Director-General of NEDO
Sir Trevor Holdsworth, Chairman and CEO, GKN

The confirmation letter sets the scene:

Mr Ray Tower, the President of FMC Corporation of Chicago, together with Mr Jim McClung, Vice-President International, and Mr. Milan Ondrus, Corporate Regional Director, Europe, together with their wives, will be in England on Monday and Tuesday, March 23 and 24, part of a European 'Tour de Force' during which they will be visiting

FMC manufacturing operations, customers and associates, including visits to Italy, Austria, Hungary and Germany.

I am arranging an informal dinner party (business suits) for them at Claridges Hotel, French Salon, on Monday evening, 23rd March, 7.00 for 7.30. Am delighted that you and your wife can join us, so that we might share our perceptions of the UK political and economic scene with them and, in return, hear their views about the American economic and political scene.

As you will probably know, FMC have been dedicated to the expansion of world wide trade for over a century and as you will see from the enclosed Annual report for 1985, they have consistently invested substantial amounts in research and development and new technology. The 1986 Report is due from the printers shortly and if this is available before March 23rd, I look forward to sending you a copy.

J. E. Bolton

All or almost all of these were personally known to JEB and it was his name which enabled him to make the invitations. On 26 February, the secretary to the Director FMC Europe phoned to say the two execs were coming and would John organize a dinner for them with five or six leaders of business or politics plus wives. John sent out letters of invitation on March 2, quite short time to find a suitable range of dinner companions

He had also organized a somewhat smaller dinner two years earlier for the same two FMC executives, again in Claridges, on 2 May 1985, following a buffet lunch for about 30 on 30 April. There was also a dinner for Bob Malott the chairman of FMC on 25 January 1984 at the Dorchester Penthouse. And John asked the Minister for Defence Procurement, Lord Trefgarne, to meet with Messrs Tower, McClung, and Ondrus, who were seeking 'an up-to-date overview of the UK defence equipment procurement situation'. All in all, FMC did well out of John since he only had an annual retainer of £2000 for a very substantial amount of work.

So far we have dealt with large companies. John was also involved with a number of smaller companies and to some of these we now turn.

Alphameric plc

Alphameric plc was founded by Dougal Craig-Wood in 1984 to engage in the development, supply, and maintenance of specialist software solutions to the bookmaking and hospitality sectors in the United Kingdom. It operates in two areas, Leisure and Hospitality. The Leisure area offers studio display systems, studio content systems, bet capturing and setting solutions, fixed odds betting terminals, and customer services terminals, as well as provides bespoke development and outsourced bureau services.

The Hospitality area offers solutions for financials, Web-based enterprise resource planning, business intelligence, central systems management, sales order captures, and electronic point of sale EPOS. Alphameric plc is based in Godalming, the United Kingdom, and in 2010 had 218 employees and a turnover of £40 million. JEB was a director from 1984 to 1990, when he was trying to pull out of his directorships.

Crellon Holdings Ltd

Crellon Holdings Ltd was a medium-size wholesale distribution company dealing in electronic components, with around 150 employees and a turn-over of some £20 million. John was Chairman from 1976 to 1978, and it appears not to have been a happy experience. As Chairman, he wrote a long and detailed response in August 1976 to an accountant shareholder complaining of poor results:

> I am afraid it is true that the final results came as a considerable shock to the Group Board because they were significantly at variance with the monthly internal accounts which cover the affairs of each of the three divisions in considerable detail . . . the expected increase in volume . . . did not take place and virtually the whole of the shortfall in profits occurred in the electrical division . . . the Managing Director of the Electrical Division failed in a number of important ways both in fulfilling his duties and in keeping the main Board fully informed of the facts . . . it is an unfortunate fact that the action which the Managing Director of the Electrical Division reported that he had taken was not taken or was ineffective.

This is an unusually frank expression of what went wrong to an outsider and the letter also included a schedule showing the contents of the monthly report and management accounts received by the main Board on a regular basis; one assumes that the Managing Director of the Electrical Division did not stay long in the company. For that matter Bolton himself did not stay long as Chairman; most of his non-executive appointments lasted much longer.

It is also interesting that the letter was followed the next month, September 1976, by the company selling its Rolls Royce for £5500 to Growth Capital, i.e. in effect to John himself. John may well have suggested this as a way of raising money/cutting expenses. In the same month the CEO, Geoff Haywood, wrote thanking John for 'agreeing to act as a referee in any of the job applications I am making'. Crellon was clearly not a happy ship.

Plasmec plc

While his main companies were household names, he did not neglect the small businesses in which he had himself grown up in industry. Plasmec Ltd, which he chaired for a long time, was a rather special case, being a small company started by ex-Solartron director John Crosse together with four foremen from Solartron. Crosse had joined Solartron at much the same time as John and became one of his closest friends. Plasmec made specialized precious metal springs, contacts for telephone exchanges and document handling machines, and it was the longest established of John's commercial company commitments, being a director from 1967 until 1994, his last resignation from a company. The reason for this long commitment was simple and personal, that Plasmec had been founded by his great friend and he had himself put money into it. It was, with one or two others such as Data Recall, one of the profitable investments that John made in his venture capital role. Eventually Monsanto bought Plasmec.

Atesmo Limited and Atesmo Contracting Services Ltd

John was Chairman from 1965 to 1988 of these very small companies. Atesmo Limited provided cold sterilization units to hospitals under licence from Germany, with ACS, the contracting services side making use of engineers' downtime in the plumbing industry. This was an instance of John backing people who came to him in his Growth Capital guise.

Other Companies

There were other companies with which he was involved over the years, including:

Crosshold Ltd, Chairman 1967–83
Development Capital Group and subsidiaries, Chairman 1973–84, President 1984–88
ICFC Consultants Ltd 1971–82
Keith Prowse Organization Reservations Ltd, 1971–82
F. J. Reeves Ltd, 1970–75
Small Business Capital Fund Ltd, 1971–82
Riverview Investments, 1968–1990.

County Sound Radio. He pulled out of his Alternate Directorship in 1986 after five years because his services weren't being used, as the Chairman appreciated, whilst still hoping that if something were to happen he could call on JEB's advice.

An advisory Board member of BDF Associates—Management Buyouts, Park Avenue, NY.

By 2000 his directorships had reduced to AMPI Trust and HR Management Software Group Ltd., run by his son Nicholas, having left most of his other directorships in 1990.

10 Personal Life and Evaluation

INTRODUCTION

So far we have dealt with John Bolton's institutional life insofar as he was an important part of major institutional developments across a wide range of activities, most notably management education and small business. But of course he had another life, with his family, friends, clubs, and a network of acquaintances connected with but not directly part of his institutional activities. It is therefore time to turn to this personal life, in which we see some important character traits and interactions which help to make up the story of the man. The first part deals with his private and family life, the second with the end of his and Gay's lives, and the third with an evaluation.

PRIVATE LIFE

We now pick up John's private life where we left it in Chapter 1 after he had married Gay and moved to Brook Place. He and Gay had an extremely happy married life, and indeed he was a strong family man, with his children and later his grandchildren also playing an important part in his life. In addition, they kept dogs, especially Labradors, golden in the early years but black after Gay died. He was involved in many local activities, especially Chobham Cricket Club, for which he played cricket as a member of the team. Thus Sunday afternoon cricket was a feature of the Bolton week during the summer in the early years, with the wives taking it in turns to provide the tea from a hut alongside the White Hart pub (which the cricket ground was behind). Gay did her stint too with the sandwich making and cake baking that preceded the game. JEB also helped to raise money for the cricket club, and in fact had the whole club to tea at Brook Place on occasion. Indeed he had a great knowledge and love of cricket, with frequent trips to the Lords test. In later life racing was another of his interests, although not one in which he was directly involved, while he always went to the Boat Race, wearing his 1st and 3rd Trinity tie. Family holidays in the early 1950s were caravanning with Gay's sister, then going annually to West Wittering until 1959, until the first holiday abroad in Italy in 1960.

But although he played cricket for Chobham, most of his other interests were in West End. Brook Place was on the border of the two quite separate parishes of West End and the far wealthier Chobham, and on first moving there JEB typically decided to support the needier parish of West End. He and Gay attended the local Holy Trinity Church where he was a sidesman; he had a strong belief in the hereafter and toward the end of his own life looked forward to being reunited with Gay. The then Rector David Davis and his wife Joan became good friends. He was also the vice-president of the West End, Windlesham, and District Horticultural Society, donating cups for photography and dahlias. In addition, he was known to play snooker at the workingmen's club in West End, at least until he installed his own snooker table at Brook Place. It was also much appreciated locally that he used mainly local firms and labour for his developments at Brook Place, and always paid them immediately. Overall, John and Gay were very much part of the community.

Brook Place itself was an important part of John's life and is worth discussing in some detail as a context for many of his activities. It was a manor house dating back to the 17th century, and substantially rebuilt in 1656 by one William Bray with priest-holes. As well as the purchase cost, it must have been quite expensive to furnish and equip. Initially it had three acres of land, but John extended this to 18 acres later, buying land from John Straver, a Dutch nurseryman who lived half a mile down the road and owned nearly all the land surrounding Brook Place. He became a very close friend of the Boltons. John spent a good deal of money on landscaping the grounds into formal gardens. This was done over a considerable period and became something of a hobby, reclaiming the waterlogged fields and setting out long garden walks with herbaceous borders and rockeries. Other features were several pieces of beautiful statuary which could be lit at night, and there were garden seats set at appropriate places. He also created a quite large ornamental lake with an island in the middle which was reached by a small bridge. Apart from being a focus to drain the land he also thought that he might be able to attract some wild duck to it for late-evening shooting. Mallards were purchased and they duly paired and bred 10 ducklings not in the little duck house on stilts in the middle of the pond, but on the bank. But Mr. Fox had other ideas and their number dwindled; the end of the story is that JEB was to be seen hiding camouflaged in a bush armed with his shotgun by the lake before sunrise in order to try and dispatch the duckling thief. On the second morning he met with success and shot the fox with three little ducklings actually in its mouth. There was no more talk of shooting ducks—they were too precious and by now part of the family! The landscaping and beautification culminated for his year as High Sheriff of Surrey in 1980, which involved two major garden parties for Surrey society. Both John and Gay adored walking around the gardens, doing this most evenings when they were at home in the spring/summer, always arm in arm.

It was not just the formal gardens; John built a suite of offices on what had been marshy land, and converted a barn into a banqueting hall for some 70–80 together with silver chandeliers and a minstrels' gallery. The barn had housed all the tractors and garden machinery and one end was once a hayloft. The pigsties on the exterior were converted to two stables for horses. Moreover John built an award-winning swimming pool as well as a tennis court. In addition, he created a separate company, Hall Bolton Estates, to make a commercial exercise out of the estate. After a few years of garden creation, Gordon Melton, the head gardener who had worked on the Sandringham Estate, was keen to try and make a business out of selling roses and rhododendrons and later Christmas trees in a small market garden venture. JEB supported this idea as it had the added benefit of being able to supply some plants for the garden at cost, and it might be seen as an early foray into encouraging the small entrepreneur. Unfortunately the might of the vast Dutch horticultural industry—with their highly competitive pricing—made it almost impossible to sell at a profit. However the vista of huge beds of roses and a field of rhododendrons, when in bloom, was glorious but Brook Place was left with a field of Christmas trees that grew so large it was difficult to uproot them!

He was fond of entertaining at Brook Place, something we will return to, and used it for various activities such as fundraising for Surrey University and other worthy causes, and hosting American businessmen visiting Britain. Fortnum and Mason were often used to do the catering on the big occasions, such as Ascot parties for 70–80, at considerable personal expense.

Brook Place was a magical place to grow up, as John's daughter Athalie reminiscences:

> I hardly remember being in the house at all except for meals in my years before boarding school (I went in Summer 1960 when I was eight). Many happy sun-filled days were spent with my brother Nick tying the dangling strands of large weeping willow trees together in a knot to make a swing, playing cowboys and Indians in the extensive gardens, building camps in the undergrowth and a den with tunnels on an old heap of soil removed from the lake. I remember that two of our cousins (John's sister's eldest boys) would come and stay for the whole of one school holiday each year and we got up to lots of mischief, quite a bit of which was directed at the gardeners as our prey! In later years when the

barn had been fully converted, the swimming pool and tennis court built we had a wonderful place to invite our friends and spend the whole day entertaining ourselves, especially in the summer. We made great use of it and from about 16/17 I had a birthday party on 23 December every year and invited all our friends and danced late into the night. It was marvellous and such a warm feeling to have the barn as a venue.

Sadly, however, after the Boltons moved out in April 1987, the Ecumenical Trust which bought it found it extremely expensive to run and after much effort to make the estate pay for itself, moved on in 2002. At the time of writing, two or three owners later, the house has gone into considerable decay while the estate has been split into four lots and sold: the barn and pool; the offices; the cottage; and the house.

Brook Place with its multiple outbuildings was an office and a place of employment as well as a home. As many as nine people were employed there: three gardeners, three dailies, a chauffeur, a cook, and a secretary/personal assistant, initially and for many years Marjorie Hudson. In addition the family venture capital company Growth Capital already mentioned in Chapter 8 was based there, and Bowman Scott worked for it after the Solartron period. Brook Place was a good place to work. One of the gardeners, Richard Long, remembering what he called 'the golden days' a quarter of a century after the Boltons had left, said: 'They were a smashing family to work for'. And Stella Pasley, who was 17 when she went to Brook Place as a nanny for the young children, later became a daily, and then after Gay died, loyal housekeeper for John until he died, having moved to Englefield Green with John and Gay when they left Brook Place. As she put it: 'The Boltons were my life', and they treated her as one of the family. John recommended her to go to the Palace Garden Party in 1991 and provided his Rolls-Royce to take her and her husband all the way to Buckingham Palace and back. Then, in his 80th birthday speech, he noted that they had known each other for over 50 years and 'never a cross word had passed between them'.

Why did John and Gay leave Brook Place in 1987? John was moving toward 70 when he would retire from most of the public non-executive and USA board appointments, which would entail a dramatic drop in income at a time of ever increasing running and maintenance costs of Brook Place not just in wage bills but because being a substantial estate the many electric meters used to literally whirl round! Gay was loath to leave as it had been such a happy house. But they also were mindful that it would be an enormous task to move after almost 40 years of accumulations of every kind and that it would be best done whilst they were fit and able to supervise it. They were looking for the perfect house to retire in Surrey/Hampshire but were not having much luck. Having received a purchase offer for Brook Place, albeit with delayed completion, they decided to move to Sunnymead, Englefield Green as an interim measure, as it was near airports/station/motorways, until JEB fully retired and that then they would move again. Gay did not like the house at all but thought that at least she could fit all her precious antique furniture that they had painstakingly collected over the years, which would make it feel like home. In the event of her sudden death JEB said he was going nowhere and would only leave Sunnymead 'feet first', which also happened!

On a personal basis, John moved from smoking a pipe to large Churchillian cigars; Monte Cristo No. 1s and No. 2s were his favourites. Cricket, golf, and other more energetic sport gave way to shooting, swimming, opera, and antiques as his main recreational interests as designated in 1989, together with financing and advising small- and medium-sized companies. His main outdoors interest in later life was shooting. There was shooting grouse in Scotland and pheasant and duck shooting in Hampshire, or indeed anywhere he was asked. He was a stalwart of the Old Park Shoot in Bosham, Sussex, from 1959 till 1976 when the syndicate was disbanded. Thereafter he joined the Tunworth Park Shoot 30 minutes down the M3 near Basingstoke and was its No. 1 for many years, still being a member at his death in 2003. Although he was unable to shoot in the final two years, one of his children would shoot his gun and he would watch from the car. Shooting was done in conjunction with both local notables and friends associated with his directorship. Sam Johnson of Johnson Wax rented a day's shooting at the Tunworth Park Shoot in December and would invite various non-executive board members from around the world to shoot. It coincided with the Johnson European AGM and was always a convivial day. As well as JEB, the Queen's former accountant Sir Gerard Peat, a Johnson Wax non-executive, always attended. One year, Prince Bernhard of the Netherlands flew over from Holland to shoot on what was called the Johnson Day!

The local friends with whom John shot on organized syndicate shoots of which he was a member were also substantial figures, such as Lesley Carr-Jones (owner of Susan Small ladies dressmaker and owner of racehorses), Eric Brinkman, Walter Garner, friend and landowner in Northamptonshire at Tansor Manor, Vincent O'Sullivan (gynaecologist, Irish, and involved with The World Hospital idea), elderly Jack Collis-Browne (of tummy upset bismuth preparation fame), and the Maharaja of Jaipur (who lived in Ascot). Beyond these there is a response to Viscount de L'Isle VC, KG for an invitation to shoot duck which he had to decline due to the funeral of the Bishop of Guildford:

> I confess to being a 'have gun, will travel' fanatic who only allows our wedding anniversary to interfere with anything so vital as shooting duck in such glorious surroundings. If it is not being forward, I do hope there is a chance I may be asked again.

Viscount De L'Isle lived at the fabulous Penshurst Place estate in Kent. And in another letter to Viscount De L'Isle:

> I will be seeing Bill Battle on Thursday 17 December at a Black and Decker Board Meeting in Baltimore and then we go off together to shoot

geese and duck in the Chesapeake Bay area, so I will have plenty of time to remember to give him your regards.

Shooting was part of networking; thus Jerry Shively in turn invited him to Ascot for Royal Ascot week in part to see if his agency might gain an entry to Black and Decker. Shiveley added in his letter: 'Still don't know how you manage to do so many things and all so well, although I guess the latter I can understand knowing you as I do. It's the busyness that baffles!'

From the early days John and Gay made significant personal friendships out of their business and public acquaintances, through both British and American contacts. The Hansens, Harry and Carolyn, from Harvard Business School and AMPI, were particular friends, with whom they used to go on holiday at Sotogrande for several years, one of the few occasions on which John would switch off. Carolyn indeed was something of a mentor and best girlfriend for Gay. The Deckers, Al and Virginia, of Black and Decker were also very good friends, with Virginia writing a poignant note after Al's death in 2002:

> When Al died, he was wearing the lovely blue cashmere sweater which you and Gay brought to him. Your lovely letter brightened my somewhat gloomy day. It also brought forth so many happy times we have spent with you and Gay. I shall never forget the wonderful trip you gave to Al and me as we motored up to Scotland for grouse hunting. Those wonderful days walking on the moors and the lunch in the middle of the Highlands with Cherry Jubilee . . . I am blessed that I have friends like you who take the time to write to honor Al.

Amongst other Americans, they were close to Sam and Gene Johnson, Jerry and Red Shively, and the Singletons, Philip and Eleanor; Philip was a very strong correspondent, keeping a range of people in touch with each other, and was involved with the Philippics dinners. Indeed John and Gay were perhaps drawn to the sort of people and values involved in family-based companies rather than professional administrator/managers.

Of his British circle of friends, a notable one from his Solartron days was John Crosse, who had joined just after John and went on to found Plasmec, with which John was associated for many years. Other local friends who frequently came to dinner / Sunday lunch were: John and Elsie Straver (lived just down the road and from whom he had bought the land to extend the estate—he was great fun and very jolly); Dr. Bill and Mary Smellie, the family GP; and Walter and Jo Garner (Gay and Jo spent hours talking on the phone). Another particular friend was Bernard (later Lord) Weatherill, the Conservative MP who became Speaker of the House of Commons but much earlier had been greatly involved with small business, making his maiden speech on the need for nurturing the small business sector. Through this connection Jack, as he was always known, became a family friend, to the extent of giving the tribute at JEB's funeral. It is nice to note that after JEB died in 2003, Eloise, then just 11, seemed to regard him as a sort of surrogate grandfather figure and, probably trying to fill the gap that Grandpa's death had left, she used to write long letters to him about what she was doing at school. He for his part used to call her every few months and ask her to tea and his special tour of the Palace of Westminster. He also kindly attended her Confirmation service at St Paul's Cathedral when she was 13.

John and Gay were excellent and gracious hosts and their dinners enabled distinguished people to meet other interesting guests. For instance on 26 May 1985 they had to lunch:

> Philip and Eleanor Singleton, friends from John's Harvard days
> Sir Peter and Lady Phillipa Scott of the Slimbridge Wildlife Trust
> Colin Corness, Chairman of Redland
> Norman and Sheila Cunningham, Chief Executive of Goldfields ARC
> Lord and Lady Nugent of Guildford.

Confirmations were sent out on April 11, original invitations presumably considerably earlier. Another lunch with heavyweights, in June 1983, was with Lords Nugent, Watkinson, and Carrington, all important political figures. And lots of other people came to Brook Place; he believed in sharing it. The Speaker's wife, Lyn Weatherill, writing to Gay in 1987, said: 'You really are a wonderful hostess and John a perfect host. Your house simply radiates kindness and friendship'.

PASSING ON

The sudden and unexpected death of Gay on 27 January 1989 was a major blow for John; they were just about to depart on a major trip when she collapsed. The anguish comes through in the letter he wrote to those sending condolences:

> In attempting to cope with our overwhelming grief at our darling Gay's passing, my family and I have been greatly moved and comforted by the wonderful written and floral tributes from our dear friends at home and around the world. The full-to-overflowing funeral service at the village church where we had worshipped for 38 years and the beautiful words and hymns will also remain vivid in our memories.
>
> Though, sadly, Gay died on the very day before we were to start a 40th wedding anniversary trip around the world, she was happy and apparently well when she just slipped painlessly away after a sudden and totally unexpected coronary attack in the hall here at Sunnymead.
>
> She was only 62, but for the unimaginable privilege of those 40 gloriously happy years together, I thank God—especially for the poignant

last 23 years after her operation in 1966, when the prognosis was 'only 1 chance in 20 of living for 5 years'. I hope that He will help me somehow to develop a cutting edge on the much less effective blade that remains of 'our pair of scissors'—and at least to continue to welcome all our friends to Sunnymead, the 'retirement pad' which Gay worked at ceaselessly to make into a happy nest comparable to our beloved Brook Place, our home for 36 years.

In watching our efforts to adjust, I feel certain Mummy will be pleased that our family is already giving close support in, for example, coaching me in the mysteries of driving a modern gas cooker. She cosseted me to the extent that my sole domestic achievement was brilliance in cooking a soft-boiled egg—and now that Edwina Currie has closed that avenue, with the salmonella scare, a period of total basic education is in prospect.

Gay so loved flowers. The floral tributes massed around the spot where her ashes are interred under the boughs of a large beech tree in the country churchyard, are still blooming a week or so after the funeral. Her memory as a unique and marvellous person will remain fresh for ever.

After Gay died John lost much of his momentum, reducing his activities, and he was never quite the same afterwards. He was in any case close to 70 and would have wanted to retire from most of his many obligations. Nevertheless he still enjoyed his family, especially doting on the youngest of his grandchildren, Eloise, who was born nearly three years after Gay died. He now had more time than when he was a parent himself building a rapidly growing business, and was able to enjoy and immerse himself in her childhood. He maintained some of his engagements, such as the Small Business Research Trust and was not beyond taking on others if not too taxing, such as the Management History Research Group, while he still attended a few events such as Royal Ascot. And he was still interested in his old clubs, greatly surprising the Chobham Cricket Club with his 'most generous gift towards the new pavilion', in spite of having moved some distance away. In addition, he did not entirely drop his community interests, and in 1991 attended and gave a witty speech at a party hosted by the relatively new owners of Brook Place to celebrate a local victory over scotching some proposals by Surrey County Council for a new bypass near Brook Place. In relation to West End he sponsored two students in Uganda for the Bisley and West End World Affairs Group. There was also a very sizeable event at Sunnymead with a guest list of 163, on 17 October 1993, his 73rd birthday, at which bronze busts of John and Gay by Sheila Mitchell RA were unveiled.

To judge by the huge number of letters received, many of them dealing with age and death, he was far from forgotten by his friends, and he himself maintained a good correspondence. Birthdays in particular were not forgotten and the recipients were most appreciative. Amongst the letter-writers were several from America—Carolyn Hansen, Purnell Hall, the Singletons, and the Deckers, but now about everyday matters of friendship and without a business dimension. There was even the occasional transatlantic phone call. More locally he still had many friends and was not without female admirers, Jo Stone and Ailsa Craig in particular.

He died peacefully at home in the early hours of 15 February 2003. The funeral arrangements noted 'much loved father of Nicholas and Athalie and adored grandfather of Olivia, Laura, Joss, and Eloise'. The service was at 11 am on February 27 at Holy Trinity Church, West End, Surrey. Donations were in aid of the Charlie Waller Memorial Trust (£2,315 was raised).

The eulogy at the funeral was given by Lord Weatherill, the ex-Speaker of the House of Commons and an old friend of the family. He inevitably focused on the Committee on Small Firms, saying: 'there are many entrepreneurs today—some of whom may never have heard of John Bolton, who owe their subsequent success to him and his Committee'. He also read a message from the then Minister for Small Firms, Nigel Griffiths, who wrote:

John Bolton's 1971 Report is his lasting legacy. He changed the nature of the Department of Trade and Industry, and in turn the success of the British economy . . . Thirty years on small businesses employ 12 million people and contribute £1 trillion pounds to our economy. John's clarity of vision is as relevant today as it was then. We all pay tribute to John's distinguished career and celebrate his life.

Lord Weatherill finished:

It was Lao Tzu who pronounced
Of the best leaders, the people only know they exist
The next they love and praise
The next they fear and revile
But of the best—when their task is
Accomplished—the people all say
'We did it ourselves'.

That is true leadership: leadership by encouragement and example. This accurately describes the man we remember today. Our sympathy goes to John's family—but I hope they are comforted by the fact that he was not only a role model to all of them but also to many others who will always hold him in high esteem, and affection and respect.

It is illustrative in a curious way that when Lord Weatherill later read the *Independent* obituary of Bolton he was shocked to learn the sheer depth of JEB's involvement and love for management education running in parallel with that of small firms. He had no idea, in spite of their long association, showing that John did little in the way of 'blowing his own trumpet'. Perhaps the last three lines of Lao Tzu quoted above were even truer than Weatherill intended?

Tennyson's 'Crossing the Bar' was read at his service, one of the four stanzas by each of his four grandchildren. Also sung was 'Jerusalem'—John believed in that hymn, as he believed that he would indeed see his 'Pilot' face to face when he had 'crossed the bar'. There were many tributes, of which the following are only a selection. Christine Napier, the keystone administrator at AMPI for many years:

> It was a privilege to work for John over so many years. His encouragement and belief in one's abilities enabled me to accomplish much in my career. I am just one of so many to be fortunate to have had his friendship and advice.

Jim Roxborough of the FME:

> He was a gentle man, in the fullest sense of that word—but also one with strong determination and a hugely developed sense of direction. He was expert in getting people to work with him in climbing mountains and in achieving both personal and corporate goals.

Sir John Mactaggart (a close friend of his son Nicholas from Trinity days):

> John was forever putting other people's pleasure and care before his own . . . He always found time to ask after me and mine, to send me a birthday card *every year* (unlike my siblings). And there was no better place to look for a word of encouragement or advice if you needed it.

Clive Edmonds, the West End rector for many years:

> He had the gift of imparting love and kindness to those around him. A family member (his former daughter-in-law Liz) has said 'Grandpa B has shown me nothing but unconditional love and kindness in all the years that I have known him'. Eloise said 'He was my inspiration'. He was also Grandpa B to many others even though unrelated. He had that gift of being as ease with other people without a hint of condescension, no matter from what walk of life.

His goddaughter (and later ward when her father died) Christine: 'Uncle John gave me so many gifts over the years but the most precious by far was his time', telling the story of when John had paddled in the pond to catch tadpoles for her while his chauffeur waited anxiously to take him to Heathrow. When prompted by the chauffeur, John said: 'But can't you see I'm doing something important'. This of course had made Christine feel important too.

Marc Verstringhe of AMPI:

> . . . to many of us John has been an inspiration, a person who opened that window of opportunity and more than that his leadership, dedication and support injected enthusiasm and the confidence to carry forward the banner of his beliefs.

His sister:

> The message on our wreath did not even scratch the surface of what he meant to us. Always and particularly since my father's death two days before John's thirteenth birthday and nearly seven weeks after my tenth, John has been a most wonderful brother in every way. He has been supportive, very good to talk to and at the same time great company with his kind wit, sense of fun and general zest for life . . . I keep thinking of Laura's excellent speech at his 80th birthday party and his advice to her to 'engage brain before mouth'. John was brilliant at following that advice. He always spoke with kind diplomacy and not once has he said anything hurtful or undiplomatic.

John's estate was valued at some £800,000, a substantial amount but hardly a great fortune. He never seemed to be able to accumulate serious wealth and always spent it on some project or other as well as enjoying a very good standard of living. His expensive daily weaknesses were good cigars and fabulous wine, while running Brook Place in the manner he did was a considerable drain on resources. He was also immensely generous. Most people probably had the impression that he was very rich indeed, partly because he always seemed very relaxed (as in not awkward) with the trappings of wealth. He also said to his daughter after the accountant had been on his yearly visit, only a few years before he died, in a wry humorous fashion 'It will be a pretty close run thing which one of us will run out first, me or the money!'

The final task of this biography is to use what has been said already to provide an evaluation of both Bolton the man and his place in history.

CHARACTER AND ABILITIES

Bolton had a very strong sense of duty and public service, qualities forged especially in wartime service. He was not ambitious for himself as much as for his country and it was in him 'to love the game above the prize'. He was a man for whom the concept of duty meant a great deal, in the best traditions of public service. The same qualities that made him successful as a team player and as a keeper of the peace in boardrooms and in the workplace also meant that he never amassed a personal fortune by running a business solely with his own benefit in mind.

He was a great risk-taker and entrepreneur, almost always taking an optimistic perspective of likely outcomes. He was also optimistic about people, giving them their heads wherever possible, indeed he threw people in the deep end. He was especially known for mentoring and supporting younger senior executives and high-flyers. The counterpart of this was that he was a man who inspired not just respect, but love and affection; in many of his roles, he created a sense of family around him.

But although he was a family man, he was certainly not in favour of nepotism and separated his work activities from his family, so that, for instance, his children did not grow up feeling part of Solartron. He also kept good links with his wider family, having his brother Nigel as his best man, being both uncle and godfather to David Bolton, and addressing his 21st party, since he was an uncle who could be trusted to make the right speech on the right occasion. He had seen only one of David's school reports; it said: 'I do not think we shall make a classical scholar out of a boy who thinks Agricola was a soft drink for farm workers' and 'Late for class Mr. Bolton, you should have been here at 9 am'. 'Why sir, what happened?' And his grandchildren all adored him. Olivia, his eldest grandchild commented: 'for someone who was surrounded by very beautiful things and had a great appreciation of beautiful things he was staggeringly unmaterialistic'. When she broke an antique dining chair during Sunday lunch, he said 'don't worry darling, we can get it fixed'.

To mention some of the terms used of him, he was quiet, courteous, modest, unassuming, and never known to be rude or angry in public. (The nearest he came to being angry in public was over Harry Hansen not being appointed to the Benjamin Franklin Medal after a landscape architect had been so honoured. But he got his way in the end). He was not someone who took credit to which he was not entitled. As Alison Rooper put it in *Accountancy Age* (March 7, 1975),

> A quiet, unaggressive man, John Bolton exudes a stable confidence in his own business competence and philosophy . . . An unflinching belief that success always rewards effort dominates Bolton's thinking . . . Somehow he lacks the panic of politicians though and radiates a quiet confidence that all will be well in the end.

He was an idealist and an optimist, the latter arguably sometimes overly so, and these derived from believing in the best of people. He had a calmness and a coolness which impressed people, even in danger. As another of the grandchildren put it: 'he was incredibly and innately fair, especially when judging someone, was always disinclined to criticise, and never bitched'.

He was willing to make time to talk to anyone and to give them personal advice if he could, and was well known for this not just on the shop floor at Solartron, but in executive circles in later life. He had strong human relations and public relations skills. He also had considerable energy, manifested in his perseverance and his willingness to take on many different activities.

He was also very much a team player, as the alphabet soup of institutional affiliations shows, together with the affection with which he is remembered in the institutions with which he was associated. He tended to be very constructive under stress and was good at sorting out the squabbles in companies in his role as a non-executive director. He was a 'big picture' man with a concern for strategy and people, not a detail man. Nevertheless he worked very hard; people consistently commented on the range and amount of work that he did, to which this author can only add 'Amen'.

Humour was important to him, and his popularity as a non-executive director was in considerable part based on his use of it to aid the transmission of his knowledge and experience. Hence the little black book in which he wrote many of his punch lines, mentioned in his obituary in *The Times*. He often allowed himself to indulge in jokes about bankers, of which the following is a sample.

> A small businessman went into a bank and asked to see the manager, Mr Smith. The receptionist replied 'I'm very sorry, sir, but Mr Smith died on Tuesday'. The man went off but came back the following week and asked to see Mr Smith. The receptionist said 'I'm sorry sir, but Mr Smith died ten days ago'. The man went off but came back again the following week and asked to see Mr Smith. The receptionist was annoyed by now. 'I've told you for the last three weeks that Mr Smith is dead. Surely you have remembered that'. 'Yes I know that Mr Smith is dead', said the small businessman, 'But I just love to hear you saying it'.

He had an economy with words; not a sentence, not a word would be wasted and what was said was therefore wise and valuable. He didn't write many letters other than those concerned with business, or at least there are no records from that source. Nevertheless, he was a brilliant letter-writer and note-writer, fluent, concise, elegant, but covering the key issues, and thus, with his feeling for people, an excellent correspondent. This was enhanced by clear, neat, handwriting; indeed in spite of having a secretary he did a good deal of writing by hand, whether drafts of talks or notes to others. There are dozens of paper-clipped 3" by 5" cards that he used for his speeches; the articles were written out, then typed. He also had a beautiful voice, clear, classless, accent-free, and well-modulated, speaking neither too quickly or too slowly. He had no difficulty in marshalling his thoughts and letting them flow on paper or in speech. He was always conscientious in responding to people, and especially very good at writing back and thanking people and at sending letters of congratulation and condolence. There are several letters of condolence from widows who say that they still treasure the letter of condolence that John wrote when their own husband died. But he was also good in the opposite context, of noticing developments and congratulating people that he knew, whether on an honour or in a new role. As an example, he wrote a charming letter to Peter Moore on his appointment as Principal of London Business School, noting that he had warned against the appointment of a businessman.

Although he was modest, he was not unaware of the value of publicity, as he showed at Solartron. He had an advance press service prepared for himself, giving a studio photograph and biographical information. He also achieved a good deal of social mobility from being the son of a railway clerk to full acceptance at the top levels of British industry and in the high society of Surrey, one of Britain's most socially conscious counties.

He was very strongly networked in industry, probably in large part due to his contacts through the BIM, the CBI, and the IOD. He was good at pulling people in, e.g. when a Thomson McLintock partner questioned his criticism of accountants in his RSA speech, John invited him to a meeting with his colleagues at Development Capital Ltd to discuss the small firm scene generally, and pushing it a bit further by adding: 'I hope I may take the liberty of asking my secretary to telephone yours to see whether we can find a mutually convenient date'. His range of contacts went well beyond British businessmen; he had especially strong links with American industry, to which he was culturally acceptable, probably more so than any other Briton of his era. He actually spent quite some time over there; in 1984–85 he spent 45 days in America, mainly with Black and Decker. He was of course very pro-American and Harvard gave him unique opportunities.

With his accumulated knowledge and experience, he achieved wisdom. As various people have put it: 'No man is born wise, wisdom cannot be learned, it is a journey of discovery where the destination remains unknown'. 'The wise always try to find the best in others'. 'The wise strive to leave the world a better place'. All of these relate to JEB, and on top of these he was a complete gentleman and a very decent human being.

So what were his weaknesses? They were few, and arguably the mirror image of his strengths: being overly optimistic, assuming the best of people, getting involved in too many things at the same time, not knowing when to say 'enough', especially to people he knew and to whom he had already given more than one chance. Eric Jones had been the commercial director at Solartron and formed a company with his son, in which John invested and kept pouring money in, never cutting his losses. Indeed he was arguably too soft and not ruthless enough to be a venture capitalist. Sometimes also he was not a good listener when being told that something wouldn't work if he believed in it. He could make mistakes, one of which was turning down the rights for Rank Xerox, although overall he had few regrets. He also ruffled feathers in Whitehall with his insistence on making the case for small business.

INFLUENCES AND BELIEFS

Bolton was not an intellectual even though extremely intelligent; the influences on his life came not from theory or reading but from experience: from family upbringing to wartime duties to American systems of management and education at Harvard. However he had a passion for management which transcended all his influences. He was not a visionary as such but concerned about the future and saw the American system as one that should be copied because of its professionalism. He was religious in a theological sense but even more in terms of its moral and social values. He was a conservative in politics but more because he believed in free enterprise than as an adherent of class-based politics. Indeed he would probably have seen himself as a 'One Nation' Tory, someone who could deal with all walks of life, and having no antagonism to trade unions or an appropriate role for the state, so long as wealth creation was a dominant objective. He was not someone who changed his mind and moved on, maintaining his commitments to his areas of particular interest to the end of his life. His attitudes toward management were not strongly capitalist but had a stakeholder rather than a shareholder perspective, viewing management as a way of serving the community and preferring benevolent paternalism in his interpersonal relations. What he did want in management was an educated cadre operating with efficiency and professionalism in the broad sense, and he strongly supported institutions such as the BIM. Education was the starting-point for his sort of management, but a practical education based on and mixed with experience. His preference for smaller organizations seems to have mainly come from his experience in destroyers, where he could know everyone personally. He was willing to pursue his interests with conviction and commitment, including a willingness to use his own money. He was also his own man. With the exception of some advice from Charles Hayward, he made his own decisions and ploughed his own furrow.

He had a very full and rich life, multi-faceted with many interests at any one time and seemingly able to compartmentalize his time according to the needs of the moment. Indeed his range of roles was remarkable: businessman; venture capitalist; benefactor; intermediary; insider; public servant; elder statesman; family man; member of the Establishment; and last but not least, campaigner, with two main missions. Few people can have been involved with so many different organizations. Of other activities not so far mentioned, John was an under-writing member at Lloyds, 1964–1981, and was a Life Fellow of the Royal Society of Arts, 1967–2003.

It should be added, of course, that he made enough money to live in very comfortable circumstances, and also had the time to do a range of things after he gave up his full-time job at Solartron (not that this stopped him while he was at Solartron!). He was named in the *Financial Times* as a possible head of LBS at a time when he was about to take over the chairmanship of the BIM, calling him 'the voice of coldly appraising sanity' in relation to management education. Management being a functional commercial activity, it is rare to find people who have a passion about it, and even more rare to find a benefactor, except in the sense of endowing chairs at a business school. Bolton was a benefactor to various management-related activities: the FME has been mentioned, as has the Advanced Management Programmes International, which brought Harvard Business School short courses to Britain, while the Management History Research Group also deserves to be noted.

He was successful with his campaigns and indeed without him, management education and small business would not have emerged in the way that they did, although it was also important that his ideas fitted with the times—the Zeitgeist was in his favour. Does that make him lucky, or aware? Mostly the latter, but he was just sufficiently ahead of the times to lead them.

LEADERSHIP

Bolton often saw himself as a catalyst rather than a leader, although he was more than willing to lead where necessary, as in Solartron, where his leadership was the essential element. We have noticed that in the management education field, although pressing for change and action, he tended to hang back when it came to play the lead role. But in the case of small business, he was more or less pushed into being the champion for the cause, a public figure, which in turn required him to write and lecture far more than in the rest of his life.

However his style of leadership can perhaps best be seen by comparing and contrasting him with his predecessor in the pursuit of management education, Lyndall Urwick who also made management his life's passion. The context was important. Both were fighting against the prevailing attitudes toward management and industry; of these Parker (1989: 118) hit the nail on the head when he said: 'we are an industrial society with an anti-industrial culture'.

Urwick was a world figure in management, arguably the only one Britain has ever had, yet his efforts at institutional development did not have the success that he would have wished. With Bolton, on the other hand, almost all that he touched was marked by success. In considerable part, of course, the difference was one of timing. Urwick had to face much more recalcitrant audiences than Bolton, for whom the tide of attitude was already turning. Urwick could have gained the same tide, but by that time had emigrated to Australia.

But there was more to it than that. Urwick was an outstanding intellectual, as well as being charismatic in his writing and his speaking. He had very clear and strong ideas about organizations and even now must be regarded as one of the great organizational theorists, largely based on his Army experience in World War I. But:

- he did not have a strong power base;
- his leadership was personal and not consensus-oriented;
- in other words he sought to be a transformational rather than a transactional leader; he had all the hard leadership skills, as well as some of the soft;
- he did not work well in committees unless he could control them;

- his ideas tended to be based in the 1930s, with links to relatively weak professional institutes and the college system;
- he did not have good links with either the employers or the universities; and
- in spite of his very strong links with America, he didn't really pursue the American model as strongly as he might have done.

Bolton certainly had strong ideas and had perfect links with the American system, both by experience and by being extremely highly regarded at Harvard Business School. When the successive deans of Harvard Business School thought of Britain, they thought of Bolton. But there were other dimensions:

- He never tried to dominate but led from behind; he was a transactional leader, with all the soft leadership skills, as well as some of the hard.
- He was happy to work with and in committees.
- Nind called him the 'primus inter pares' of the FME, but he was more than that; it just wouldn't have happened without him.
- He recognized the need for universities rather than colleges to provide management education because that was how he had done it in America.
- He worked the critical interface between academia and business to great effect.
- But he also accepted the need for professional institutes; his leadership of the BIM was to take it to the managers, rather than concentrate on big business, as had been the case in the 1950s.
- He had the money to help to make things happen and, critically in some instances, he was willing to use it.

Great men, both of them, with many similarities but also some key differences. Urwick, in spite of being born into the Establishment and having all the attributes of intellect and leadership, was an outsider, at least in Britain. Bolton, the son of a railway clerk, became one of the most influential people in industry, the ultimate insider (although not to the point of honours). Urwick did not make the system work for him whereas Bolton did, using the right sort of leadership for the occasion, even if this meant using his own money. Thus he pushed hard to make the FME a reality at key points, he underwrote the AMPI, while on the Committee of Inquiry he initially sought consensus on the Report and to make it acceptable to Government, while in the following decade he saw the need for taking a more aggressive line. The legacy of the Bolton Report and its aftermath has been a permanent increase in appreciation of small firms and their prominence in policy. Without Bolton's leadership, small firms could have been ignored for many years further, while the AMPI and the FME might not have got off the ground. Considering counterfactual history, what would have happened without him? At the very least he was a critical catalyst in both management education and small firms. At the most his absence could have meant little or no action, certainly at the time and maybe for some years to come.

BOLTON'S PLACE IN HISTORY

There are obviously many people who play a wide range of roles in British public life, many of whom he was acquainted with, such as Sir Peter Parker and Sir Monty Finniston who are mentioned in this biography. But not many have managed to change Britain to the extent that John did, or provide the leadership to change situations. Playing a key role in institution building is perhaps not now ranked with developing new theories or dominating a major company, but it is an important part of creating a total system. The books that attempt to measure contributions in these different ways are the two volumes of *The Golden Book of Management* (Urwick 1956 and Urwick and Wolf 1984), which provided a roll of honour of the great management figures of the past, and on an international stage. The first one covered 70 pioneers who had died before the first volume was finished, the second a further 38 who died between 1956 and 1984. Lyndall Urwick edited the first volume and included many who played a role in their countries not unlike Bolton in Britain. Bolton, in this author's opinion, would have been part of that first roll of honour, had the time of his death permitted him to be part of it. The second volume, edited by William Wolf with Urwick's assistance, concentrated more on writers and academics than institution-builders and Bolton would probably not have been chosen. Yet he deserves recognition in such company.

This of course raises the question of why did he not receive a higher honour than the CBE given to him after the Committee of Inquiry? Possibly because that was his last major activity in the public service. Possibly because he was not head of a sufficiently important organization for sufficiently long. But it also seems possible that his persistent activities on behalf of small business grew to annoy the Government of the time. He did of course achieve other awards, honorary degrees from Bath and Surrey, and the Bowie Medal from the BIM. He thought he received the Bath award for retiring after 25 years as Chairman of the FME, and the Surrey one was of course for his many contributions in the University's early days, while the Bowie Award was for contributions to management education.

However bringing a work like this to an end must finish as it started by emphasizing the importance of people and reminding ourselves of Emerson's aphorism that there is no history, only biography. It is perhaps appropriate to finish with two descriptions of John's contributions. One is by Professor Ray Thomas at the presentation of his honorary degree at Bath

University in 1986; after noting the decades of emphasis on economies of scale, he went on:

> Yet the British retain an inner independence, even a willingness to 'have a go'. This all too often finds its outlets away from work, or perhaps today, in that new dimension of our society—the 'do-it-yourself' economy . . . This submerged entrepreneurship has, at long last, become the 'white hope' of the revival of activity and employment as society adapts to a new pattern of organising activities. But how has this change of attitude come about? Surely it has come with a realisation of the interdependence of large enterprises and individual entrepreneurs. The value of the small firm as innovator, facilitator and catalyst even in the age of giant internationals is at last being accepted, even stimulated, in this country. Yet a change of 'received wisdom' owes much to the outstanding report which bears the name of its chairman and architect, John Eveleigh Bolton, whom it is our privilege to honour today.

However the last word should go to one of his peers. Sir Peter Parker had a not dissimilar career to Bolton, overlapping at Harvard and in the FME, and in his autobiography he said of helping to 'form a small war-party to start to fight the case for management education' (1989: 116):

> An entrepreneur, John Bolton, took the chair; and of that set of crusaders he was the most original of managers. I cannot think of a businessman who has worked harder for the cause of management education in Britain in his time: he chaired all the key centres of initiative, the BIM, the Business Graduates Association, the Foundation for Management Education. In business he was a pioneer in the sunrise valley of electronics, setting up his own company there in the early Fifties, straight from his Harvard Business School training. His name only went public in the Sixties when, as chair of what came to be called the Bolton Committee, he championed the cause of small businesses, years before it was fashionable. And, not incidentally, it is saddening that John Bolton has never received that full public recognition he deserved long ago.

References

Ambrose, S. (1992) *Band of Brothers*, New York, Simon and Schuster.

Auletta, K. (1984) *The Art of Corporate Success: The Story of Schlumberger*, New York, Putnam.

Bannock, G. (1991) *Small Business Policy in Europe: Britain, Germany and the European Commission*, London, The Anglo-German Foundation.

Bannock, G. and Peacock. A. (1989) *Governments and Small Business*, London, Sage.

Barnett, C. (2001) *The Verdict of Peace: Britain Between Her Yesterday and the Future*, London, Macmillan.

Birch, D. (1979) *The Job Generation Process*, Boston, Mass., MIT Program on Neighbourhood and Regional Change.

Bolton, J.E. (1971) *Report of the Committee of Inquiry on Small Firms*, Cmnd. 4811, HMSO.

Brech, E. (2002) *The Concept and Gestation of Britain's Central Management Institute, 1902–1976*, Bristol, Thoemmes Press.

Brech, E., Thomson, A., and Wilson, J. (2010) *Lyndall Urwick, Management Pioneer: A Biography*, Oxford, Oxford University Press.

British Institute of Management, *Annual Reports 1964–66*.

Caves, R.E. (ed) (1968) *Britain's Economic Prospects*, London, George Allen and Unwin.

Chandler, A.D. (1990) *Scale and Scope: The Dynamics of Industrial Capitalism*, Cambridge, Mass., Belknap.

Coleman, D.C. (1973) 'Gentlemen and Players', *Economic History Review*, 2, 2.

Coopey, R. and Clarke, D. (1995) *3i: Fifty Years of Investing in Industry*, Oxford, Oxford University Press.

Curran, J. (1986) *Bolton Fifteen Years On: A Review and Analysis of Small Business Research in Britain 1971–1986*, London, Small Business Research Trust.

Douglas, R. (1991) *Surrey, The Rise of a Modern University*, Guildford, University of Surrey.

Franks, Lord. (1963) *British Business Schools*, London, British Institute of Management.

Galbraith, J.K. (1967) *The New Industrial State*, Princeton, Princeton University Press.

Heavens, S. (2006) *Advanced Management Programmes International: A Contribution to Management Education in the United Kingdom*, Cambridge, Judge Business School, University of Cambridge.

Hill, R. (1975) *Destroyer Captain*, London, Kimber.

Kotter, J. (1990) *A Force for Change: How Leadership Differs from Management*, New York, Free Press.

Learned, E., Christensen, C., Andrews, K., and Guth, W. (1969) *Business Policy: Text and Cases*, Homewood, Illinois, Richard D. Irwin.

Macmillan, H. (1931) *Report of the Committee on Finance and Industry*, Cmnd. 3897, HMSO.

McNulty, T. and Pettigrew, A. (1996) 'The Contribution, Power and Influence of Part-Time Board Members', *Corporate Governance*, 4, 3, 160–179.

Nind, P. F. (1985) *A Firm Foundation: The Story of the Foundation for Management Education*, London, Foundation for Management Education.

Parker, Sir P. (1989) *For Starters: The Business of Life*, London, Jonathan Cape.

"Profile: John Bolton. It Is the Team That Matters." (1958, May 22) *New Scientist* (newspaper) 24–26.

Quail, J. (2000) 'The Proprietorial Theory of the Firm and its Consequences', *Journal of Industrial History*, 3, 1, 1–28.

Redcliffe-Maud, Lord (1969) *Report of the Royal Commission on Local Government in England*, Cmnd. 4040 and 4040–1, London, HMSO.

Robbins, Lord (1963) *Report of the Committee on Higher Education*, Cmnd. 2154, London, HMSO.

Rubinstein, W. (1994) *Capitalism, Culture and Decline in Britain, 1750–1990*, Cambridge, Cambridge University Press.

Sampson, A. (1965) *Anatomy of Britain Today*, London, Hodder and Staughton.

Schumacher, E. F. (1973) *Small Is Beautiful: A Study of Economics as if People Mattered*, London, Blond and Briggs.

Shattock, M. (1994) *The UGC and the Management of British Universities*, Buckingham, Society for Research into Higher Education and Open University Press.

Spencer, A. (1983) 'Non-Executive Realities', *Management Today*, May, pp. 64–69.

Stanworth, J. and Gray, C. (1991) *Bolton 20 Years On: The Small Firm in the 1990s*, London, Paul Chapman.

Stanworth, J., Westrup, A., Watkins, D., and Lewis, J. (eds) (1982) *Perspectives on a Decade of Small Business Research, Bolton Ten Years On*, Aldershot, Gower.

Stone, N. (2010) *The Atlantic and Its Enemies*, London, Allen Lane.

Storey, D. (1994) *Understanding the Small Business Sector*, London, Routledge.

Takizawa, K. (1974) *A Comparative Study on the Problems of Small Business in the United Kingdom, the United States and Japan*, pamphlet published privately.

The History Guide: What Is History? (n.d.) www.historyguide.org/history.html (accessed 15 December 2014).

Thompson, E. P. (1970) *Warwick University Limited*, Harmondsworth, Penguin.

Thompson, FML (2001) *Gentrification and the Enterprise Culture, Britain 1780–1980*, Oxford, Oxford University Press.

Urwick, L. F. (1956) *The Golden Book of Management: A Historical Record of the Life and Work of Seventy Pioneers*, London, N. Neame.

Urwick, L. F. and Wolf, W. (eds) (1984) *The Golden Book of Management. New Expanded Edition in Two Parts*, New York, American Management Association.

White Paper (1970) *Reform of Local Government in England*, Cmnd. 4276, HMSO.

Whyte, W. H. (1956) *The Organization Man*, New York, Simon and Schuster.

Wiener, M. (1981) *English Culture and the Decline of the Industrial Spirit*, Harmondsworth, Penguin.

Williams, APO (2010) *The History of UK Business and Management Education*, Bingley, Emerald.

Wilson Committee (1979) *The Financing of Small Firms*, Cmnd. 7503, HMSO.

Wilson, J. F. (1995) *British Business History, 1720–1994*, Manchester, Manchester University Press.

Wilson, J. F. and Thomson, AWJ (2006) *The Making of Modern Management: British Management in Historical Perspective*, Oxford, Oxford University Press.

Wingo, W. (1967) *Pattern for Success: Presenting the Harvard Business School Advanced Management Program*, New York, Doubleday & Company.

Wood, B. (1976) *The Process of Local Government Reform 1966–74*, London, George Allen and Unwin.

Yamey, B.S. (1972) 'The Bolton Report on Small Firms', *The Three Banks Review*, September, No. 95, pp. 20–38.

Young, D. and Scott, P. (2004) *Having Their Cake: How the City and Big Bosses Are Consuming UK Business*, London, Kogan Page.

Index

234   *Index*

234   *Index*
234   *Index*